Everything Women Always Wanted to Know About Cars

But Didn't Know Who to Ask

Books by Lesley Hazelton

Everything Women Always Wanted to Know About Cars
    (But Didn't Know Who to Ask)

Confessions of a Fast Woman

England, Bloody England

Jerusalem, Jerusalem

The Right to Feel Bad

Where Mountains Roar

Israeli Women

A Main Street Book Doubleday
New York London Toronto Sydney Auckland

Everything Women Always Wanted to Know About Cars

But Didn't Know Who to Ask

Lesley Hazleton

A Main Street Book
Published by Doubleday

a division of Bantam Doubleday Dell Publishing Group, Inc.
1540 Broadway, New York, New York 10036

MAIN STREET BOOKS, DOUBLEDAY, and the portrayal of a building with a tree are
trademarks of Doubleday, a division of Bantam Doubleday Dell Publishing Group, Inc.

Technical Illustrations by Dan Saultman/Art Staff, Inc.
Spot Illustrations by Jim Torok
Book Design by Gretchen Achilles

Library of Congress Cataloging-in-Publication Data

Hazleton, Lesley.
  Everything women always wanted to know about cars : but didn't
know who to ask / Lesley Hazleton. — 1st ed.
       p.   cm.
  Includes index.
    1. Automobiles—Popular works.   2. Women automobile drivers
—United States.   I. Title.
TL146.5.H39   1995
629.222—dc20   94-46601
                                                                   CIP

ISBN 0-385-47621-3
Copyright © 1995 by Lesley Hazleton
All Rights Reserved
Printed in the United States of America
September 1995
1   2   3   4   5   6   7   8   9   10
First Edition

**For every woman who ever wished for
more control over her life.**

All statistics quoted in *Everything Women Always Wanted to Know About Cars* are taken from original research conducted by the author in focus groups. These groups were comprised of 150 women from cities throughout North America.

Acknowledgments

Especial thanks to Rosemary Allenbach, Rosellen Brown, Sheryl Carlson, Lynn Freed, Vicki Glembocki, Clare Gibson, Hilary Haselton, Cindy Hillis, Annie Howell, Kathryn Mac-Neil, Barbara McFadden, Gigi Marino, Mary-Jo Mehl, Lorna Schnase, and Joan Shipley for hosting focus groups; to my automotive-journalist colleagues Peter duPre, Larry Hall, and Keith Martin for their help, advice, and encouragement; to Ann Basetti and Gene Nutt for food for both thought and belly; to Sandy Nelson and Dan Saultman of Art Staff for their patience; to Mike Geylin and Fred Mackerodt for their time and ideas; to my editor Lori Lipsky and her assistant Frances Jones for their enthusiasm and help in shaping the manuscript; and as always, to my good friend and agent, Gloria Loomis, for being there.

Contents

1.

Living with Cars

Talking Cars

I remember everything about the day I bought my first car. The pride, the awe at the financial responsibility, the way I stroked the paintwork. It was the cheapest car on the market—a Citroën 2CV—and I loved that car with an intensity that still persists, years later. It was simple, it was basic, and it always, always worked. And even after all the fancy cars I've driven since then, if you gave me half a chance—and if they still made that car—I'd buy it again.

I remember that day so clearly because while men take for granted the independence that cars bring, women do not. Our own car means freedom. It means control of our own lives. It means, in short, far more to us than it does to most men.

Yet for years, automakers thought of women as the poor relations of the car world. We were a "niche market," not half the population. So far as they were concerned, women were in the bleachers, men in the grandstands.

Not anymore.

Women now buy nearly half the cars in the United States (48 percent, to be precise). That's close to sixteen million cars a year, eight million of them new and eight million used. So what we think about cars and what we know about them is suddenly of prime importance. In Detroit, in Japan, in Europe, automakers are trying to figure out "what women want."

4

They could try listening.

Women talking about cars is something else altogether. Men may talk about them more, but women have a lot more fun doing it.

I discovered just how much fun when I ran a series of focus groups in six states and one Canadian province, with a total of 150 women of all ages, incomes, and ethnic backgrounds. Some drove spanking new cars, some lovingly kept-up vintage cars, some beat-up old clunkers. Often, the smaller and older the car, the more women were attached to it.

These women were dynamite. They were both savvy and frustrated, forthright and funny.

Each group began with the questionnaire reprinted on page 277, and lasted up to three hours. And those three hours were in turn riotous and intimate, humorous and touching, raucous and revealing. They were evenings of shared memories, intimacies, calamities, insults, high points, low points, dreams, fantasies, and information. We talked sex, relationships, our lives, and yet we were still talking cars.

I have spent hours on end talking with men about cars since I became an automotive journalist in the late eighties, but I have never had such fun doing it as in these groups. As a result, this book was written by 151 women—myself, and the 150 women in the focus groups, who speak in direct quotes throughout these pages.

Women talk differently about cars than men. Since we come newer to cars—we've only started buying cars in proportion to our numbers in the last two decades—we come without all the clutter of what we're *supposed* to say about them. We come with requirements of quality that apparently never occurred to men until women started demanding them. We come with fresh eyes and fresh hearts.

Here are the main differences. They don't apply to all women or to all men, of course, but they do represent a very distinct trend.

Women	Men
see cars as an integral part of their lives	see cars as machines
focus on reliability	focus on power
are honest and forthright when they talk about cars	feel they have to pretend to know all about cars
know more about cars than they think	know less about cars than they think
are serious about cars but also have a sense of humor about them	are *too* serious about cars, can't allow themselves to be funny about them
are more pragmatic about cars	are more image-conscious
think of cars in terms of a relationship (which might be why they have a sense of humor about them)	think of cars more in terms of a romance (which might be why they have no sense of humor about them)
talk cars by their experience in them: what happened in and around them, people and places	talk cars by the numbers: cylinders, horsepower, 0–60 mph, all that tech talk
take great pride in ownership	tend to take ownership for granted
see cars as symbols of freedom and independence	tend to see cars as status symbols

➡ "A boyfriend once told me you had to redline a car to see how fast it could go. It was kind of an exercise thing."

➡ "Sounds like a guy thing to me."

—New York group

Certain words surfaced time and again in the groups:

reliability

freedom

independence

relationship

security

These words are the key to what women want from cars, so we'll take a closer look at them in this first part of the book.

In the second part, we'll deal with buying cars—threading the maze of making the choice, negotiating, and being a smart buyer.

The third part gets on the road, looking at driving, breakdown, safety, and security.

The fourth part gets into the fun of cars, both serious and frivolous.

And the fifth part gets under the hood, looking at how cars work, and removing the totally unnecessary veil of mystery about these simple mechanical creatures.

I didn't grow up knowing about cars. I remember what it was like to open up the hood and be frustrated because I didn't have the faintest idea what I was looking at. I knew next to nothing about cars at the time; I only knew I liked to drive them. I could check the oil and, if I really had to, maybe change a tire, though I tended to wait for a man to come along and do that for me. But if anything went really wrong, I was at a total loss. And dealers rubbed their hands in delight when they saw me walking into a showroom.

So I asked a lot of dumb questions and got good answers. I apprenticed myself to a mechanic and found out how engines work. I hung out in Detroit and listened and observed. And when I wrote about cars, I had a different take on them than my male peers.

I wrote about them, without even intending to, from a woman's point of view. That is, I was more interested in the feel of a car than in the numbers, in the experience of driving it than in its performance on paper. And I saw an acquaintance with the hardware as a matter of self-respect—it seemed a good idea that I understand this thing I depended on and drove every day—and also as self-defense against breakdown or emergency.

Why a woman's book of cars?

Because we do think differently about cars than men.

Because we place greater stress on reliability, safety, and security.

Because we now have the money and the market clout to make automakers listen.

Because women are tired of being talked down to about cars. Tired of having our concerns labeled "women's concerns" and considered marginal. Tired of the pointless male obsession with numbers instead of quality.

We've had enough of mechanics who assume we're idiots. Enough of all the old stale myths about women drivers. Enough of being condescended to and ripped off by dealers. Enough of being treated like children just because the subject is a machine that makes noise, goes fast, and has grease in it.

Knowledge is power. This book lays it on the line, clearly and honestly. Mysteries will be revealed, secrets laid bare.

Thinking about cars, buying them, driving them, understanding them, caring for them: It's all here, in plain language.

Enjoy!

➡ **"Does anyone ever feel like a car is a safe place to cry?"**

➡ **"Yes, and yell!"**

➡ **"Definitely: I can cry better in a car than anyplace else."**

—Texas group

The Reliability Factor

In the late eighties, automakers eager to expand their sales to women began scratching their heads trying to figure out what women want in a car.

All this head-scratching by mainly male Detroit (let alone mainly male Coventry, Munich, Tokyo, and so on) may have helped promote premature baldness, but it seems mainly to be a sign of blindness to the . . . well, to the blindingly obvious.

Simply put, there are three rules to what women want most in a car:

Number 1. Reliability

Number 2. Reliability

and

Number 3. Reliability

This puzzlement at the obvious was particularly strong in Detroit, where I was told repeatedly, as late as 1990, that the only reason women prefer import cars is that they hate being broken down on the highway.

"Why, of course," I'd reply. "What a dumb feminine reason for buying a car! Just because it works! Pfooey!"

I also began to wonder about male sanity, since the clear implication was that men just love breaking down on the highway.

To Detroit's credit, it's been closing what became known as "the quality gap" with commendable speed. But too late for many women, who need only one bad experience with a car to reject both that car and that automaker forever. Women do not tolerate unreliable cars. The only wonder is that men did for so long.

When the women in the focus groups ranked the importance of nine qualities they might look for in a new car, reliability ranked by far the highest, followed by handling and safety close together, then style, comfort, and price at some distance behind, with horsepower and fuel economy bringing up the rear, and prestige lagging so far behind, it didn't even qualify.

If this sounds like horsepower is not so important, that's deceptive. When I asked the same women what most pleased and what most annoyed them about the cars they owned, power figured high on the list of what most pleased them, in second place only to reliability. And the lack of power figured equally high on the list of what most annoyed them.

What women are saying, then, is not that some things are important and others aren't. We're simply establishing priorities. The message is:

First give me reliability. Then give me safety, style, and comfort, all at a decent price. And make sure it has good power too.

"Women want it all," one Detroit vice-president told me, in an aggrieved tone of voice that suggested this is most unreasonable of us.

But what is unreasonable about this? Except for prestige, which seems to be of greater importance only to professionals such as lawyers who have to dress and drive to match their jobs, all the other factors are the basic elements of a quality car. What a shame that we still have to spell this out. And that anyone should even think it unreasonable.

➡ **"A good car performs reliably, handles well, is safe, is good-looking and comfortable, is good value for the money, has enough power to accelerate and climb easily, and does not guzzle gas. And so far as I'm concerned, these are not luxuries: These are the basics."**

—Business owner, New York

Trust and Loyalty

Most women are absolutely unforgiving when it comes to cars. So long as the car performs well, trust is complete. And we *want* to be able to trust our cars—to rely on them completely.

We are not willing, as men have been for so long, to tolerate drips in the driveway from leaking engines, or anxious, iffy starts on cold mornings. When we pay up to half a year's salary for a machine—the average price of a new car is just over half the average annual income—the least we expect is that this machine will work without fail, each and every time we switch it on, and each and every mile we drive it.

So if the car fails, even once, we'll turn away not only from that car but most likely from any car by the same automaker. If a car breaks down, that's a betrayal of trust. And trust once given and broken will not easily be given again. There are no second chances with women and cars.

➤ **"I drive my husband's car right now, because I had a Prelude and the timing belt went out on the freeway. I felt like it was a betrayal, a breach of trust. It only had 38,000 miles on it, and it had no business doing that. I wanted nothing more to do with it because it had let me down."**

➤ **"That's like the time we got locked into our Cadillac. The battery died suddenly, and the power locks and windows wouldn't work. My husband finally got my window open wide enough for me to squeeze through and unlock the car from the outside, but I never trusted that car again. That was it for that car."**

—Washington group

Domestic automakers still have a long way to go to earn women's trust: 82% of women in the groups mentioned non-American makes as the cars they most trust, and only 18% named American makes. But when it came to cars they most distrust, they were far more egalitarian: There was a clean fifty-fifty split between American and non-American makes.

Yet sometimes a woman loses trust in her car through no fault of the car itself. Because of an accident, for instance. Or theft. Or life itself intervenes, and she loses trust in the car by association with some bad event. Such experiences can make or break a car in its owner's eyes, regardless of the quality of the car itself.

The Customer Satisfaction Index

Cars have gotten much better in the last ten years: safer, better-handling, more reliable. In fact, this past decade has seen a revolution in cars. The name of that revolution is Quality.

It is absolutely no coincidence that this was the same decade in which women began to buy cars in proportion to our numbers in the population. Women went for those makes we saw as delivering on quality, and it showed in the sales figures. With women half the new-car market, automakers had no choice but to respond by raising quality.

But how do we recognize quality? One increasingly popular measure is the customer satisfaction index, or CSI for short—a fancy name for market research on people who've recently bought new cars. And the key figure in automotive market research has been J. D. Power III (call him David, not John, and never J. D.), whose outfit is usually referred to as "an independent market research firm in California."

But the fact is that J. D. Power and Associates make most of their money from automakers. They sell their reports to them, and then charge them licensing fees to use the Power ratings in advertising and promotion. And in recent years they've coached automakers—for a fee—on how to score higher on the Power surveys.

This places the impartiality of J. D. Power's ratings in some question, especially when compared to those of *Consumer Reports*, whose researchers won't take so much as a cup of coffee, let alone money, from automakers. Yet J. D. Power has not only set standards for quality, but has also made quality—as measured by customer responses—a major issue in today's auto biz.

Each automaker does its own customer-satisfaction surveys for internal use, of course, but who's going to believe those? J. D. Power's are the ones most quoted and therefore the ones automakers most covet.

So who is J. D. Power? He's a former Ford manager who started up his own market-research firm in the seventies, as a service to automakers. Only those automakers who subscribe can receive the full reports; otherwise, he releases only the top ten cars in each category.

This is convenient: Those who do badly on the surveys

are shielded, while those who do well pay a licensing fee to advertise the fact. And since licensing fees are highly profitable, there are, as you may have guessed, a lot of different categories of J. D. Power surveys. So many that it's downright confusing.

To start with, there are awards for the best car, the best truck, the best sport-utility, and so on. And the best import or domestic. And the best make of car. And the best car or truck in its price and size . . .

Then all these are measured several ways. There is what Power calls initial quality but what the rest of the auto biz calls TGW, or "things gone wrong." Translation: defects. (Alas, the best cars do not have zero defects; right now they have about 50 defects per 100 cars, or a one out of two chance that your new car will need something fixed.)

Then there's customer satisfaction after three months of ownership. After a year of ownership. And after five years of ownership. As well as satisfaction with what Power politely calls "the dealership experience."

There are even more categories, but you get the picture: Just about every automaker, one way or another, can lay claim to a J. D. Power award.

Despite the confusion of categories, however, the Power surveys are absolutely consistent on one thing: The top three makes for overall customer satisfaction in the early nineties are the three big newcomers to the market: Lexus, Infiniti, and Saturn.

Lexus and Infiniti make luxury cars, while Saturn makes economy cars. Yet clearly, buyers of all three feel that they're getting value for their money.

Lexus is the luxury division of Toyota, Infiniti is the luxury division of Nissan. They were the first to devote themselves first and foremost to quality—not only of the car itself, but also of service at dealerships. Their aim was to make owning one of their cars a pleasure, and they succeeded.

Saturn took a very different tack. A semi-autonomous division of General Motors, it took advantage of its Tennessee location far from the stifling GM bureaucracy in Detroit to introduce a major innovation in how cars are sold: the "no-dicker sticker," where instead of the buyer having to negotiate the dealer down from an inflated "sticker price," a low sticker price was established and the haggling session cut out. The result: Although Saturn cars didn't do that well on the level of things-gone-wrong, they did so well on overall satisfaction that they trailed only Lexus and Infiniti.

Driving Your Image

➡ "In other parts of my life I don't like to stand out, but with the car I'm still protected in some way because it's not *me* that's standing out, it's the car. The car becomes an extension of me: I stand out, but not too far."

—Computer programmer, Washington

Cars do move us, not just physically but also emotionally. Anyone who's ever climbed behind the wheel of a full-size pickup knows the big grin of instant power that comes over her face the moment she looks out over that expanse of hood. Any woman who's ever slid behind the wheel of a sports car knows the quickening of the heartbeat. And few can resist the surge of confidence, even invulnerability, that comes from driving a luxury car, surrounded by leather and power controls on everything.

➡ "I drive a Pontiac station wagon, but at one time I had an old Corvette, and I sure felt sexy in that."

➡ "You *were* sexy in that!"

—New York group

We simply feel good in such cars, and very aware of how we look in them. We may like to think of ourselves as ultra-practical in our choice of car, but there's an undeniable emotional element too.

➡ **"There are some days I really do want a car that would express me, and then there are other days when I'm being good and practical and know I shouldn't be involved in such superficial things. But most days I do want a car that makes a statement."**

—Physiotherapist, Pennsylvania

➡ **"People say my car is a fun car. But my car is not fun if I'm pissed off. Nothing that car can do to me is fun if I'm pissed off. So to what extent does it depend on me, and to what extent on the car?"**

—Teacher, Oregon

A car that would express her? Yes: Because we are only human, we infuse our cars with identity. They are *ours*, and therefore they become part of us—part of who we are.

Of course there's no identity inherent in a car. That's why advertising whiz kids exist: to try as hard as they can to stick on an identity. "An identity is a car I can recognize from a hundred yards away," said one famed automotive designer, and that's probably still a good definition, although it covers only maybe two percent of all the cars on the road today. (The good news is that the cars with the clearest identity are often not the most expensive: the Mazda Miata, the VW Bug, and the Jeep Wrangler, for instance.)

For most of us, a car's identity is a mix of both the car itself and the driver.

A car's identity changes according to the owner. A Mazda Miata, for instance, means something very different to a brand-new college graduate than it does to her mother, who has just seen the last of her kids graduate and can now kick over the traces, sell the minivan, and get the dashing little convertible she always wanted.

➡ **"My youngest daughter graduates high school this summer, and I can't wait to trade in the Explorer and get myself a two-seater. I don't want anyone to ride with me anymore. It's funny, you raise children for** twenty-five years and then suddenly you get to have your own car."

➡ "It's like getting your identity back gain."

➡ "I'll be able to drive with the music I want. It'll be like being 17 again, except better."

➡ "Yes, we're all waiting for that day when we can let loose again, like a new stage of freedom. It's almost like when you were a teenager and starting to drive. It's so exciting! We've raised our children and they're great kids, but from here on in, the cars are for us!"

—Texas group

If we can afford it—and older women generally can—we use cars to express our lives. But it's also a two-way street: Our cars, no matter how new or how old, how desirable or how plain, change the way we feel about our lives. They make many of us feel more in control.

When I asked if their car made them feel more in control of their lives, or less, the majority of the women in the groups said more:

58.3% say their car makes them feel more in control.

Only 2.4% said the car made them feel less in control—these were young suburban mothers who felt trapped in child-ferrying schedules—while the others said it made no difference.

But cars can do more than give us a sense of control: They may even change our image of ourselves.

Every woman has different priorities, depending on where she is in her life—in feeling as well as age. We have many different aspects to our personalities, so ideally, we'd have many cars. I've driven every type of car there is in my work as an automotive journalist, and each one brings out something different in me. There are times when I love the smoothness of a

➡ **"You feel different in different cars. With the van, I have a real sense of power and safety. I'm higher than the rest of the world, and I know that nobody's going to mess with me on the road, because I can do them a lot more damage than they can do me. And then, by the same token, I look at my new convertible and I feel happy."**

—Retiree, California

17

good sedan, times when I want to raise hell and turn heads in a sports car, and times when I want to play macho in a pickup truck or outdoors woman in a sport-utility.

Yet no matter what type of car they drove, the women in the focus groups answered quite consistently when I asked them to rank ten words for how their cars made them feel (on a scale of 1 to 4, 4 being high, 1 being low).

Feeling	%	Feeling	%
Independent	3.71	Happy	3.13
Capable	3.34	Carefree	2.77
Free	3.30	Aggressive	2.66
Safe	3.18	Classy	2.28
Responsible	3.15	Sexy	2.11

Independent, capable, and free. The car itself is the statement—almost any car. The specific image is, you might say, merely the icing on the cake, the thing that makes you happy when you look at it.

The Color Chart

Auto dealers nurture the fond illusion that if they can get a woman to confide what color car she wants, they've clinched the deal. This, of course, says far more about the state of mind of auto dealers than that of women.

Detroit designers also have strange ideas about women and car colors. They tell me that women hate red cars and love white ones.

But in fact, not once, in all the focus-group discussions about what women want from a car, was the color mentioned as a deciding factor. Color simply didn't matter.

Still, I did ask the women in the groups what their favorite car color was. For the record (and so that Detroit can start adjusting its color charts), the main colors mentioned were:

➡ "I'm ready for a Jag."

➡ "Me too."

➡ "They're so classy-looking. Not showy."

➡ "They don't *have* to be showy."

—Pennsylvania group

18

Green	20.3%
Blue	19.5%
Red	18.8%
Black	15.0%
White	13.5%

Do I need to add that nobody gave a single vote to pastel pink or powder blue? Consider it mentioned.

The Male Mystique

Women give men a pretty bum rap when it comes to cars. The reason lies in a male problem of image: the male mystique.

We all know there's a male mystique of cars. Some way in which a car adds to a man's sense of his own masculinity. Not all men subscribe to this mystique—in fact, I'd like to think most no longer do—but the proportion who still hang onto it is high enough that women react with irony and disdain.

In reality, most men are driving exactly the same cars as most women—sensible, safe cars that are highly functional, comfortable, and pretty reliable. And they're driving them for the same reasons as women. But the male mystique blurs this fact. The result is that cars have become part of the gender wars.

➡ **"I think it's a possession thing. I have three brothers and I've watched how they react with cars, and for a lot of guys I know it's a possession thing versus an expression-of-self thing. I think guys tend to look at cars as an extension of their personality, while women try to *make* the car their personality."**

—Student, Pennsylvania

➡ **"What *is* this thing with men and cars?"**

—Legal assistant, New York

➡ "Do you ever play the do-you-want-to-drive game? I love to drive, so do-you-want-to-drive becomes a very loaded question, because I'm unwilling to give up the driving, even on a long trip. It's a power situation, I think."

➡ "Oh, yes, the driver's seat is definitely a position of power."

—California group

➡ "I remember a Sadie Hawkins dance and I was driving my Mom's car, her little Datsun or whatever it was, and I drove this guy way up into the mountains, and it was a rush, this sense of power at having this man in my car, and me being in control."

—Engineer, Texas

20

Women of all ages seem to agree with this student. Most women are convinced that men are irrational about cars—and that we, of course, are rational. Three-quarters (75.1%) say that women want something different from a car than men: first and foremost reliability, followed by utility/functionality, safety, style, and comfort.

Ten Things Women Say We Want in Cars *as opposed to men*

Reliability; men want to drive a jet fighter

Something practical, but we dream about cars that aren't

Dependability, not a phallic symbol

Comfort for our body size

Less ego attachment, more dependability

A car we can have an understanding with

A look

Safety *and* sexiness

Less sex, more class

Safety, speed, and lots of makeup mirrors

Part of the male mystique of cars is expressed in the language. Until not so long ago, men inevitably referred to their cars as "she," as in "she goes like a dream." I don't pretend to know why men feminized their cars—perhaps because they wanted to feel in control of them—but it seems to me an excellent sign that few still do so.

Then there is a certain late-night drunken-winking-leering possibility in mechanical terms such as push rods, ball bearings, pumps, power strokes, drive shafts, vibration, lubrication, bodies, couplings, and friction.

And consider the macho names of many car models: fast animals such as jaguars, mustangs, bearcats, and broncos, or masculine icons such as rangers, chieftains, and troopers. It's clearly time for women to start naming cars.

Until quite recently, a visit to any auto show was like entering a time warp: back to the fifties, when men were men and women were girls. There were dancing girls, shivering through their pancake makeup, bathing beauties draped seductively over hoods and steering wheels, and a distinct aroma of testosterone as the almost exclusively male crowd pressed around the fastest and showiest cars.

But perhaps the real reason why cars are so much part of the male mystique is that they do indeed, as women suspect, represent power.

True, women may well be less concerned than men with power in terms of engine size and performance. But there are many other, far more important, kinds of power. Women know that cars are empowering. That with a car, we feel more powerful, more capable.

When I lived in New York City, I didn't have a car—sensibly, I rented whenever I needed one—but I missed having one of my own. Owning my own car, I realized, made me feel more grown-up. People laughed when I told them this; after all, I looked grown-up enough. But what I meant by grown-up was that sense of being in control of my own life, of not being dependent on the schedules of others in the forms of buses and taxis and friends, of having not just the freedom to come and go as I wanted, but the sense of power and control that we all feel, some more consciously, some less, when we're at the wheel of a car.

Women know where the real power is. We know that engine size is as irrelevant as penis size. Power is not in the numbers, or even in the performance, but in the sense of control and independence.

➡ **"It's the car itself that's empowering. It can be any car at all, so long as it's *my* car."**

—Artist, British Columbia

What's Love Got to Do with It?

➡ "I suffered separation anxiety when I traded in my old BMW. I bought a new one, and this one and I are finally getting to be friends. It's like a new dog. It takes awhile to get the bond going, for the car to feel like mine; it's not instantaneous."

➡ "I've had separation anxiety with all my old cars—except for the Chevy. After I'd traded them in I'd go to the lot and see if they were still there. I'd keep thinking I saw them around town, and I'd find myself looking for them and wondering how they were."

—Texas group

A vice-president of one of the major car companies told me recently that the secret to selling cars to women was that women develop a kind of romance with their car.

His remark struck me as ironic. Traditionally, it's men who have had a romance with cars, while women have remained ultra-practical. A car is just a car, they'd say. Just metal and rubber. What's the romance about?

Even more ironic, though, was that he'd gotten it wrong.

"It's not a romance," I told him. "It's a relationship."

"That's what I mean," he said.

"No," I replied, "there's a world of difference between a romance and a relationship."

He looked puzzled, and for a moment I had a vision of psychologist Deborah Tannen hovering in the wings, whispering "You just don't understand."

Women's relationships with cars can be as complex as their relationships with men. In fact, the more I listened to the women in the groups talking, the more it struck me that many of the terms we use to talk about cars are also the terms we use to talk about our relationships with men: We're looking for long-term, steady relationships, not passing affairs.

Those of us who can afford it do indeed look for romance in a car—a car we can be madly, passionately in love with, like that snappy little convertible. That's the romantic lover, for sure. But it usually comes only after everything else is in place—after we're sure we have a solid, reliable car in the garage.

What we look for in a car is not so very different from what we look for in a man. What's love got to do with it? Everything that romance does not. When we love a car, it's rarely because it's the best-looking thing on the road. We may love it for its homeliness, or simply for the fact that it's served us so well, that it's stood by us and never let us down.

In fact, the closest relationships are very often with the oldest and ugliest cars—cars that could best be called funky, with no flashy components.

One of the first things many women with older cars say about them is the number of miles they've traveled in them. "It's an '86 Honda Civic and I've put 120,000 miles on it," or "I have an '88 Subaru with 95,000 miles on it." These are cars that go the distance. And though the paintwork is dull and the style outdated, we hate the very thought of parting with them. Those miles aren't just anonymous miles of road;

➡ **"I drive a ten-year-old Subaru wagon, and I call it Old Buddy, because there's nothing sexy or fun about it, it's just there for me. I can go anywhere in it and know that I'm going to be okay. It's been such a good friend."**

—Administrator, Oregon

➡ **"I love our old Nissan even though it's ugly. It's so safe, and besides, it loves me! It's like family now. We've become very attached."**

—Artist, New York

they're the miles of our lives, and the cars have taken us through. They've been there literally every inch of the way, so separation can be wrenching.

➡ **"My '89 Mazda pickup was just totaled—I was hit by someone running a stop sign—and it has to be replaced. I'm heartbroken. I'm attached to my truck, and a new one just won't be the same."**

—Production assistant, British Columbia

We hope for this kind of attachment, but we can make do without it. Most of us don't expect a car to make us happy; we do expect it to sort of sink into the background of our everyday lives—to be there, and never to obtrude by being unruly or uncooperative. An anonymous kind of car, right?

Well, maybe not. Ask women who own such cars what's the best thing about them, and a large number will say "It gets me there."

"Right, it does the job," said that male vice-president when I repeated this phrase to him.

"No," I said, "that's not quite the same thing. 'It gets me there' is personal. It's a relationship, even if not the most loving one. But the way you just put it is impersonal. The two sentences may mean the same thing, but they have a completely different slant."

This is the core of it: Women have more of a relationship with their cars than men. Cars are not merely objects, but part of the process of our lives, and that's reflected in how we talk and think about them.

And how we talk to them.

Yes, talk to them.

45% of women talk to their cars.

Of course, many women don't like to admit it. Talking to your car ranks down there with talking to yourself.

➡ **"Oh, no, don't tell me you talk to your car. . . ."**

➡ **"Are you sure *you* don't?"**

➡ **"Ah . . . Yes, well. . . ."**

—Texas group

24

One woman compared it to talking to a cat or a dog. Another, to a baby. You can see why:

39% of those who talk to their cars praise the car when it performs particularly well.

32% encourage the car when it's facing a cold start or a steep hill.

13.6% greet the car when they get into it.

13.6% plead with the car, begging it to come through for them.

Only 6.8% ever swear at their car. "That," as one woman said, "is bad karma."

➡ **"I used to talk to my bicycle when I was little, and I still talk the same way to my car— little murmurs of appreciation when I first get in, that sort of thing, like talking to a horse. I think when we're young we ride horses, and when we grow up we drive cars."**

—Software consultant, California

What Women Say to Their Cars

Praise

You're a good baby.

Good car.

Good kid.

Good job.

Good girl.

You swim well!

Encouragement

Come on, let's go.

Atta girl.

Come on, you can do it.

Just get me there.

It's okay, baby, it's okay.

Greeting

Hi, cutie.

Hi, car.

How are you doing today?

Hey, baby.

Let's go.

Pleas

Don't run out of gas now. Not now!

Please work!

Don't break down now!

Please don't die.

Thanks	Swearing
Bless you, little car.	Goddamn it, start!
Thanks!	Stop that damn noise!
You beauty.	Unspecified
Love	Chatty things, like to my cat.
I love you.	I keep it posted on where we're going.
I'll love you forever if you take care of me.	I sing to it.

The image of a girl and her horse comes to mind again when you consider that a third of all women pat their cars on occasion, and some do more:

33.1% pat their car.

11.3% stroke their car.

3% kiss their car.

Relax: Car-kissing is not a new fetish. The car gets kissed on the steering wheel after performing especially well—avoiding a potential accident, for instance, or passing the hundred-thousand-mile mark on the odometer.

And just as we name horses, so too we name cars.

Nearly a quarter of all women (24.1%) name their cars.

The most popular name by far is Betsy and its variants, Bessie and Betty.

Relatively few women give their cars male names—only 18%—while 44% give their cars female names, and 38% gender-neutral names. Color names are popular, like True Blue, Blue Streak, Blue Goose, for instance, or Red Racer, Scarlet, Vino, and Big Red.

"I think women tend to name their cars more than men," said one woman, "because of the kids. Kids like naming things." Another said her car had no name yet: "It's still too new." A third: "Most of my other cars have had names, but this one doesn't because I don't feel it has a lot of personality." And a fourth: "It's personal what I call the car. It's between me and the car. Sorry."

Okay, I confess: I've never had a name for any of my own cars. I've never kissed one either, though I did kiss the propeller of the plane I did my first solo flight in.

But I have patted cars. On the steering wheel when a car performed in some stellar manner—starting every morning on a cross-country trip in zero-degree weather, for instance, or getting down a mountain without brakes. Or on the hood as I get out of a car whose lines I particularly like, or that has just performed particularly well on a lap around the track.

Why do I do it? It just feels right. A gesture of appreciation. A sign. An acknowledgment that what's just happened is, one way or another, something special. That there is indeed a bond between me and this car.

Home, Haven, Sanctuary

They used to say that a man's home was his castle; it may be that a woman's car is hers. For many women, the car is where she is her own person, the place that is hers and hers alone. Where she can just be herself.

That kind of freedom is particularly important to women, perhaps because it's still relatively new. It's the freedom that comes with a certain amount of economic independence— with the wherewithal to buy a car, no matter how old or how beat up, and to run it wherever and whenever she likes.

➡ **"My Saab is a haven. It's invulnerable, and I'm invulnerable in it."**

—Social worker, Oregon

➡ **"I think in the car. It becomes my study. It's full of all my books and things, and I close the door and it becomes the one place where I can really think, without interruption. It's my haven of quietness."**

—Graduate student, Pennsylvania

A haven is a kind of home away from home, a place you can retreat to. But for women with children, the car is no haven: It's an extension of the house. As a homemaker in Washington put it:

➡ **"The car is literally part of my house. It's like the nursery. Nancy goes to sleep in the car, and I'll leave her there to sleep, in the garage, rather than wake her."**

Several women listed the things they keep in their cars—children's books, toys, diapers, dirty clothes, clean clothes, candies, newspapers, shoes. The contents of their houses sort of gravitate toward the car. "It's as though I take my house with me when I drive," said a Pennsylvania hotel receptionist. She ticked off everything from condoms to junk food, and concluded with:

➡ **"It's my kitchen, my den, my living room, my dining room, even my bedroom. There are times when I think I spend more time in my car than I do at home. Sometimes, in fact, I think my car *is* my home."**

Her bedroom? Yes indeed, and she didn't mean sex.

Several women talked about sleeping in their cars. The car was often seen as a last refuge, something that was theirs no matter what—a place where, if they had to, they could even sleep.

These were not destitute women. One Californian was in fact extremely wealthy, but clearly, like most women, she did not take money for granted. She found it comforting to know that she could always sleep in her car if she had to. For another, it was a matter of freedom rather than survival.

➡ **"There's a tremendous freedom in knowing that I can sleep in my car if I want to. I have two foam mattresses in the back of my van, and sometimes if I'm on a long trip I'll pull over and take a nap. I love the freedom of being able to take off and be self-sufficient."**

—Photographer, California

28

One graduate student had actually lived in her station wagon for three months, driving out of her Utah hometown each night to sleep up in the canyons.

➡ **"It wasn't real homelessness, just a college kid who couldn't get along with her mother. It was after I'd had green hair, but I was still a punk. There was definitely a certain romance to it. I was so tortured at the time anyway, and I'd tell people in coffeeshops 'I live in my car.' "**

Totems

A few women described their car as "my sanctuary." This word kept echoing in my head as I realized how many totems women carry in their cars—small items of special personal significance. Just over 20 percent keep a totem in their car, and some keep more than one.

This is far less strange than it may sound. Most pilots, for instance, carry some form of totem with them when they fly. They don't tell anyone about it, of course—at least, very rarely. Perhaps that's because most pilots are men, and they're embarrassed to be seen as superstitious.

But the totems aren't so much superstition as a means of making the car yours, investing it with something that is particularly meaningful to you—something, in fact, *of* you. Perhaps that's why only one woman had a Saint Christopher medal in her car, and only two had fuzzy dice. The most popular totems by far were either gifts or found items, such as beads, toy animals, and natural objects (stones, crystals, seashells, feathers). Nearly all these totems had, as totems should, some special meaning. Stones from a seashore or a river where the driver had been in the car with someone special; Mardi Gras beads or a bracelet made by a young daughter or niece; toy animals that made her feel safe as she drove, like a yellow protector alligator, or a snake.

- ➡ "I love stones—quartz and sea glass and so on—so I pick them up and keep them in my car."

- ➡ "So your car's kind of like your little sanctuary? Where do you keep them? On the floor?"

- ➡ "All around: in the glove compartment, in the side pockets. I sort of keep the places the car's been."

- ➡ "I love that. I'm going to do that."

—New York group

Some totems were exotic, like an African travel god given one woman by her 103-year-old aunt. Some were nostalgic, such as a purple satin ribbon from another woman's very first car. (The ribbon had been tied to the steering wheel when she was given the car.) Some were, well, eccentric; one woman kept birth-control pills on her dashboard. ("It's the only place I'll be sure to see them every day," she reasoned.)

I understand the impulse. I keep totems on my desk rather than in my car, but when I drove cross-country alone a couple of years ago, I took with me a cuddly toy frog. (I just liked the *idea* of a cuddly toy frog.) It sat on my lap the whole way across America, and from time to time I'd stroke it. Okay, yes, I also talked to it. That frog got me safely to Seattle. I admit the car helped too. But I still have that frog, and I'd never attempt another cross-country trip without it.

Intimate Spaces

- ➡ "When you're in a car, you're thrown up against each other, and everything else is screened out. So you get these enclosed moments. Like when I was driving my mother back to San Francisco recently, and we began to talk about sex. We told each other real things, such as we never had all the years we lived together in the same house. And as we drove on, I had this wonderful awareness of us as two women moving together through the world."

—Homemaker, California

Enclosed moments of intimacy—of frank revelation as opposed to the comforting chitchat that takes up most of our talk—often happen in a car because it is a small, defined space that enfolds its occupants safely against the world. It's a sort of metal womb, a comforting counterpoint to the ridiculous cliché of the car as phallic symbol.

30

Automotive intimacy lies in conversation, not sex.

➡ **"The car is the only place my husband and I are really alone. It's where we can have a truly private conversation, with no fear of interruption from the kids. Sometimes I think we're so busy with work and family life that we forget how to really talk to each other. So I look forward to the times when it's just the two of us, coming back from some function late at night. Sometimes we'll just sit in the driveway and keep on talking, staring ahead at the garage door."**

—Lawyer, Texas

Note that this couple look not at each other but out the windshield. The strange thing about intimacy is that it's often easier if you're *not* looking at each other. In a car, you're both looking at the road ahead, the surface of your minds occupied with the business of driving: the driver steering and braking, accelerating and shifting, the passenger registering the road, riding shotgun as it were. The conscious self is otherwise occupied, leaving the subconscious free to emerge.

People have told me things in cars that they said they'd never told anyone before. Come to think of it, I have told other people such things too. And not just to friends and lovers. Comparative strangers know things about me that close friends don't, simply because, by chance—"I'll give you a lift home"—we were enclosed together by metal and motion.

"That's it—something about the motion, perhaps," said the lawyer. "Like the way you can lull children to sleep in the backseat by driving them around the block."

But I think it's more than that. There's something in it of the old psychoanalyst's trick: Take away eye contact and the words and the associations flow more freely.

It may sound odd to think of the car as some kind of therapeutic environment, but several women say they use it that way, as do many men. They get into their cars and just drive, anywhere and nowhere, as if the physical driving could drive out the problems besetting them. Others insist that it works better when the problem is sitting right there beside you.

➡ **"The car is by far the best place to talk out differences with your husband or your lover. Not bed, not the kitchen. The car. There, he's got nowhere to run to. He can't get up and go get a drink, he can't pick up the newspaper, he can't evade the issue. Especially if it's you who's driving."**

—Writer, California

➡ **"We'd gone out to this wonderful restaurant, candlelit dinner and all, and then afterward we got into his car and just drove around, and it was as though if we stopped driving we'd break something between us. And after we'd been driving an hour or so like that, not going anywhere in particular, that's when he asked me to marry him."**

—Architect, Oregon

But it works the other way too. A sizable percentage of marriage proposals seem to have been made in a car, perhaps because a man finds it easier to garner his courage when he is side by side with the woman he loves instead of face to face.

Sometimes it seems that the whole cycle of life takes place in cars. One woman says her Volkswagen became all the more precious to her after it became the site of "the near birth of my first child." The baby was born just ten minutes after she and her husband reached the hospital.

Night encourages enclosed moments. That's when the darkness wraps itself around you, and on a long trip, it's as though you are traversing a mysterious emptiness. It's easy to imagine then that you and your passengers are the only living creatures in the world, bound to each other in this metal cocoon traveling through the void.

One of the most moving of such moments, shared by a New Hampshire teacher, could have happened only at night.

➡ **"When my youngest daughter was about eight, she had just discovered death, and she was spooked, having real terrors. One night we were driving home from Boston, my husband and I in the front of the car and** she in the back, and she began asking us questions about dying, and what happens. You couldn't see anything outside; there were just these questions, the kind of questions you're afraid to ask in the light, and our answers. It was as though we were in a perfectly sealed capsule, safe and protected against the outside."

Dreaming Cars

➡ "I always have car dreams. It sort of parallels life stuff."

➡ "Yes, it's like a symbolic feedback of how you're taking care of yourself. So if I have a dream that I'm driving too fast or I run out of gas, I know I haven't been getting enough sleep or haven't been eating right, and it's time to pay attention."

➡ "Or maybe you're just making things come right in a dream. Like it's stressful riding with someone who won't ask for directions, so I have dreams in which he actually does pull over and ask!"

—New York group

Cars play such a major role in our everyday lives, it should come as no surprise when they turn up in our everynight lives too.

Over a quarter of the women in the focus groups (27.8%) have dreams about cars and driving.

Most of these dreams are one of two kinds: either being anxious and out of control, or being relaxed and in control.

One of the great things about car dreams is that you

don't have to be a psychoanalyst to figure them out. There's a clear symbolism, for instance, in the fact that the out-of-control dreams often involve steep hills. In the downhill dreams, the brakes are the culprit, and the driver is hurtling along way too fast.

➡ **"I have a recurring dream of trying to make it over the hills to my friend's house and the brakes failing on the downhill, with me maneuvering in and out of school areas, trying to avoid the children. . . ."**

➡ **"I once dreamed I was at the wheel of a huge eighteen-wheeler, and on a long downhill the brakes went, and I'm hurtling down the hill, totally out of control, and then this herd of schoolgirls on bicycles, all in flowing white dresses, crosses the road ahead of me. . . ."**

—California group

Uphill dreams are dreams of backsliding.

➡ **"Right now I'm having a recurring dream of driving up a steep hill, so steep that I'm lying back in the car and I'm going, 'Oh, God, help me make it to the top of this hill because it's so steep I'm afraid I'm going to slide back down.' [She grins.] But I make it."**

➡ **"I dream again and again of things going wrong as I'm driving, but especially of suddenly finding that I'm going backward, very fast, and I can't stop the car."**

—Pennsylvania group

Other out-of-control dreams involve a driverless car.

➡ **"Somebody else is driving and they're taking me some place, and I'm in the backseat, and suddenly I realize that there's nobody at all in the front: The car's still moving but nobody's actually driving it."**

—Stockbroker, Texas

Dreams of crashes also involve issues of control.

➡ **"I have scary dreams about going very fast, someone else driving and me the passenger, and I can see the crash coming and there's nothing I can do about it."**

➡ **"I'll be driving through the desert and there'll be a huge fiery crash that I just avoid."**

➡ **"I remember childhood dreams of being in cars where my parents were driving and something horrible happened. In retrospect it was directly symbolic of what was going on, since they were going through a really rough time and I was scared they were going to split up."**

➡ **"Did they?"**

➡ **"No, they didn't. I guess I worked it out in my dreams for them."**

—British Columbia group

And dreams of bridges need no interpretation.

➡ **"When I first learned to drive, I had a dream that I was about to drive off the top of the Fremont Bridge, this very high bridge in Portland."**

➡ **"I have a recurring dream about being in a car on a high bridge—I don't know which bridge—and the bridge swaying, and I can't move."**

—Oregon group

Dreams of being in control are less dramatic, but they can be very seductive: The sensations of driving—the wind, the scenery, the sounds—are vivid, and nothing can touch you.

➡ **"I'm just going really fast, cruising along on one of those coast roads, the wind blowing in my hair, a wonderful sensation."**

➡ "That's like when I dream I'm at the wheel of a gullwing Mercedes, the one car I really lust after, and I'm driving it very fast down this long straight road with no end, going someplace but no place in particular."

➡ "And absolutely in control of your fate."

➡ "Absolutely."

—Washington group

Many dreams have a strong element of escape fantasy, of being free of the usual world and its constraints, and taken into another, more romantic world.

➡ "My car dreams are so romantic. I'm zooming around the French Riviera on the Grand Corniche. Nothing much happens but it's very glamorous."

➡ "Somebody must be watching."

➡ "Oh, *everybody's* watching . . ."

—California group

Sometimes dreams deal very directly with driving.

➡ "I usually dream about cars after I've been on a long road trip, so I'm back in my own bed but my mind is still on the road. The landscape shifts and I'll find myself at the edge of some precipice or driving along in desert canyonlands. After a long road trip it's like you're still moving, so I have these sort of dislocated dreams for a few nights. They're more about disorientation than anything."

—Photographer, California

Sometimes, well . . .

➡ "I learned to drive a shift stick around the Bennington monument in southern Vermont, and I used to dream about lurching around this obelisk trying to figure out how to engage the gears. I guess it doesn't take much to find the phallic symbolism there."

—Therapist, New York

And sometimes they're about people. They may be about potential relationships.

➡ "I've had a whole group of dreams about a man I know. He's not a man I'm interested in or anything like that, at least not that I'm aware of, but often he'll appear in the dream in a car. Some car that it looks like he should have. Sometimes he just arrives in the car, sometimes he offers me a ride. I don't know if I accept or not. I don't even know why I'm dreaming about him. . . ."

—Office clerk, Pennsylvania

Or they may be about existing relationships.

➡ "Just last week I dreamed I had four flat tires, and my boyfriend and I are out there—we're sort of on the skids right now—and he's scratching his head trying to figure out what to do. There's all these people offering help, and I'm saying 'Let's take their help,' but he's like '*I* can take care of this, missy. . . .' "

—Administrative assistant, Texas

What's most noticeable is that women rarely dream about specific cars. The precise piece of sheet metal is unimportant; it's the driving that is the essence, because the very act of driving is still a loaded symbol for most women, one full of possibilities. Of control and loss of control of your own life, for instance. Of autonomy lost and found. Of independence. And of mobility and freedom.

38

2.

Buying Your Car

Making the Choice

Some people just *know* which car they want. They march on into a dealer's showroom, negotiate the price, and drive the car home with the deal done.

Most of us, whether female or male, are not possessed of such fine decisiveness. Yet women make other purchasing choices with no problem. While most men can dither for ages over buying a new suit, for instance, most women are quite businesslike about it. The reason is simple: They know what they want.

If you want to wear a suit to work, you're not going to get an evening suit. You know the length you want, you know you don't want it overtly sexy, you know you don't want frills or froufrou. You also know it has to wear well all day, it has to be comfortable, and it has to be professional-looking. And of course it has to be within your budget. The rest is taste—and that certain something that tells you: Yes, this is you.

With a car, you need to be equally specific. Equally certain, that is, about what you want it for (what kind of driving you do, on what kinds of roads, in what kinds of weather). And about your budget. And your taste.

But of course there are two major differences when it comes to buying a car.

One: A car usually costs a lot more than a new suit.

(I say "usually," because at the upper reaches of designer clothing, you can indeed spend more on a suit than on a small car.)

Two: Your car has to be, first and foremost, utterly reliable.

So it's worth doing a bit of self-questioning and a little research before deciding on a car. You probably worked hard for the money. Don't be in a rush to let it go.

People in the car business tell me that most car buyers spend no more than an hour or two shopping for a car, and usually buy the first car they test-drive. I find this shocking. How often have you bought the first suit you tried on, without trying on a few others?

In fact, those people in the car biz are wrong, at least when it comes to women. Most women are pretty tough buyers.

Myth: Women know less about cars, so tend to buy them on impulse.

Reality: Nearly half—43%—of women do a lot of research before buying a car, another 35% do some research, 14% do a little, and only 8% do none.

This helps explain why car dealers now worry when they see a woman walking into a showroom. Time was, they rubbed their hands in anticipation of an easy sale at a high markup. Now they know that very often, she has a sheaf of information and numbers tucked away in her purse. And they know that a well-informed buyer is going to get a better price, no matter how much of a sales job they try on her.

So be that well-informed buyer.

Know what you want and how much you're willing to pay for it.

Here's how.

First, narrow your choice of car to three, four, or five models. These are the cars you'll test-drive. Ask yourself some basic questions about what you want from a car, and the answers will help you decide.

The Questions

1. *How do you use your car?*
   - Do you use it mainly to run errands in town, in and out of the car all the time, or for a daily commute?
   - Do you take long trips by car?
   - How much "stuff"—luggage, sports equipment, papers, professional equipment—do you carry in your car?
   - Do you usually drive alone or with passengers? How many passengers?
   - Do you carry children often?
   - Do you carry animals?

2. *How do you drive your car?*
   - Do you enjoy the act of driving?
   - Do you enjoy the sense of being in control of a car?
   - Do you like to drive fast?
   - Do you enjoy zipping in and out of traffic?
   - Do you think of your car as just a means of getting from Point A to Point B in relative comfort and safety, or do you believe in the joys of the road?

3. *How do you think of yourself in a car?*
   - Do you want to cut a fine figure, or do you simply not care?
   - If you do care, what kind of fine figure? Elegant? Sporty? Daring? Sensible? Independent-minded? Wildwoman?

4. *Where do you live?*
   - A cold climate or a warm one?
   - How much rain, snow, and ice do you have?
   - How hilly or flat is it?

5. *What kind of body do you have?*
   - **Are you short or tall?**
   - **Do you prefer a narrow seat or a wide one?**
   - **Do you have back trouble?**

6. *And of course the most important question of all: How much can you afford?*
   - **What is your absolute cutoff point?**
   - **Can you afford to maintain the car you want, including registration, insurance, and maintenance?**

Answer these questions honestly and then keep the answers in mind while you consider the nine different types of vehicle on the market. You might also want to refer to "How to Talk Engines," on page 210, and to "Tech Talk Translated," on page 285.

The Nine Car Types

The Sedan

This is the most popular type of car: a four-door passenger car with a separate trunk. Sedans may be subcompact, compact, midsize, or large. Engine size and physical dimensions vary within each category. So does the degree of luxury, and, of course, cost.

Pluses You can carry three or four passengers in comfort. The rear doors give easy access to the backseat. Low liftovers on the trunks of most new sedans make getting things into and out of the trunk far easier than in the past.

Minuses For some, the sedan has too many associations with the word "sedate." Many of us may indeed be sedate, but we don't like to admit it. Sedans rarely catch your eye on the road.

Some automakers make "sports sedans"—there's even a Volvo sports sedan. These have larger engines, stiffer suspension, and a more sporty driving "feel," and don't feel at all sedate—a clear case of having your cake and driving it too.

The Coupe

The word coupe comes from the French *coupé*, meaning "cut," because it's like a sedan except with the rear doors cut out. This means that coupes have sportier styling than sedans—more swoop down to the trunklid. Coupes are generally subcompact, compact, or midsize.

Pluses Coupes are generally more stylish than sedans.

Minuses The backseat problem: Passengers may find it hard to climb in and out of the back. And getting children in and out of child seats in the back is a back-wrencher.

The Hatchback

This may be a sedan or a coupe, but without a separate trunk at the rear. Instead, the whole of the back opens up. (It's known as a third or a fifth door.) Backseats fold down to create lots of cargo room.

Pluses Three-door hatchbacks are generally very stylish. (Five-door ones are a bit clunkier.) There's lots of room for carrying everything from animals to luggage. You can also sleep in the car in a pinch.

Minuses Fold-down rear seats are not as comfortable as regular ones.

The Sports Car

A sports car generally has two seats (though there may be room for two people without legs in the back). It's lower to the ground than a sedan, is sometimes but not necessarily a convertible, and tends to have a stiffer suspension and higher horsepower, thus making it more of "a driver's car"— that is, fun to drive. Most sports cars are rear-wheel drive, but front-wheel-drive ones are gaining ground.

Men go in for lengthy discussions on what is a "true" sports car. The general idea seems to be that it's designed to go fast and sacrifices everything else—comfort, economy, common sense—to that principle. But the advent of the Mazda Miata in 1989 proved them wrong: Sports cars can be fun and pretty and fast *and* reliable and comfortable and easy to drive.

Pluses They're head-turners. You look great in them. They look great on you. They're lots of fun to drive, and the convertibles are downright romantic. They may or may not be faster than a sedan, but they certainly feel that way since they're smaller and nippier.

Minuses They're harder to get in and out of than a regular car because they're lower to the ground, and there's generally little room for luggage. They are the least practical of cars, which might be why they're the most fun.

Myth: Women don't like flashy red sports cars.

Reality: 26.1% love them, 33.1% like them, 30% are so-so about them, and only 10.8% hate them.

The Sport-Utility

These used to be called Jeeps, and they were strictly utilitarian vehicles until someone had the brainstorm of putting four doors on them instead of two, and presto—you had a family vehicle. Sales took off.

When Chrysler took over Jeep, it began to enforce the trademark. The word "jeep" couldn't be used generically anymore. This was a problem for Chrysler's competitors, who saw a new market and began to make similar vehicles. Unable to call them jeeps, since only Jeeps were jeeps (if you follow me), some Detroit genius came up with the moniker "sport-utility vehicle" (SUV or sport-ute for short). Despite the incredibly clumsy name, sport-utes quickly became hot sales items.

Most come with macho names—Ranger, Bronco, Pathfinder, Cherokee, Explorer, Wrangler, Rodeo, and so on—and have four-wheel drive. They're higher off the road than regular cars (in fact, some are typed in the car biz as trucks, not cars at all), and this means they can handle rough unpaved tracks that regular cars can't. It also means they're marketed as outdoors-wildernessy vehicles, even though 95% to 99% (depending on who's spouting figures) are never driven anywhere tougher than a gravel driveway. Despite the macho image, or perhaps because of it, women now buy one-third of all sport-utes and half of the luxury ones.

The latest thing in sport-utes: USUs. No relation to UFOs, these are "urban sport-utes." They are four-door sub-compact sport-utes, baby siblings of the Cherokees and Explorers, and far less expensive. They look rather like overgrown Tonka toys, and are just plain cute (as well as practical). Suzuki paved the way with the four-door Side-kick. In 1995, Kia followed with the Sportage, Geo introduced a four-door Tracker, and Toyota began selling the RAV-4, a bestseller in Japan.

Pluses Drivers love the height off the road, because it provides better traffic visibility. You feel big, bad, and beautiful. And you have lots of cargo space.

Minuses Full-time four-wheel drive is really not necessary unless you're driving through jungles or Antarctica. You generally have to clamber up into the driver's seat, though some are now coming with steps, while the new urban sport-utes are just the right height. Most sport-utes are heavy vehicles, so have bad gas mileage. And small, two-door sport-utes have a particularly high percentage of rollover accidents due to the combination of height off the road (known in car-biz lingo as a high center of gravity) and a short wheelbase (the distance between the front and rear wheels). Note that sport-utes are more expensive than comparably powered sedans or coupes.

➡ **"I want a Jeep, a Cherokee Limited."**

➡ **"Yes, I would have guessed you as a Jeep. There's something about your packaging that makes you look like you'd fit one of those."**

—British Columbia group

Buying Your Car

47

Myth: The majority of minivan drivers are women, because this is the Mom-with-kids vehicle.

Reality: Over half of all minivan drivers are men. It seems men have kids too. And hobbies. And businesses.

The Station Wagon

Usually known simply as wagons, these look like sedans with an extra section added onto the back, which is what they are. Instead of a rear window curving down to the trunk lid, the roof continues back to create a larger luggage compartment.

Pluses Lots of cargo room. More economical to run than a sport-ute or a minivan.

Minuses Something of an image problem, though since minivans have taken over as the prime I'm-just-waiting-till-the-kids-are-grown vehicle in recent years, wagons are making a comeback.

The Minivan

The modern answer to the station wagon: taller, higher off the road, with a lot more interior space. Minivans began as a kind of cross between the old Volkswagen vans and a station wagon, and have taken the place of the station wagon as the one type of vehicle that signifies "Mom with kids," despite the fact that over half of minivan drivers are men.

Like sport-utes, minivans are not cars but trucks. And although most safety standards for regular cars will apply also to minivans, sport-utes, and pickup trucks by 1997, they still have a higher center of gravity than regular cars, and you can't power them round corners like you can a regular car.

Pluses Most minivans have some form of step, which makes them easier to get in and out of than a sport-ute. And they can carry an immense amount of passengers and luggage. Kids love them because it's like riding inside a moving rec room. Interiors are getting downright luxurious, with seats as comfortable as Barcaloungers.

Minuses Still typecast, despite the facts, as a Mom-with-kid vehicle. Not for someone who loves the art of driving.

The Pickup Truck

At least there's no doubt that a pickup is a truck. The pickup has an open bed behind the cab, which has a single bench seat seating two or three (though some "extended cabs" can seat a couple of kids behind). The open bed makes the pickup the ideal vehicle for hauling stuff, which is why it's so popular with farmers and builders. In fact, Ford's F150 is the best-selling vehicle of any kind in the United States.

Compact pickups, with shorter beds, became fashionable in the eighties as the latest fun vehicle with the surfing set, who throw the boards in the back and make for the water.

Pluses Lots of room in back for hauling stuff. A different image for a woman.

Minuses Lots of wasted room in the back if you don't haul stuff. Poor handling when compared to a regular car.

The Convertible

Any car whose top can be lowered onto or into the trunk lid, or taken off all together. Most have canvas tops, thus the word "ragtop," though some hard-top convertibles are also available. Some tops are raised and lowered by hand, others by power controls. It usually takes anywhere from a couple of seconds (as with the manual Miata) to seventeen seconds (with some of the fancier power-controlled tops) to lower or raise the top. On a Jeep Wrangler, it can take ten minutes.

Most ragtops have plastic rear windows, though some more expensive ones have glass (giving clearer vision and allowing a built-in defroster). The accepted wisdom has it that ragtops are for the South, not for the North. As often, the accepted wisdom is wrong.

Pluses Romance. Image. Fun.

Minuses Open-top driving can be tiring: Wind and sun take their toll on your brain as well as your hair and face. You're also giving up a certain amount of safety for image, unless you have a very expensive convertible with a pop-up roll bar.

➡ **"When the shooting stars were out, my husband and I took the pickup over to my grandfather's farm, put two lawn chairs in the back, and drank Wild Turkey as we watched the stars and had this great conversation about God and the cosmos."**

—Office manager, Pennsylvania

➡ "It took me until my mid-forties to realize I was a top-down kind of girl. Then I saw a little silver Miata and was absolutely smitten. I said to my husband, "We really have to talk," and he was very relieved when he realized it was just a car. He bought it for me, and he was fine with that until one night he caught me sneaking into the garage and patting the taillights. He didn't think this was the sign of a healthy woman."

—Administrator, California

➡ "There's one guy at work who's such a jerk, and he has this gorgeous red convertible Porsche. And I see him getting into it at the end of the day and I think, 'Yeah, you've got a great car, but you're still a jerk.' "

➡ "It's true: Guys drive these cars because they think it makes them look good. But it doesn't work that way. If anything, they make the car look bad."

➡ "And women make it look good. It's so exciting when you see a woman driving a really great car."

—New York group

Now that you know what you want from a car, what type of car you want, and what you can afford, it's time to narrow the choice down to three or four models. How? Look, talk, and read.

Look at other cars on the road.

Talk to friends, family, and acquaintances about their cars.

And read: *Consumer Reports* puts out a new-car issue every April that covers most of the market, or you can go to the automotive section of the library or any good bookstore and look through reputable new-car reports, such as *Edmund's Car Buyer's Price Guide*, the *AutoIntelligence New Car Decision Maker*, or *The Complete Car Cost Guide* from IntelliChoice.

But first, if whether you buy an import or a domestic car is important to you, you'll want to read the next section, since in this as in so much else with cars, all is not quite as it seems.

Who Makes What, Where

American-made cars are far better than they were ten years ago; in fact, they're better than Japanese cars were ten years ago. But of course Japanese cars have also improved, so the "quality gap" is still there, though narrowed to the extent that it no longer plays a major role in most women's choice of car.

Nowadays, a Japanese car may in fact be American-made, and an American car Japanese-made. Not just the parts, but the whole car, down to the last button. Let alone made in Mexico, Canada, or Korea.

Confused? I don't blame you. So here's a quick look at who makes what, who owns who, and the whole new world of transplants, joint ventures, automotive twins, and the idea of "the world car."

Who Makes What

Each of the Big Three—the three Detroit-based American automakers—makes cars with several brand names (known as "marques" or "badges") by dividing its operations into different divisions. The Japanese followed suit in the eighties by setting up luxury-car divisions with different names.

Company	Brand names
Chrysler	Dodge, Plymouth, Jeep-Eagle, Chrysler
Ford	Lincoln-Mercury, Ford
General Motors	Chevrolet, Pontiac, Buick, Cadillac, Oldsmobile, Saturn, Geo, GMC
Honda	Acura, Honda
Nissan	Infiniti, Nissan
Rolls-Royce	Rolls-Royce, Bentley
Toyota	Lexus, Toyota
Volkswagen	Audi, Volkswagen

This means that eight automakers produce twenty-four brands between them, more than half of the forty-three currently sold in North America.

Who Owns What

Large automakers, like large companies in every other business, tend to buy smaller ones. The smaller ones retain their separate corporate identity, so unless you read the business pages carefully, you'd never know that in the early nineties, for instance, Ford bought Jaguar, BMW bought Land Rover, and General Motors bought Saab.

Sometimes, instead of buying the whole thing, or even a controlling interest, the larger company will buy a sizable percentage of shares of the smaller company's stock. Ford owns a large percentage of both Kia and Mazda, GM owns a percentage of Isuzu and Suzuki, while Chrysler used to own part of Mitsubishi. These percentages often accompany joint-venture projects, where the two companies produce cars together, each one selling the same car under its own badge. (See "Twins" on page 55).

The Koreans and the Japanese play the same game with each other: Mitsubishi has a stake in Hyundai, for example, Nissan in Subaru, and Mazda in Kia.

Transplants

Trying to figure out exactly *where* a car was made can be tough. The old distinction between import and domestic cars no longer applies. Nearly all cars are now, one way or another, international.

To start with:

Not all cars with import nameplates are imports.

Most of the Japanese automakers are now designing and producing cars in the United States. The American plants, and the cars they produce, are called transplants. Some of these are classified officially as domestic cars since they contain over 75 percent American-made parts. The transplants include Hondas (made in Ohio), Toyotas (made in Kentucky), Mazdas (made in Michigan), Nissans (made in Tennessee), Mitsubishis (made in Illinois), Subarus (made in Indiana), Suzukis (made in Ontario, Canada), and Isuzus (made in Indiana). In 1994 the Europeans joined the transplants with BMW starting up an assembly plant in South Carolina, and Mercedes-Benz in Alabama.

Then again . . .

Not all cars with domestic nameplates are domestics.

Some are made in Canada or Mexico at plants belonging to American automakers. Others are made in Asia and "rebadged" by domestic automakers, such as the Dodge Stealth (Mitsubishi) and the Ford Aspire (Kia).

In 1992 Congress passed the American Automobile Labeling Act, which said that every car sold in the United States must show its percentage of domestic-parts content on its window sticker. This was intended to clear up some of the confusion. Instead, it makes the confusion worse.

Why? First, the stickers ignore where the cars were assembled—that is, where all the parts were put together into the finished car. Second, the law counts parts differently, giving higher weight to a parts supplier owned by the automaker, for instance, so that a car with 53% of its content made in the United States may be labeled as low as 11%.

Best advice: Ignore domestic-parts content. It's misleading.

Coproductions or Joint Ventures

As if transplants hadn't muddied the import/domestic waters enough, many automakers are now involved in coproductions across national lines. General Motors and Toyota produce Geos together in California. Other Geos are rebadged Suzukis and Isuzus made either in the States or in Canada. Chrysler and Mitsubishi were partners for many years in Diamond-Star Motors, which produced the Eagle Talon and the Mitsubishi Eclipse in Illinois. Mazda builds some Fords in the States, and Ford builds some Mazdas.

The international waters get muddier still when you consider a vehicle like the Mercury Villager minivan, which is also known, under the Nissan badge, as the Nissan Quest. These were designed and engineered by Nissan in Japan, but are built and assembled by Ford in the States.

The only sensible conclusion is to forget about what's domestic and what's imported, and to start thinking about all cars as international, or world cars. Making cars is big business, and big business doesn't care about national borders.

➡ "I got on my high horse about buying American-made a few years ago, but I came down off it when I realized that though it may have been assembled in America, there were parts from here and parts from there, and most of the parts did not have a zip code within the United States."

➡ "But American cars *are* getting better."

➡ "Yes, because they're being made of foreign parts."

—Washington group

Twins

Yes, cars too can be twins. This happens in three ways:

1. **An American automaker makes the same car—that is, same engine, same chassis, same body, with different exterior and interior touches—and badges it two or even three different ways for its different divisions.**

2. **A joint-venture car is badged differently for each of the partners in the venture.**

3. **One automaker simply makes the car for another and puts the other's badge on it.**

Here's a list of some of the more popular twins. Some are identical except for the badges, while others are fraternal twins, with slight changes in outward appearance and interior design. Sometimes one is slightly more expensive than the other. Compare prices carefully. You might be able to get a better price at one make's dealership than at the other, because even though the cars are twins, most people don't know it. One twin might sell well and the other slowly, making dealers of the slower-selling model more willing to accept a lower negotiated price.

Chrysler Cirrus/
Dodge Stratus

Dodge Intrepid/
Chrysler Concorde

Dodge Neon/
Plymouth Neon

Dodge Stealth/
Mitsubishi 3000

Eagle Talon/
Mitsubishi Eclipse

Ford Contour/
Mercury Mystique

Ford Explorer/
Mazda Navajo

Ford Probe/
Mazda MX6

Ford Taurus/
Mercury Sable

Geo Prizm/
Toyota Corolla

Geo Storm/
Isuzu Impulse

Geo Tracker/
Suzuki Sidekick

GMC Jimmy/
Chevy S-10 Blazer

Isuzu Rodeo/
Honda Passport

Mercury Villager/
Nissan Quest

Pontiac Firebird/
Chevy Camaro

World Cars

Ford was the first to call open attention to the irrelevance of national origin in today's automaking world by calling the midsize car it introduced in Europe in 1994 the Mondeo, or "world car." (Evidently deciding that North America was not ready for the worldly truth, Ford made the American version into twins: the Ford Contour and the Mercury Mystique.)

For the first time, the same basic model, with only cosmetic changes, was being sold the world over. That sounds so rational that the only real question is why on earth international automakers insisted on doubling and tripling their costs by making separate cars for Europe and North America all these years. But the Mondeo is not only sold the world over, it is also *made* the world over, with design, assembly, and parts supply in different parts of the world. Rather like a reverse-direction transplant car, in fact.

The Four Prices of a New Car

The little matter of cost is far more pertinent to most people than where a car was made.

Make that the very large matter of cost.

Americans spend an average of twenty-nine weeks' pay—over half the average annual income—on a new car. I think that's outrageous.

A car is important, true, but not *that* important. If you're spending more than a third of your annual income on a car, you're buying one that's too expensive for you to maintain with ease. You don't want car payments to become a millstone around your neck. What pleasure is there in having your own car then?

Still, even a third of your annual income is a lot of money, so do some research before you fork it over. Cars, you see, do not have a single price. In fact, car pricing is a consumer nightmare: Each and every car on the market (with the exception of Saturn cars, which sell at the same price everywhere) has no less than four prices.

Yes, four. And they're all variable.

Infuriating? You bet.

Irrational? Absolutely.

Legal? I'm afraid so.

But once you get a handle on these prices and know what they represent, you can use them to your advantage in buying a new car. It's the time-tested principle: Know thine enemy.

The four prices are the sticker price, the dealer invoice, the true invoice, and what you pay.

The Sticker Price

The sticker price is based on the Manufacturer's Suggested Retail Price, or MSRP. This is exactly what it says. It is not *the* price of the car, merely the amount the manufacturer suggests the dealer sell it at. It allows for a hefty profit for the dealer—anywhere from 7% to 25%, depending on the car, with an average of 17–18%. (Generally the more expensive the car, the higher the profit margin.)

The MSRP is displayed, by law, on a window sticker known as *the Monroney*, after the congressman who got it declared mandatory in the interest of consumer protection. The sticker also gives EPA mileage estimates, the specifications of the car (make, model, engine configuration, and size), a full list of all standard and optional equipment on the car, destination or delivery fees, the VIN number (vehicle identification number), and domestic-parts content.

The Monroney was a good idea, but as far as price goes, it does little to protect the consumer other than publish the MSRP, which should be—but isn't always—a cap on the price.

Of course dealers would like to have you believe that the MSRP *is* the price of the car. This figure is used in all the automotive magazines and in all newspaper stories about cars. Even *Consumer Reports* uses it in its reviews.

But it is *not* what you should pay.

Too many people assume that because the sticker says a certain price, that is *the* price of the car. It is not.

It's way too high.

Courtney Caldwell, editor of the magazine *American Women Motorscene*, calls the willingness to pay sticker price Sticker Sucker Syndrome. Both men and women suffer from it, but women tend to have it worse.

Here's the cure:

Never pay sticker.

And of course never pay more than MSRP either. That

sounds obvious, but believe me, some people do. Cars that are "hot" when they come to market, like the redesigned Mustang in 1994 or the Miata when it first came out in 1989, are in high demand, so dealers stick on extra markups, thus fleecing those willing lambs who have to be the first on their block to own a hot new car.

Dealer Invoice

This is the wholesale price of a new car. It's anywhere from 7% to 25% lower than the MSRP. Generally, for a mid-size car, it's about 15% lower.

Books such as the *Edmund's New Car Price Guides* and the *AutoIntelligence New Car Decision Maker* give both MSRP and dealer's invoice prices for every make and model of vehicle and for every option. These books are issued by the year and are an excellent primary source of ballpark pricing information. But automakers may increase the MSRP slightly two or three times a year, so the services listed on pages 61–62, "Tirekickers for Hire," are a better bet for absolutely up-to-date pricing.

Does this mean the dealer's invoice is the rock-bottom price? No dealer is going to sell at a loss, after all.

Well, no, it doesn't. Because dealer's invoice is often not what the dealer actually paid.

True Invoice

This is what the dealer actually paid for the car, and unless you have excellent lines into the car business, you'll never know how much it was. Sometimes it really is dealer invoice. Often it's less.

What the dealer pays for a car is the outcome of business practices so arcane they're downright Byzantine. There are three main ways dealers pay less than dealer's invoice.

First, if dealers sell a certain number of cars, they may get a larger allotment of hot-selling cars the following year. It sometimes even pays dealers to sell a car below true cost so that they can raise their turnover volume to a higher level of bonuses and preferential treatment from the automaker. This is known as "pullback"—an additional profit of 3% to 5% on the invoice price.

Second, slow-selling cars often have *rebates and incentives* attached to them. Usually these are a few hundred dollars, but sometimes they are a few thousand. Figures like that may well affect your choice of which car to buy. Customer incentives are passed on to the customer directly from the automaker. Dealer rebates should be passed on to the customer by the dealer, but rarely are. To find out what rebates and incentives are in operation, go to the library and ask for the weekly *Automotive News*, which runs a continual update on rebates and incentives on the page before last. Or more expensively, call 1/900/AUTOFAX. (This costs $2 a minute, and the average call is ten minutes.) All the services in "Tirekickers for Hire" also have up-to-date figures on rebates and incentives.

Third, if a dealership has good ratings on customer-satisfaction questionnaires sent out by automakers soon after purchase, the automaker may reward the dealer by rebating up to $500 a car.

All these factors explain why dealers sometimes advertise great prices on new cars. However good these prices seem, you can still often negotiate them down some more.

What You Pay

What you pay depends on the research you've done, the car you've chosen, and the way you negotiate. *Consumer Reports* recommends a general rule-of-thumb of 3% over dealer's invoice. If you're a good negotiator, you may pay less. (I'll go into negotiating techniques in "Dealing with Dealers" on page 94.)

One question a lot of women ask is "What's a fair profit for a dealer to make?"

It's a question no man has ever asked me. Only women.

And while it seems to be true that women do indeed have

a greater sense of fairness than men, fairness is not the issue here. The issue is getting the car you want at the best price you can get.

The money you're spending was hard-earned, so let's get hard-headed about this: There *is* no fair profit. Your job is to get the car at the lowest price. The dealer's job is to sell it to you at the highest price. To settle for midway between the two is to settle for a bad deal. So once more:

Pay no more than 3% over dealer invoice.

Preferably, of course, less. Believe me, the dealer still makes a profit.

Monthly Payments on Loans in dollars, per $1,000 of loan amount

	2 yrs	3 yrs	4 yrs	5 yrs
5%	43.87	29.97	23.03	18.87
6%	44.32	30.42	23.49	19.33
7%	44.77	30.88	23.95	19.80
8%	45.23	31.34	24.41	20.28
9%	45.68	31.80	24.89	20.76
10%	46.14	32.27	25.36	21.25
11%	46.61	32.74	25.85	21.74
12%	47.07	33.21	26.33	22.24

Tirekickers for Hire

Today's professional tirekickers are comparison-buying services. These are particularly useful once you've narrowed your choice down to three or four models.

All offer pricing—dealer's invoice as well as MSRP—and a

variety of additional information, in reports that can be mailed, faxed, E-mailed, or FedExed to you.

Consumer Reports New Car Price Service

This includes *CR*'s own ratings, which are probably the most independent assessments available, since *CR* remains absolutely aloof from any kind of financial dealing with the automakers. (It does not accept review cars from automakers, as all automotive magazines do.) The cost is $11 for one car, $20 for two cars, $27 for three cars, and $5 for each additional car. Tel: 800/933-5555.

AutoIntelligence New Car Report

This service also publishes an annual guide to new cars. Its reports cost $27 for the first car and $22 for each additional car. Reports include data on recalls, theft rates, and safety. Tel: 800/445-6111.

IntelliChoice Armchair Comparison

You can order a side-by-side comparison of any two cars you want for $19, and the report includes the value of your trade-in vehicle as well as the resale value of the cars you're considering. Tel: 800/227-2665.

Car/Puter

Used-car pricing as well as new is covered by this service, with discounts for AAA members. Costs $20 for the first report and $16 for each additional one. Tel: 800/722-4440.

Car Price Network

Run by Pace Publications, which publishes several automotive price guides, this service faxes reports on both new and used cars. Cost is $7 for each new-car report, $4 for each used-car report, plus a $4 transmission fee. Tel: 800/227-3295.

The Used-Car Market

In 1993 used-car sales exceeded new-car sales for the first time ever. The only wonder is that it took so long.

There are some terrific used cars on the market now, thanks to new-car leasing. The cars come off lease at two or three years old, in good shape and with moderate mileage.

But whether you're buying or selling a used car, how do you check its value?

You keep hearing of the "Blue Book value." Well, the Blue Book is indeed blue: it's called the *Kelly Blue Book*. This and the *NADA* (National Automobile Dealers' Association) *Used Car Guide* (also blue) are the bibles of used-car values, though *Edmund's Used Car Prices* offers much of the same information in an inexpensive TV Guide–size paperback. All these books provide wholesale and retail value: that is, what the dealers will pay for a car and what the dealer would like to resell it for, both of which, of course, are . . . yes, negotiable.

Your library, bank, and credit union will all have copies of these books, which are reissued constantly to keep up with price changes. Make sure the one you're consulting is the latest one.

Values are given by model, year, and options. Don't forget to factor in the options; things like air conditioning that are now standard on most midsize cars were often optional just a few years ago. These values assume reasonable wear and tear and average mileage. If your car is in particularly good shape and has very low mileage, it will be worth a lot more.

Alternatively, you can check the prices by phone. Two of the services listed in the previous section provide pricing on used cars as well as new. *Consumer Reports* also has a special used-car price line (900/258-2886). Two others are *Edmund's* at 900/786-AUTO and *Auto Priceline* at 900/999-2277.

The fee for these services is up to $2.50 a minute, and the average call lasts five minutes.

You'll also want to check the value of your car if you want to trade it in when you buy a new one, though you are *always* better off selling it privately. (See page 122 for how.) No dealer is going to offer you anything other than the wholesale price. If he does, then you can be sure he's playing the numbers game and is making up the difference somewhere else in the pricing of your new car.

If you're buying a used car from a dealer, rather than on the private market, demand a warranty so that you have some protection, since few states' lemon laws cover used cars. **And *always* take the car to an independent mechanic to get it checked *before* you close the deal.**

Worst Bet for a Used Car

Ironically, this is one that's often recommended as a best bet, and that's buying a car that's been in a rental fleet.

It's true that they look very tempting: usually less than a year old, often with as little as 10,000 miles on them. But remember, these cars have taken a lot of abuse in their short lives. They've been driven by dozens if not hundreds of different drivers in ways that those people would never dream of driving their own cars. I've heard too many stories of people taking rental cars drag-racing on dirt roads to ever even think of buying one. And most rental companies do only minimal maintenance: They're interested in quick turnaround, not in long-term staying power.

Best Bet for a Used Car

One that's just come off a lease. It will be in good shape since leasers face heavy penalties for abnormal wear and tear, and at, say, three years old, it should cost no more than half of its original sticker price. In fact, as more and more cars come off leases, the used-car market will be better than ever before, and you should be able to get great cars, relatively new, at terrific prices.

Best Sources for Deciding on Which Used Car

The *Consumer Reports* auto issue, every April, runs two lists by make and model year: one of reliable used cars and the other of used cars to avoid. And *Edmund's* now puts out a book of *Used Car Ratings*, scoring used cars on safety, reliability, performance, design, fun to drive, and value.

The True Cost

What? All this about prices and now I'm talking about true cost?

I sure am. Because what people tend to forget is that the price you pay for a car is not the full cost of owning it.

Consider the following annual costs, all of which must be met when you own a car.

Insurance

Insurance costs vary depending on a number of factors.

The Age and Model of Your Car The older a car is, the more it depreciates in value. And since it's worth less, it can be insured for less.

But insurance rates also vary widely depending on the type and model of car. The Chevy Camaro, for instance, is a sports car with very high accident rates, probably because the bulk of its ownership is young men who tend to use it as an outlet for testosterone buildup. In general, convertibles and sports cars cost more to insure than coupes, and coupes cost more than sedans. Check out the insurance cost of the car you want before you buy it, or you may suddenly find yourself having to pay several hundred dollars extra a year.

Where You Live I know this sounds unfair—it *is* unfair—but if the crime rate is high in your neighborhood, your insurance company will know about it and will charge you more. Sometimes a lot more. When I moved from New York City to Seattle, my insurance went down to almost half *(and* my car was broken into the night I arrived, but that's a different story).

Your Age This is one place where it pays to be older. Older drivers tend to have better judgment and take less risks, so they pay less accordingly. (Women also pay less than men, for exactly the same reason.)

The Safety Features of Your Car Insurance companies offer discounts for antilock brakes, dual airbags, antitheft systems, and, in big-city areas, cars parked in a closed garage.

Your Driving Record Insurance companies seem convinced that anyone with a speeding ticket is more likely to be in an accident. The statistical evidence for this is sketchy at best, but it is true that an accident at high speed will result in heavier injury to both people and metal. So be warned: If you have even one moving violation in the last three years, your insurance can rise drastically. If you have two, it can double. That definitely makes it worth your while to go to court to challenge a moving violation.

Registration

Registration or licensing fees vary from state to state, and generally vary according to the value of the car. They can be as high as $500 a year. So check out your state's fee and add that in to your annual cost estimate.

Gas

Estimate the number of miles you drive per year, divide by the mileage per gallon of the car you want to buy, and multiply by the cost per gallon of gas. This is your annual cost of gas.

Maintenance

Oil and filter changes every three to five thousand miles, depending on the car and the type of driving you do, usually cost anywhere from $15 to $40, depending on where you live.

Your owner's manual will tell you what else needs to be done when, but you can generally estimate $100 to $250 a year for regularly scheduled maintenance.

Repairs

You don't expect any repairs on a new car, but you may be faced with some anyway. Tires do wear down and need changing. If you ding your car in a parking lot or if a window is broken, either by accident or by a thief, you may not want to claim it on your insurance and see your rates go up, or the repair bill may be below your deductible. So even for a new car, add a possible $250 a year for repairs (not everything is covered by warranties), and a minimum of $500 for an older one.

Parking

For most people, this is not an issue, but if you live in a large city, you may have to pay for regular off-street parking as well as for downtown parking. Factor in these costs. *And* the cost of parking tickets.

I admit this is a lot of calculating to do, but believe me, it's worth your while. So remember:

Never go anywhere near a dealership without your trusty pocket calculator.

This will enable you to figure out your real annual cost of ownership. That is:

twelve monthly payments, *including* applicable state retail taxes + down payment + insurance + registration + gas + maintenance + parking

Most analysts say that you should spread the down payment over five years and deduct the residual value of your old car (that is, its resale value). The way I see it, they're wrong. We're talking actual outlay. Resale money down the road is no help when you have to pay your bills this month. Besides, that resale money will most likely go as a down payment on another car.

As a general rule, the annual cost of owning a car should be no more than 15% of your after-tax income. And preferably, of course, less.

The Time to Buy

I hear lots of stories about the best time to buy a car—the time, that is, when you're most likely to get a good deal. They include a rainy day, the day before Christmas, the day after Christmas, the end of the month, the end of the year—who knows, maybe the end of the millennium.

There's some truth in all of these—perhaps one or two hundred dollars' worth of truth, but probably no more. In fact, if business is slow for a dealer (the idea behind rainy days), then that dealer may be looking for more profit from a car rather than less.

The end of the model year, however, is one time when you can indeed get good buys. Automakers bring out their new models several months ahead of the year. Rather like magazine publishers bringing out a December issue in mid-November, automakers will trot out their 1996 models anywhere from July to October of 1995. Dealers will still have 1995 models in stock, but the 1996 models are "newer" and therefore hotter. This is when you start to see ads with great prices on the 1995 models, and TV commercials full of balloons and hyped-up "big-sale" talk.

Buying the previous year's model has clear advantages: You'll get a better "best offer" from the dealer (the later you wait in the year, the better that offer will be), and you can use this to negotiate for an even lower price. Plus your insurance rates will be lower than if you bought the brand-new "next year's" model.

But every silver lining has a cloud, and there are also clear disadvantages: You'll have less choice as to options, since the dealer really is clearing stock, and you're buying a car that has one year's depreciation on it, even though it only has twenty or thirty miles on the odometer. If you intend to keep it only two years, say, you'll have lost up to 25% of its value (the first year's depreciation) the moment you sign for it. But if you intend to keep the car at least five or six years, that first year's loss will amortise itself over the years, so go ahead.

Figuring the Options

Options are wonderful.

They're also infuriating.

You finally choose the car you want, and then you have to make sense of a vast array of optional extras—each of which adds to the car's final price.

You could, of course, simply buy the *base model*—the model that is supposedly the standard car, with all extra details being optional. That is, if you can find it.

Beware of those low base prices in automakers' commercials for economy cars: They're often for cars without sound systems, let alone air-conditioning, and even if you wanted one, you'd be hard put to find it on a dealer's lot. There's hardly any profit for a dealer in the cheapest base cars: They *want* you to get lots of options. A case of deceptive advertising? You bet.

Luxury cars tend to include just about everything as *standard equipment*. They offer very few options, because all the luxury details are included in the price, down to the leather seats and the CD player. But luxury is only a small part of the car market. Most cars come in a sometimes bewildering array of models and option packages—two different ways of marketing the same thing.

Different models of the same car sometimes really are different models—a four-door instead of a two-door hatchback, for instance, or a six-cylinder engine instead of a four-cylinder one. But often they're simply the same car with different options made standard. One model may have a regular sound system and manually operated seat and window controls, while another may have a much better sound system and power controls for seats and windows. Automakers generally differentiate their models by the letters or numbers added onto the name—the Honda Accord LX and the EX, for instance. Pay attention to which one includes what as standard equipment. And to the price difference.

Option packages help simplify the choice of options by packaging a number of them together. Buy one, and you buy the whole package. And pay for it, of course. Still, option packages are popular: The automakers have done their market research and know that someone who wants power seats generally also wants power windows, a better sound system, and a rear-window defroster, for example.

You don't have to do this: You can order the car with only the options you want direct from the factory, and wait a couple of months for delivery. But this means you probably won't get such a good deal on the car: The dealer doesn't have to stock it in inventory, and there's no incentive for him to come down on the price.

You can also *option up* your car to the state where it's *fully loaded*—that is, you've got just about all the available options on it. But beware: These can add up to half the final price of the car.

Don't let yourself be pressured into getting options you don't really want.

To help make sense of the vast array of options, I break them down into five categories:

- Must-haves
- Good-to-haves
- Nice-to-haves
- Neat, but . . .
- No thank you

Must-Haves

The three things in this category *should* be standard on all cars. Infuriatingly, this is not yet the case. This is where you should not even think of saving money.

1. *Antilock brakes*
(ABS for antilock braking system)

Though ABS is standard on most cars over $20,000, it is still only optional on many cars below $20,000. But if you can afford only one option of them all, let this one be it.

Upside ABS helps you avoid accidents by allowing you to stop in a shorter time and distance, and without swerving.

How It Works When you stomp on the brakes in an emergency, you're braking so hard that your wheels lock. That is, the brake pads come down so hard on the wheels that they stop turning altogether. This sounds good but isn't, because the whole weight of the car—a ton or two of metal—is still careening forward due to momentum. And since the wheels have locked up, you can't steer them: You have no steering control. This is when you go veering all over the place and end up doing circles in the middle of the highway. Antilock brakes, as you might suspect, stop the wheels from locking up. A small computer senses the point of lock-up and feathers the brakes ten to fifteen times a second—far more times than even the most expert human foot can manage. This keeps the brakes just the right side of lockup, which means that you have maximum braking power while still retaining control. You can understand why insurance companies offer discounts if you have ABS.

How to Use ABS You'll do it automatically. In an emergency, you just stomp on the brake pedal. If you feel vibration, *don't* lift your foot: The vibration is the ABS working.

Downside Dangerous if you think that because you have ABS, you can tailgate or get yourself out of anything. Regard ABS as an emergency aide, not as part of your everyday driving.

2. Dual Airbags

Why haven't I put dual airbags in the number-one place? First, because driver's-side airbags are now standard in nearly all new cars, and as of 1998, dual airbags will be mandatory. Second, because though airbags can help avoid serious injury in an accident, ABS can help make sure you don't get into one in the first place.

Upside Airbags help save lives. But bear in mind that they are *supplementary restraint systems*, which is why you often see SRS, for short, on an airbag cover. This means that though not as effective as seat belts, they are a valuable additional safety measure.

How They Work Sensors at the front of the car register a sudden impact, and detonate a chemical charge inside the airbag well. The airbag explodes, inflating in a split second—which just happens to be the same split second that your body is hurtling forward due to the sudden impact. The airbag cushions you. It deflates almost as quickly as it exploded. There'll be some "smoke" in the air, which is actually the talc that the bag was packed in. The bag will be hanging out of its casing like . . . well, like a used condom. Once used, it has to be replaced professionally.

Downside Dashboard airbags work only in a frontal collision (or any collision within 15 degrees of head-on). They do not work in side or rear collisions. Volvo introduced side airbags built into the front seats in 1994, and other automakers will soon follow suit.

73

Many people fear that airbags will go off when they're not supposed to. It has happened, but it's extremely rare. Some complain of side effects of airbags: broken glasses or a rash from the powder. Question: Would you rather break a pair of glasses and have a rash, or be in a coma in the intensive-care unit?

3. Rear Window Defroster

Yes, even if you live in Florida.

Upside Clears frost and/or condensation off the rear window, allowing you full vision. Obviously, driving without being able to see out the rear window is dangerous.

Downside It takes a minute or two, sometimes three, to work—the filaments have to heat up, then melt the frost or evaporate the condensation. But it's worth waiting those two or three minutes before you put your car into gear.

Good-to-Haves

These options are essential to many better-heeled buyers and are indeed extremely helpful. But not completely necessary.

1. Central Locking System

Upside Lets you lock and unlock all the doors at once. Best systems lock all the doors automatically when you start the car or it goes over 5 mph. Others are controlled from the driver's seat. From the outside, when the car is parked, the best systems work on a remote control, also known as keyless entry.

Downside Check exactly how the system works in the car you're interested in. In some, when you open the driver's door, all doors open. This may be convenient, but it's also a security risk.

A word of caution on systems that operate by a switch on the door: Make sure the driver's door stays open when you get out, or you may find yourself locked out with your keys inside. Look for a mechanical antilockout device, which disables the power lock on the driver's door. This also addresses the common fear of being trapped inside a car in the rare but possible event of sudden battery failure.

Automatic power locks sound better but also create problems: First, many people dislike trying to get out of the car when it's parked but the engine is still running, only to find that the door is locked; second, there is a possible security concern if all the doors automatically unlock when you turn off the engine. Again, check that you can disable the power locks mechanically.

2. Traction Control

Especially valuable in rear-wheel-drive cars, which are trickier to handle on slippery surfaces than front-wheel-drive ones.

Upside Improves traction—the grip of the wheels on the road—and steering in rain, on ice, or in snow.

How It Works A sensor at the wheels figures if a wheel is losing traction, and sends a message back to the engine to reduce power to that wheel until traction is restored to normal. In less expensive systems, the antilock brakes are applied to the wheel on the verge of slipping.

Downside Expensive systems work at all speeds, others work only below 25 mph. Dangerous if you use it as an excuse to drive less carefully in slippery conditions.

3. Height-adjustable Shoulder Belts

Upside Wonderful for women, who tend to be somewhat shorter than men and not at all the same shape or size as most automakers' experimental dummies. Belts can also be adjusted so that they don't cut into the breasts. Best news: A new law makes adjustable shoulder belts mandatory in all new cars from 1996 on.

Downside None.

4. Height-adjustable Driver's Seat

Upside Especially for women, this is a boon, since cars are still designed mainly for male shapes and sizes. You can raise the seat for better vision through the windshield, or lower it for a more racy feel. Power controls make the adjustment very easy. Manual controls are somewhat clunky, but just as effective.

Downside None.

5. Adjustable Steering Column

Upside Lets you adjust the steering wheel to the height and distance from you that feels comfortable for your body size. This is especially valuable to women, who are generally different sizes from automakers' standards. The best systems tilt up and down, and also telescope toward you and away from you. Power systems are available on luxury cars but are completely unnecessary; a manual control is just as effective.

Downside None.

6. Rear-Window Wiper and Washer

Yes, even in the desert, where dust and sand can do as thorough a job of obstructing vision as rain and snow.

Upside Clears grime from rear windows and provides better vision out the rear in rain.

Downside Generally available only on hatchbacks, station wagons, sport-utility vehicles, and minivans. Sedans and coupes rarely get the option, though they often need it.

7. Air-Conditioning

Upside Sounds like a luxury, but if you consider the state of your nerves and your driving when you're hot and bothered, it's not. Sinfully wasteful but fun: driving a convertible on a hot day with the top down and the air-conditioning on full blast.

Downside Reduces fuel economy.

8. Integrated Child Seats

Upside Mothers of young children love them: no hauling bulky seats around, no installation, no slippage once they're in place. Because they're built into the rear seat, they provide better protection than portable child seats.

Downside Integrated child seats are available only in a few vehicles, mainly minivans, thus reinforcing the Mom-with-kids image of minivans. There is no reason such seats could not be optional for every car on the market.

Note that seats with built-in child seats are generally less comfortable than regular seats when the child seat is folded up and an adult is sitting there.

Nice-to-Haves

This section is very much a matter of personal preference. Some people consider these options very important, but others can easily do without them.

1. Power Windows

Upside Convenience, especially if you do a commute with a lot of tolls. Most systems have a one-touch control for the driver's window—touch it once and the window goes down all the way.

Downside On most cars, it's easy to confuse the switches, especially at night, when you may find yourself lowering the right rear window instead of the driver's one.

2. Cruise Control

Upside A great aid if you're traveling long distances on an interstate. It reduces driver fatigue, and specifically reduces stress on the thighs and hips. For lead-footed drivers, it also helps you stay within the speed limit.

Downside Cruise control can lull a driver into inattention—even, on a long, straight highway, into an almost hyp-

➡ **"The radio is more important than power to me. Just to be able to play the radio and feel good."**

➡ **"I agree: I could do without air-conditioning, but there *has* to be a good stereo."**

—British Columbia group

notic state. In an emergency, it takes far longer to get the foot on the brake. Cruise control is a clear case of trading safety and control for convenience, so use it with caution.

3. Automatic Transmission

If you regularly drive in stop-and-go traffic, this may be a must-have. The same, of course, if you don't drive a manual transmission. For most of us, it's a matter of preference, but be aware that you pay extra for automatic transmission.

Upside Makes it less tiring to drive in heavy traffic and on urban hills. Demands less driving skill than a manual transmission. The best automatic transmissions can now be programmed for "sport" or "economy" driving as you prefer.

Downside Some drivers feel that an automatic transmission takes away some of their control over the car.

4. Upgraded Sound Systems

Upside These systems can be truly amazing, with a sound quality approaching living-room acoustics despite the vibration and sound of the car on the road. A cassette player allows you to listen to books on tape as well as the music of your choice; a CD player provides superb sound quality.

Downside No second guess as to what most attract thieves to a car.

5. Lumbar Support

Upside A boon to anyone with back problems, which by some accounts is a third to a half of the adult population.

How It Works Either manually, with a lever that adjusts the amount of air in an inflatable cushion inside the seat back, or with a power control, which does the same thing more easily.

Downside None.

6. Theft-Deterrent System

Upside In theory, should make your car less liable to be broken into or stolen. Insurance companies offer discounts if you have an antitheft system.

How It Works Some systems sense movement inside the car and set off an alarm or start the horn honking while at the same time flashing the car's lights. Others protect the radio, deactivating it the moment it's yanked from the dash. Yet others deactivate the ignition system. The best do all three.

Downside Car alarms go off so frequently with false alarms that passersby pay no attention. The sound infuriates neighbors. Even car thieves often pay no attention and calmly go about their work. Remember, these systems are theft-deterrent, not theft-proof. Still, given the choice of two cars parked next to one another, one protected and one not, thieves will go for the unprotected one.

7. Cellular Telephones

Upside In an emergency, you can call the police, an ambulance, or a tow truck. The best car phones work with hands-free operation—that is, you don't need to hold the receiver as you talk—and mute the radio when the phone is in operation.

Downside Monthly and per-call charges are high, and clarity can be iffy. Since most people use their car phones for everything *but* an emergency, they are also a major distraction to driving: The mind tends to be focused on the person you're speaking to, not on the road. And if it's not a hands-free system, you only have one hand on the wheel. Also remember that in long-distance driving, you may often be out of range.

8. Sunroof

Also called a moonroof, depending, I suppose, on whether you're a night person or a day person.

Upside Improves ventilation without the blast of air from an open window, and also makes the interior lighter.

Downside Reduces head room.

➡ **"You put the moonroof back, and you put the stereo on, and the sound and the air surround you and you're cruising and all is well."**

—Student, Pennsylvania

Buying Your Car

79

9. Double Sunshades

Upside Anyone who's ever driven on a winding road in late-afternoon sun knows how the sun can blind you from the front at one turn and from the side at another. Ford paved the way in 1993 by putting double shades—one for the front window and one for the side window—in its Explorer sport-utility. Others quickly followed suit.

Downside None.

10. All-Wheel Drive or Four-Wheel Drive

Upside Improved traction and steering in snow and mud as well as on rough road surfaces. Good to have if you live in the snow belt and drive a lot on unplowed roads.

How It Works Most cars are driven by two wheels, either the two front (front-wheel drive) or the two rear (rear-wheel drive). In all-wheel drive, power is delivered to all four wheels full time. In four-wheel drive, power is delivered to all four wheels only when you want.

Downside The system adds to the vehicle's weight, so it reduces fuel economy. Traction control is less expensive and lighter; though not as good as all-wheel drive, it provides many of the benefits, and, except for those driving in the toughest conditions, may be an acceptable alternative.

Neat, But . . .

1. Larger Engines

Upside More power, more speed.

Downside Do you really need more power and more speed? Unless you tow boats or trailers, collect boulders, or like to race your car on weekends, you generally don't need a larger engine. Multivalve technology on all modern cars (see "Tech Talk Translated," p. 285) improves the performance of smaller engines, and besides, performance is often a matter of how you drive rather than what's under the hood.

2. Power Seats

Upside Convenient.

Downside Too tempting to adjust the seat when you're driving, which distracts your attention from the road and lessens your contact with the basic driving controls. Manual seat controls are just as good and less liable to malfunction.

3. Power Side Mirrors

Upside Convenient, especially if more than one person drives your car, so that the mirrors need to be adjusted constantly.

Downside None, but you can easily live without them.

4. Leather Seats

Upside Luxury.

Downside Expensive. And very hot if you leave the car in the summer sun.

5. Automatic Climate Control

Upside Convenience.

Downside Expensive. Manual controls work just as well.

6. Ride Control

Electronically adjustable suspension systems provide a smoother or harder, more "sporty" ride on demand.

Upside Fun to play with.

Downside Most people can't tell the difference.

7. Trip Computers

Usually only in luxury cars, these are electronic dashboard displays that, at the press of a button or two, tell you everything from your average fuel economy to distance traveled in miles or kilometers.

➡ **"I think the wooden dashboard and the leather seats of a vintage Mercedes make it one of the most beautiful things in the world."**

—Hotelier, California

Upside Useful when they warn you that the oil is low or a taillight is burned out. Otherwise, useful as something to keep your front-seat passenger occupied. Men love playing with them.

Downside Infuriating array of mainly useless information. Useful information, like how many miles' worth of gas you have left in your tank, is gained quicker and more directly from looking at the fuel gauge.

8. Navigation Display

Still in the experimental stage but already available as an option on a few car models. A computer screen is set into the dashboard; you program in your destination, and the computer follows the distance traveled and the turns you make, showing you both where you are and where you should go. The jury is still out on how good these systems are.

Upside Could replace maps.

Downside I love maps! Also, these systems mean that you're looking at the dashboard screen instead of at the road, which makes them dangerous, though systems with audio directions are now in the testing stage.

No, Thank You

1. Rustproofing

This, together with paint and upholstery preservatives, is one of the things dealers love to talk you in to.

Upside None.

Downside Expensive and unnecessary. New cars today come with all appropriate underside coatings.

2. Paint Sealant

Upside None.

Downside Expensive and totally unnecessary. Modern car paint is far tougher than the paint used just ten years go.

So unless you intend to make a major Arctic expedition or let your kids polish the car with steel wool, forget it.

3. Extended Warranty

This is often offered by dealers, and it extends the automaker's warranty by another three years.

Upside Covers you for all repairs covered by the warranty, which does not mean everything. Most such warranties cover only certain parts of the car.

Downside Dealers have invented an amazing array of exceptions built into the small print of extended warranties. They are expensive and generally not worth the money unless the car you are buying has a lousy reputation for reliability—in which case, why buy it?

4. Routine Maintenance Warranty

Upside None.

Downside You're paying up front for work to be done as far as three years into the future. Why would you want to do that?

Options We're Thankful They Don't Make Anymore

1. Talking Cars

These had a brief vogue in the eighties. The voice was usually a woman's voice, and it chimed in to tell you that the door was open when you knew damn well it was open because you'd opened it. Usually you wanted to throttle the voice. Most owners settled for disconnecting it.

2. "Ladies' Styling"

This was big in the fifties. It usually meant pinks, lavenders, and other pastels. And in one case, matching umbrellas.

No surprise that even then, the ladies did not buy it.

Being a Test-Driver

➡ **"What should I look for in a test drive?"**

➡ **Look for? What should I _do_ in a test drive?"**

—Texas group

I've been test-driving dozens of cars a year for the past seven years, in order to review them. And I find that most of what I need to know, I can find out in the first half hour.

A lot of it is common sense. It requires no expertise. You look at the car, you touch it, you drive it, you listen to it.

But first, let me stress:

Always test-drive the car, whether it's new or used.

In fact, you should:

Test-drive at least three cars.

This is the most fun part of buying a car. You simply walk in to the dealership, say you'd like to test-drive whatever model it is you're interested in, drive it, and walk out.

You can develop a sudden interest in that Mustang convertible or that Jaguar your boss drives. Or you can be practical and test-drive only the cars you're seriously considering. If the dealer has any sense, he'll be only too delighted to get you into the car. If he objects, he has no sense, so you wouldn't want to deal with him anyway.

But remember:

You are there *only* to test-drive the car. You are *not* there to buy it. Not yet. Not today.

The salesperson will ask if you're interested in buying the car. (It sounds like a stupid question, and it is—does he really expect you to say "No, I'm just here to have some fun," even if it's the truth?)

SAY "Yes, I'm considering it, but obviously I want to test-drive it first."

The salesperson will ask what color you want.

SAY "It doesn't matter." (Coming from a woman, this really unnerves them, since they're convinced that women buy cars according to color.)

The salesperson will ask how much a month you're paying on your current car, or how much a month you want to spend.

SAY "That's really not relevant. First, I'd just like to test-drive the car."

If you're just playing, remember to dress for the game. It's good to look as if you can afford a Porsche if you want to test-drive one. Tell the salesperson that the battered old pickup you drove up in is just a friend's runabout and that your BMW is in the shop for repairs.

If you're doing serious test-driving, give the salesperson as little personal information as you can. The more they know about you, the easier it is for them to manipulate you into buying a car on the spot. Make it quite clear that this is only one of two or three cars you're considering, and that you intend to test-drive the others as well.

After you've driven the car, the salesperson will invite you into the showroom to discuss it.

SAY politely but firmly that you really have to leave now.

A new-style dealership will let you go with the minimum of hassle. An old-style one will try to keep you there.

The salesperson might say that if you buy today, they can cut you a special deal since they have to meet their quota, or clear the lot, or some such reason.

SAY "I'm sorry, I have an appointment, I really have to go now."

So what if you don't have an appointment? As a friend who loves test-driving cars said, "Just lie like a man."

The salesperson will ask for your card or your phone number. Do not give it.

SAY "Why don't you give me *your* card, and I'll be in touch."

Then take the card, say thank you, and leave.

NEVER buy the car on the spot.

And if any dealer says, "We can't let you test-drive the car because of our insurance," or "We can't let you take it on the road until you've made an offer," or any other excuse for keeping you out of the car, you know what to do: WALK.

The test-drive, you see, is a means of testing out the dealer as well as the car.

The Step-by-Step Checklist

This checklist applies to both new and used cars. Note that nearly half these steps are checks done before you even start driving the car.

___ **1. The body.** Walk around outside. Check the alignment of doors with the body, trunk with the body. Make sure everything matches up perfectly. You don't want shoddy workmanship.

___ **2. The door.** Open the driver's door. Does the handle feel comfortable? Does the door open wide enough to get in and out easily? Try it a few times. Shut the door a few times: Does it close firmly each time?

___ **3. The seat.** Sit in the driver's seat. You'll be spending years in this seat; it's the most expensive seat you'll ever buy, and it should be the most comfortable

Adjust the seat to the distance from the steering wheel that fits your size (your wrists should hang over the top rim of the wheel when you sit with arms outstretched, and your foot should be able to go all the way down to the floor on the brake pedal without stretching).

Adjust the seat height, if you can, and the tilt of the steering wheel. (If they are power-controlled, you may have to turn on the ignition to do this.) Can you reach the shift easily? The pedals? The handbrake? The lights? The radio? The glove box?

Does the seat feel right? Does the back fit your back? (Adjust the lumbar support if it's available.) Does the back of the seat push your shoulders uncomfortably forward? Does the seat cramp your thighs?

Is the seat easy to slip in and out of? You're going to be in and out of this car a lot if you buy it; if you notice that it's an effort to get in and out now, it's going to be far worse once you're living with it.

Can you open and close the door easily when you're seated, or is it a stretch?

Just as important, can you see all the gauges fully? (In some cars, I find that if I get the seat and the wheel where I want them, the top rim of the steering wheel hides part of the gauges. This is not good. The highway patrol will not accept your argument that you couldn't see how fast you were going because the steering wheel hid the speedometer.)

__ **4. The smell.** Ignore the dealer's suggestion that you enjoy the new-car smell. All new cars have the new-car smell. Even used cars are sometimes sprayed with it.

__ **5. The interior.** Take a good look around. How does the car look inside? Plasticky? Check the fit and finish of details like the cupholders, the glove box latch, the belt buckle. (I once got into a brand-new test car, pulled out the lighter to put in a radar detector, and found that I'd pulled out the whole of the lighter fixture.)

__ **6. The mirrors.** Adjust the rearview and side mirrors. Does the rearview mirror give you a clear view? Do you have to stretch your head to see out the side mirrors? How big is the blind spot? Can you tell where the front of the car is? The back?

__ **7. The hood.** Open the hood. (The lock is usually under the dash, to the left of the driver's legs, and this pulls it slightly open; to open it all the way, feel under the center of the hood for a lever and press it either up or to one side or the other.) Is it easy to open? Check that the dipstick is easy to get to, and that all caps for fluid checks and filling are clearly marked. (See "Tender Loving Care," p. 222, for which ones are which.)

__ **8. The trunk.** Open the trunk. (The trunk lock is often down to the left of the driver's seat, alongside the fuel-cap lock.) Check the whereabouts of the spare tire, jack, and lug wrench. Is it easy to reach into the trunk? Would it be easy to get heavy things into and out of it? Is the trunk big enough for your needs?

___ **9. The seat belt.** Get back into the driver's seat and put on the seat belt. If it adjusts for shoulder height, adjust it. Is it comfortable? Is it easy to buckle and unbuckle? Again, does it feel right?

___ **10. The controls.** Run through all the controls: The gearshift, whether manual or automatic, should be smooth. The lights, climate control, sound system, indicators, cruise control, defrosters, door locks, window controls and locks, and moonroof controls should all be easy to reach and operate. Make sure you like the feel of them.

___ **11. The locks.** Get out, and lock all the doors before you close the driver's door. Does the driver's door automatically stay unlocked? This may sound like an inconvenience, but it's not. Imagine if you'd left the keys inside the car.

___ **12. Ignition.** Get back in and start the car with the door open. If the car has antilock brakes (ABS), does the ABS light come on for a second or two, as it should, together with the battery light? (If it doesn't, the car doesn't have ABS, no matter what the dealer says.) Let the car idle. It should be smooth and quiet.

___ **13. Climate control.** Check both the heat and the air-conditioning. Adjust the directional flow to make sure you're not going to get hot or cold air blasting right into your face or onto your knees and nowhere else.

___ **14. The first few minutes.** The dealer will probably insist on driving the car for the first few minutes, with you in the passenger seat. This is to get you feeling comfortable in the car without having to worry about driving an unfamiliar vehicle. It's a waste of time, and a condescending move, but most dealers still insist on it, for both women and men.

At this stage, the dealer will probably ask which radio station you prefer, so that he can tune the radio to that station. Say you'd prefer the radio off. You need to hear the sound of the engine on a test-drive, and you do not need to be distracted by music. You'll test the sound system later.

__ **15. The route.** Always choose a route you know. That way, you're concentrating on the handling of the car, not on finding your way or listening for directions.

You want a route that lasts about twenty minutes and that includes both heavily and lightly traveled roads. If the dealer won't let you drive that long, leave. If you can, choose a route that includes as many different kinds of road as possible: urban, suburban, freeway, country.

Tell the dealer politely but firmly that you'd rather not talk while you're test-driving the car and that you can get into a conversation about it later.

__ **16. Handling.** Does the car shift smoothly? If it's a manual shift, check the pressure you need on the clutch pedal. Heavy pressure will wear on you after a very short time. If it's an automatic, check that it shifts gears smoothly, without clunking or pulling or lagging. Do you feel that you have full control? That the car will respond promptly and smoothly to your every input?

__ **17. Vision.** Now's the time to recheck that you have the vision you want—that you can see well out the windshield and through the rearview and side mirrors. If you find yourself peering, that's a bad sign.

__ **18. Steering.** Check the steering by moving the wheel slightly from side to side. Is the car responsive, or is there travel in the steering wheel? Do you feel you have to haul on the wheel?

__ **19. Noise.** How does the car sound? Does it purr or does it tend to roar? Can you live with this noise level?

__ **20. Cornering.** Take a few sharp corners. How does the car feel? It should hug the road.

__ **21. Parking.** Drive into a parking lot and reverse into one spot. If it's an automatic shift, make sure there's no clunk when you engage reverse. Go head in to another parking space, and reverse out. Now parallel park. How does it feel? If not good, ignore dealer suggestions that "You'll get used to it." Why get used to something that doesn't feel right?

__ **22. Windshield wipers.** Try them out. Press the washer, and let the wipers work a bit. Are they smooth, or can you hear them? How much of the windshield do they cover?

__ **23. Emergency braking.** Drive to a low-use road, check for traffic, and when you're sure there's nobody behind you, do two sudden stops. (Warn your passenger first.) Does the car stop smoothly and quickly? Does it swerve? Does it feel in control?

__ **24. Acceleration.** Check for traffic, and do two quick bursts of acceleration from low speed. (Better warn your passenger again.) Does the car accelerate smoothly, or does it lag? Again, does it feel in control?

__ **25. Sound system.** By now you'll start heading back, so this is the time to try out the sound system. Check both talk and music. Does it sound tinny? Hollow?

__ **26. Conversation.** You want to check the conversational level in the car, so turn off the radio and start talking to the dealer. I know you've said you'd rather not talk, but the dealer will be only too happy to forget that. Can you hear the dealer clearly and easily, or do you have to strain?

27. Think. When you get back, sit in the car a moment or two after you turn off the engine and ask yourself if you really *like* this car. "Okay" is not enough. Any car that runs will be "okay." But does it feel right for you? Did you enjoy driving it? Ask yourself if you'd want to spend five hours in it. Or five years in it.

28. LEAVE. Once more for good measure: Do *not* commit yourself to anything the same day as a test-drive. Take the dealer's card. Do *not* give the dealer your number unless you enjoy getting a stream of phone calls from one salesperson after another all the following week. Say you want to test-drive other cars and you'll be in touch.

➡ **"I test-drove several convertibles, and it was down to the Audi and the Mustang. And I looked at the Audi and thought "This is a really safe car and I should buy this." And every time I walked up to the Mustang I just started smiling. . . ."**

—Homemaker, California

Extra Steps for a Used Car

If you're buying a used car, you'll be getting an independent mechanical evaluation (see p. 123), but you can save yourself unnecessary time and expense by doing a few preliminaries yourself. So in addition to the preceding checklist, you should:

1. Check for misaligned body panels. These indicate that the car has been in an accident serious enough to require replacement of a whole body panel.

2. Check for different color tones in the body panels. This indicates that the car's been repainted after an accident.

3. Check for bubbles in the paint. These indicate rust beneath.

4. Check, of course, for obvious rust.

___ **5.** Under the hood, check for rust, and make sure the hoses are firm, connections are tight, the battery terminals are not corroded, and the wires have not been painted over. Check that the oil is clean (honey-colored, not dark).

___ **6.** Start the car with the hood still open and the hand brake on, then walk to the front of the car and check that the engine is running smoothly. Put your hand on the open hood and see if it's shaking badly. Listen for any tapping or knocking noises. Then walk round to the back and check that the exhaust is clean (no smoke, no noxious—or obnoxious—smell).

___ **7.** Check all the electrical controls: lights, defrosters, all power windows, mirrors, and seat controls.

___ **8.** Check the tires for tread depth and even wear.

___ **9.** With the engine still idling, but before you start driving the car, check the brake pedal. If it gets hard about two-thirds of the way down, that's good. If there is no resistance all the way to the floor, get out of this car and do not drive it at all.

What about kicking the tires?

Unless you want a sore foot, don't.

It's a hangover from the days when tires had inner tubes, and was of doubtful use then. Today it's just another of those meaningless phrases that make guys feel like guys.

Dealing with Dealers

➡ **"I love the ritual dance of buying a car. I think it's fun."**
    —**Production assistant, New York**

➡ **"My experience with dealers was a joke, a total joke."**
    —**Homemaker, Oregon**

Dealing with dealers is really quite simple for a woman. All you have to do is be firm but polite. It's not that different from dealing with children.

And know what you want. Again, not that different from dealing with children. Don't let yourself be talked into something else. Just be firm, but polite.

Dealers are easier to work with if they see that you know something about cars. After reading this book, you'll know a lot about cars. And about dealers.

Never forget these three things:

The price of every car is always negotiable.

No matter how nice he or she may be, the dealer is there to make as big a profit as possible.

**Until you actually sign for the car, you can always
walk out.**

The "niceness" factor is tricky. Especially in the new-style dealerships, appealing young men aim to strike up a relationship with you. This is a pseudo-flirtation. It lasts as long as the buying process lasts, and not a second longer, though it can be hard to remember that. You find yourself liking them, thinking things like "It's only fair to let this nice guy make some profit."

RESIST such impulses. They may be worthy of you; they are *not* worthy of your pocketbook.

Unfortunately, niceness is often not a factor at all. Arrogance, take-what-we've-got-or-leave-it, and rudeness too often are.

Both men and women detest what J. D. Power calls "the dealership experience," which for most people ranks on the scale of pain somewhere close to having a root canal treatment. It's small wonder that the number-one item on consumer complaints in state attorney-generals' offices throughout the country is new and used motor vehicle sales.

Women in particular ask Why?

Why can't there just be a fixed price?

Why do we have to play the haggling game?

Why the waste of time and energy?

Why does the whole thing have to be so **infuriating
demeaning
insulting
maddening
exhausting?**

Answer: It doesn't have to be that way. It should be enjoyable, and it can be.

This section, then, is a guide to making the car-buying experience less painful—to making *you* the one in control, instead of the salesperson, and to restoring some sense of fun and free choice to the whole affair.

But first things first: Know thine enemy.

The Old and the New

There are two kinds of dealers out there these days: the old-style ones and the new-style ones.

New-style dealers are simply good businesspeople. They have grasped one of the most basic principles of good business, which is that a satisfied customer will return for more business. Thus the better they treat you now, the more likely you are to come back for regular maintenance, as well as for repairs, whether under warranty or not, and to buy another car a few years down the road. (That repair business is important to them: Dealers make two-thirds of their income through their repair departments.) New-style dealers exert relatively low pressure on you, respect you as a customer, and actually do seem to value your business.

All this may seem obvious, but in fact it represents a revolutionary change in dealers' style of doing business. Many dealers, the old-style ones, still seem to imagine they're selling snake oil, not cars.

Old-style dealers behave as if they're about to go out of business (which with justice, consumer know-how, and a touch of luck, they soon will). They are high-pressure salesmen. They treat all customers, but especially women, as if they are idiots; they seem convinced that women are incapable of spending their own money; and they are full of strange ideas, such as "If I can get a woman to tell me the color of the car she wants, I know I've sold her the car." Go figure.

All the major carmakers now run training programs for their dealers that focus on dealing with women, stressing respect and courtesy. This is an excellent sign. And it has raised the number of new-style dealers immensely.

Unfortunately, participation in such programs is voluntary. Dealers too often send junior personnel as a gesture; the owners and the real managers pay no attention. Simply put, not all dealers are educable. While many are making honest efforts to improve their relationships with potential customers, others are clearly bogged down in some mythical age when a man did what a man had to do (buy a car, for instance) while a woman sat by and said "Yes, dear."

The Sleaze Factor: Twenty Things Women Say About Dealers

Patronizing
Extremely patronizing
Insulting
Extremely insulting
Outrageously insulting
Worthless
Genuinely worthless
Sleazy
Liars
Sleazy lying bastards
Neanderthal
Irritating
Annoying
Pathetic
Creepy
Losers
Jerks
Sleaze
Slime
The unmistakable odor of
snake oil

Straight from the Horse's Mouth

I sat down for an afternoon with a car salesman in the Midwest: in his thirties, good-looking, seductive voice. I plied him with drink, and got him to give me some straight answers. Since he's still in the car business, he talked on condition that he remain anonymous. You'll see why.

There's a lot to be learned from what he said, because

what he described was the workings of an old-style dealership. Forewarned is forearmed: once you know their tricks, you won't fall for them. And do they have tricks. . . .

Q.: Why does it take hours and hours of sitting in the dealership to buy a car?

A.: I call it the Stockholm syndrome. After a while, in a hostage situation, the hostage begins to identify with the terrorist. The idea is to keep you there so long that your resistance is worn down and you say, "Oh heck, I'll take it," no matter what the price. That's why you get things like "I'm sorry, we need to go check your credit" or "We need to run these numbers through." What happens then is that the guy goes back to his assistant sales manager and they sit and b.s. for a while, and then they say, "Oh, better go out and tell her something."

Q.: What's this business with handing you over to somebody else?

A.: At some dealerships, they have a rule that says there have to be three "turns" before a person is allowed off the lot. A turn is, if I don't get you to buy, then I say, "Oh, maybe Billy can help you on this." Then Billy gets to work his tricks on you, and if his tricks don't work, then Jimmy.

Q.: Why do they always ask how much I want to spend?

A.: That's the key phrase they're taught. Let's say you offer me $11,000 for a car. The next key phrase is: "If I can get it for you at that price, ma'am, will you buy it today?" You always say "Yes," because after all it's a $20,000 car. So I say, "Okay, I'll write it up and take it to my manager and see what he says." Then I come back and say, "I'm so sorry, but he really won't go for it. But I *can* get it for you for $19,895. How does that sound?"

Q.: What's this business about writing up an offer?

A.: What happens is that I write up your offer, then you sign it. It has no legal status—it's really just a piece of paper—but it makes you feel committed. It draws you into the process, keeps you engaged. And it also tells me what you can spend, because the offer includes your social security number, so we can run that through the computer and within ten minutes of that offer being submitted, I know what your salary is and what your credit rating is and how much car you can afford to buy.

Q.: So it's a kind of fake formality?

A.: Right.

Q.: What other tricks do you use to keep me there?

A.: We'll keep trying to show you cars. Some dealers will take your car to have it appraised, which means it's gone for half an hour, an hour, and you can't leave even if you want to. Not many still do that, but some do.

Q.: A friend who once worked in a dealership said she was told, "Ignore what they want, sell them what we've got."

A.: Exactly right. You get them committed to the sale, and then at the last moment, "Oh, that one's gone, it'll take months to get it in again, but look you can take this one here home today." That's what I'd do. If you wanted a red car with gold wheels and all I had was a gold car with red wheels, I'd say, "Sure we can get what you want, let's put the deal together." And then at the last minute, "Oh, damn, I've called all over the country and can't find one, but look, I'll knock five dollars off this one, even though it's the car you hate."

Q.: And if it's more expensive?

A.: I'll say, "This car will be another $30 a month, and you have to ask yourself, every morning you go out to the other car, will you think about the dollar a day you're saving by being in a car that doesn't make you happy, or will you be glad you got the dull upholstery instead of the fine Corinthian leather?"

Q.: And what about all those negotiations with your manager?

A.: Once, when I was new to the business, the customer was sitting right there and I'd called the general manager on the phone. The manager said, "Tell me how much she wants to pay," and I said, "$18,500." And then he said, "Now, say out loud 'Really, the invoice is $21,000?'" And it went on like that, with him guiding me through every sentence. Meanwhile the customer's eyes are getting wider and wider as she hears what I'm saying. At one stage he said, "Say out loud, 'I'm sorry, I'm not going to tell her that, I can't tell her that.'" By the time we'd finished, she was convinced that a high price was a fantastic bargain. The best salespeople, the old-line pros, will bring you stories like "Look, the manager's having a bad day" or "We're one away from the quota, and I know if we sell you this car we can make the quota." Any time you hear anything personal like that, it's b.s. It's all designed to sucker you in to feeling like you're getting a great deal. And if they tell you a hard-luck story, ignore it. Never, ever, feel sorry for a salesperson. It's all part of the deal.

Q.: What happens when a woman walks into a showroom alone?

A.: Easy mark. We're hoping we'll just quote the sticker price and she'll say "Cool" and that's it.

Q.: So how come women complain that dealers ignore them in showrooms?

A.: That's just stupidity on the part of those dealers. I was trained to view a single woman as a potential large-gross profit. Some of my best sales are to women.

Q.: Is it true that men get better deals?

A.: Often they do, but not always. Women are coming in better prepared than they used to be, and dealers are actually learning to fear women who come in armed with sheets of paper full of research. Men detest dealers as much as women, and for much the same reasons, but because of this, they tend to come in as though they're the hunter out to get his prey, ready to bag the last great woolly mammoth. It's more of a poker game with men. With women it's more of a pseudo-romance, and more and more women are realizing that this pseudo-romance is really no different than picking someone up in a bar and saying "I'll love you forever if you stay the night with me."

Q.: So I come in with my research, and . . .

A.: Say you offer two or three hundred above dealer's invoice, which is what *Consumer Reports* recommends. A good salesman will try to get you to throw your sheet of paper away. You then say, "Look, I understand you've got problems or new fees or whatever, but this is what I'm really prepared to pay." Then we'll probably come back and dicker with you and you'll get it for close to what you want. Because we do want to sell the car. We have a lot of credit riding on it. Dealers floor their inventory: We borrow money from the automakers for the cars on the floor, then when we sell the cars, we pay the automaker back and keep the profit. But we're paying interest on that money—flooring charges, they're called—so that's a terrific motive for us to blow a car out and get a fresh one in. We're in business to move our merchandise, so a smart guy will put a deal together with you.

Q.: The general wisdom is, never tell a dealer how much you can afford to pay per month.

A.: Absolutely right. Because then you have no idea what you're really paying for a car. We call them "payment buyers," and when I get someone to agree to a payment, that's the best. I get more money for the same car, because I get them paying $281 a month, say, for six years instead of five.

Q.: How big a profit can a dealer make?

A.: As big as he can get. If I do make a big profit on a sale, I'll say, "I laid her away in a car" or "I really laid them away on that deal" or "I grossed their face off," meaning I made so much gross on that deal it was really unbelievable. That's the backroom talk.

Q.: Any more of it?

A.: Another term is "grinding." A customer may "grind" on me by continually asking for a lower price, or we may say in the back room, "Let's go grind on them for half an hour and see if we can bump their offer, and if we can bump them ten bucks a month, we've got a deal here." What we say is "Go for the bump."

Q.: So it's the old bump and grind?

A.: In this case, grind and bump, yes.

Q.: And what about all those extra things that tend to get added on once I think I've made the deal?

A.: You have to remember you're dealing with not just one but an array of professional negotiators. After you've been sold the car, then we send in the chemicals man to try to sell you paint sealant, rust-proofing and so on, and then the F&I person—finance and insurance—who tries to sell you expensive insurance policies. And all of them make a profit off these things, so you're really getting run through a car wash, going through one set of brushes after the next. If you're not prepared for it, it's very difficult to say "No, I don't *want* floor mats, I don't *need* rustproofing, I'll bring my own financing, I have my own insurance." It's like a giant pile of piranhas, and you just have to realize that you're very attractive bait, and dangle yourself around until you get the best deal.

How do such sleaze tactics survive? The main culprit is the commission system.

Too many car salespeople still work entirely on commission. So when you go to a dealership, try to find out if the salespeople get a salary, as they do at all Saturn dealerships, for instance, as well as at many dealerships offering fixed prices on certain models, or if they work entirely on commission. Those who work solely on commission—still the majority—are likely to be far sleazier.

It is a crazy situation: While cars themselves are getting better and better in response to consumer demand, the way they are sold lags far behind.

How Women Rank Dealers

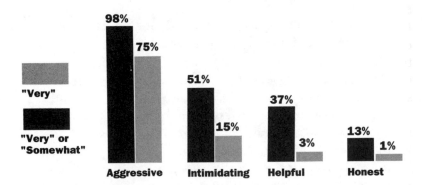

Just about everyone is sick and tired of old-style dealers. Some senior automaker executives dream publicly about a system where a buyer could order a car direct from the factory, custom-tailored to her desires, with all the options she wants and none of the ones she doesn't want, and the factory could have the car made and delivered within three days. Don't hold your breath on this, however. Though many automakers would like to do away with dealers altogether, federal and state laws won't allow that.

Auto dealers are franchise operators. By law, automakers cannot sell directly to the public, for fear of price-fixing. Dealers usually have franchise agreements with several automakers at a time. And they hold the upper hand, since the law makes it is almost impossible for an automaker to terminate a franchise agreement. Many of the agreements now come up for renewal every five years, but even then, it is almost impossible not to renew. The dealer can have the worst customer-satisfaction reports in the country, yet the automaker cannot terminate.

Instead, many automakers are now trying the carrot approach. If dealers have consistently high customer-satisfaction scores, for example (in research done by the automaker), they may receive a bonus on each car sold, up to $500 a car. If they have low scores, they may receive none. It's an approach that seems to be working: The new-style dealerships with good customer-satisfaction ratings are on the rise. The old-style ones either will have to change, or go out of business. But they won't change unless we, the consumers, insist on it.

So when you are sent the customer-satisfaction questionnaire after buying a car, fill it in honestly. Ignore any dealer who tells you to check everything as excellent because it's just a formality, or the automaker is trying to squeeze him, or some previous customer is crazy and has a vendetta against him. Tell it like it really is.

But remember too that new-style dealers are also out for profit, and as much of a profit as possible. They're just more subtle about it. Saturn dealers, for instance, can afford to play down the pressure tactics not only because Saturns have fixed prices, but because they get a built-in profit of some $1,000 a car—a large profit for that price range of car, and one that means that General Motors are selling Saturns to dealers at comparatively little over cost. New-style dealers are far more pleasant to deal with, but never forget that they're still businesspeople.

Out of the Mouths of Babes

How *Not* to Do It

- ☞ "I just had to have a car that week, because I was going on a cross-country trip the following week."

- ☞ "It was the only car in town that had all the options I wanted."

- ☞ "When my husband and I filled out the credit application, the salesman came back with it and ripped it up in front of us. He said he was so sorry but his boss wouldn't accept it. We were really embarrassed, and that put us in a situation where we felt we really had to prove ourselves. We knew we could afford the car, so we ended up paying too much for it and driving it home."

- ☞ "I just saw that red car sitting there and knew I had to have it."

- ☞ "My husband and I went to look at a car, and we really liked it, but the salesman wouldn't negotiate at all. He said this car was in hot demand and this was the last one on the lot and he didn't know when he'd get another one, and if we didn't buy right now we'd lose the chance to have one. And we walked out and went to get some lunch and talked it over and came right back because we were afraid we'd lose it."

Horror Stories

- ☞ "Dealers treat women like we don't know anything, like we're really dumb, a bunch of bimbos."

☛ "Every time we went shopping for my car they'd hand the keys to Nick, and Nick would turn round and give them to me."

☛ "I was looking around at an auto mall and said, 'Give me your best price.' He said, 'What do you mean?' And I said, 'Just give me your best price.' And he wouldn't. He wouldn't give me a price at all. Instead he said, 'Shouldn't your husband be here?'"

☛ "The last time I bought a car, my husband came with me, and the salespeople kept addressing questions to him. I was saying 'Hello? Excuse me? *I'm* buying this car.' It was really annoying."

☛ "I walked into a dealership just before a holiday weekend and there were four salesmen standing there, but nobody came to help me. Other people came in, couples or men, and the salesmen started talking to them, but nobody came near me. It was like I had a communicable disease or red letters on my back. I began looking under the hood, and still nobody came. So I went to another dealer, my three kids in tow, and he said, 'Hey, take the car for the weekend, try it out, see how you like it.' And of course he'd sold me the car then and there."

☛ "I walked into the sports-car place thinking I'd trade in my two-year-old BMW for a sports car, but nobody would even talk to me. They could see I had a car of some value, but they were clearly thinking 'Hey, she's not going to be the decision maker, so why bother with her?'"

☛ "I walked into one dealership and this salesman walks up to me with a silly grin on his face, saying 'Looking for a new car, are we?' Like I was five years old. He was actually rubbing his hands together as he talked."

107

- "I've gone in with my mother and had a salesman come out and say, 'Can I show you little ladies something?'"

- "After a month of searching and talking to every lamebrain idiot in this city and being called Babe and Honey and Dear and Where's-your-husband and Why-don't-you-have-your-husband-come-back-and-help-you-do-this, I was so frustrated I bought the same car as the boring company car I'd had for the past four years: I knew that if I couldn't trust any of the salespeople, I could at least trust the car."

- "One salesman kept putting his hand on my knee as he was talking to me. It made me really uncomfortable. In the end I just walked out, but I wish I'd said something."

- "I have a friend who's twenty-three but looks sixteen, blond hair, buxom, pretty, and she went to a dealership and the guy literally said, 'If you go to bed with me, I'll lower the price on this car.' She complained, of course, and he was slapped on the wrist, but he's still there."

Driven to Anger

- "They did this hustle they do with the figures and they took it to the manager, and there was this little covert operation going on, and I just looked at my husband and said, 'We're out of here, I'm not taking this b.s.'"

- "I honest-to-God never thought I could be pushed to anger when buying a car. I think of myself as low key. But I found myself screaming at the guy I bought a car from. I said, 'Do you want to sell this car or don't you?' It was a horrible experience, even though

I did get a good deal in the end: the sticker price was fourteen thousand and I got it for ten."

☛ "This should be fun—you're spending a lot of money on something you really want. Instead, it's so stressful and insulting, it's ghastly."

☛ "It's humiliating to be reduced to their terms when you're paying good money."

☛ "I'm in sales, and I was really mad. I would never treat my customers this way. It was an insult to my intelligence. You just don't insult customers by trying to manipulate them into something they don't want to do. The salesman actually told me that I wasn't being reasonable with my offer. And I blew up. How dare he tell me I'm not reasonable!"

☛ "When I asked the dealer how much it was, and he said, 'How much do you want to pay?' I got into a shouting match with him. I said, 'Anywhere else I go and ask for a price, they tell me. What's wrong with you?' He said, 'It doesn't work that way with cars.' In the end, I used some very bad language and walked out."

☛ "We went to a dealer through our credit union, which had already established the price, but the guy starts in with 'Tell me how much you're ready to pay each month and I'll tell you if you can afford this car' and so on. The price was supposed to be preestablished. I was furious. I said, 'We have money, we have it today. We're buying a van, we're buying it today. We can buy it here or we can buy it somewhere else. So you tell me the bottom line, right now, or we go somewhere else.' My husband of course is dying meanwhile. We did finally get the right price and we bought the van, but why did I have to blow my top to get it?"

➡ **"Have they all been to car-dealership school, class of '58? Their attitude toward women is like a real time warp."**

—Lawyer, Texas

☛ "This whole negotiating thing is b.s. I don't have time. I want my car, I want it at a fair price, I want it now, and I don't want it to be a whole game."

Playing the Game

☛ "My husband and I actually enjoy going to dealerships. He went to business school and took courses in negotiation. Because I'm a woman and look like I'm eighteen, they think they can manipulate me, and we let them think that. We play good guy/bad guy, and it works. It's fun."

☛ "My husband was willing to settle for a much higher price than I was. Men are really pushovers compared to women. We're the tough ones, and the dealers don't even know it—probably because most of them are men!"

☛ "It's sort of like playing chess. Whenever I've bought a new car, I haven't needed it immediately, so I've had plenty of time to shop around. It's almost a form of entertainment, especially since I'm quite ready to walk out at any point. The last time, my husband came with me, and when the dealer started talking to him, he said, 'No, you don't understand, I'd buy it for what it says on the sticker. You've got to deal with her.' And sure enough, an hour and a half later I got a great buy on it."

☛ "Either you walk out when they start with their nonsense or you laugh and say, 'This is the price I had in mind.' And then you just sort of dialogue. I think the problem is that women are just not used to negotiating. Most of us don't realize that negotiating can be fun."

When It Works

☛ "We bought through our credit union, and it worked perfectly. The dealership manager walked us out to the lot, said 'Pick whichever color you want,' and that was that."

☛ "We bought through a buyer's agent. First we checked out the cars and test-drove a couple, then told the agent exactly what we wanted—make, model, options, everything. And he got it for us at a really good price."

☛ "We had a good experience with a local dealer on the car we have now. They advertised the car at a good price, we went in, it was what we wanted, and we bought it. They fulfilled their part of the bargain, but when we told them we'd been around pricing other cars, they came down even further, and we bought it for less than it was advertised. It was easy."

☛ "I just hung in there and kept negotiating. I basically ignored everything they said and just kept coming back with my original offer. Every time I said, 'I'm sorry, I have to leave now,' they'd come back with a number closer to mine. Finally I got the car for just two hundred dollars over my original offer, which was actually below what I thought I'd have to pay for it. It took a couple of hours, but it felt good. In fact it was fun."

➡ **"Negotiate! The worst they can do is say No. The worst you can do is say 'Bye!"**

—**Courtney Caldwell,** *American Woman Motorscene*

Bitter Lemons

Cars now are more reliable, better built, longer-lived, and safer than ever before. But here and there, a lemon still slips through, leaving a bitter taste in your mouth and your pocketbook.

All states now have lemon laws in place. They won't get rid of the bitter taste, but they will protect your pocketbook. Most cover leased cars as well as outright purchases, and some also cover used cars.

Generally, a lemon is defined as a new car, van, or light truck that has not been repaired successfully after at least four attempts, or is in the repair shop a total of at least thirty days within a defined period, which varies from state to state. You can get a copy of your state's law from your state attorney-general's office.

If you do have a lemon, here's what the Center for Auto Safety, a non-profit organization set up by consumer-affairs advocate Ralph Nader, recommends you do:

1. Give the dealer an opportunity to make repairs. Keep copies of all repair orders.

2. After the second unsuccessful repair attempt, or when your car has been out of service for fifteen total days, write to the automaker's regional office.

3. After three repair attempts, or when the car has been out of service for twenty days, write to the automaker's headquarters. Say you will invoke your lemon-law right to a refund or replacement unless your car is successfully repaired.

4. After the fourth unsuccessful repair attempt, or when the car has been out of service thirty days, write again to the automaker demanding a refund or replacement. Keep copies of all correspondence, of course.

5. If the manufacturer refuses your demand, apply for arbitration. Your state attorney-general's office will tell you how. In most states, you also have the right to go directly to court. Demand an independent arbitration program rather than arbitration procedures offered by the automaker.

Do Women Get Worse Deals?

The vast majority of women in the focus groups—83.6%—felt they'd gotten a reasonably good deal on their cars.

Well, maybe not. After all, it's hard to admit that you got grossed. And difficult to know if you get a good deal unless you have done the research and have all the figures in hand.

The truth emerges when nearly a third of those who said they got a good deal—31%—said they could have done better if they'd been male. And this percentage would clearly be higher if most women hadn't taken the precaution of bringing a man along with them.

Of those who felt they got a bad deal, 33% thought it was because they were women—only 2% more than those who thought they got a good deal. So it appears that the outcome has nothing to do with it: Whether the deal is good or bad, about a third still feel that being female is a liability when they set foot in a dealership.

In 1991 the American Bar Foundation commissioned a study in which six "buyers," all in their twenties, college educated, and dressed like young professionals, bargained for cars in dozens of dealerships in and around Chicago.

They all negotiated the same way. They offered to pay dealer's invoice; then, when the dealer came back with a "best offer" of a higher number, they split the difference between their original offer and the dealer's counteroffer, and went on doing this until the dealer either accepted or refused to continue bargaining.

The results: For the same model car with exactly the same options, with a sticker price of $13,465 and a dealer's invoice of just over $11,000:

White men paid an average of $362 above dealer invoice, white women paid $504 above invoice (a 39% greater markup), black men paid $783 above invoice (more than double the markup), and black

women paid an astounding $1,237 above invoice, or more than triple the markup for white men.

The director of the study, Ian Ayres of Northwestern University, said he thought that rather than outright or intentional bigotry, these numbers reflected a shared and perhaps subconscious assumption among many salespeople that blacks and women are less knowledgeable or less adept at the bargaining process than white men and are therefore more willing to accept a higher offer.

Despite his attempt to play down the racism, he has a point: In a 1992 study by the Consumer Federation of America, 37% of people polled did not know that the price of a new car was negotiable. Broken down by race, 61% of blacks said they didn't know this, as opposed to 31% of whites.

Even more disturbing: The "buyers" often received the worst offer from salespeople of the same sex and race.

And more disturbing still: While someone can sue under civil rights laws for racial discrimination in a retail transaction, there are no such laws on discrimination against women.

That leaves knowledge as your best protection.

Are Women Dealers Better?

Many women are so disgusted with how they're treated as women in dealerships that they are convinced that women salespeople—currently 7% of the automotive sales force—can't be any worse and will most probably be better.

42% said they'd trust a woman salesperson more than a male one, and 58% said either that trust would depend on the dealer, not on gender, or that they'd trust women and men equally. Nobody said she'd trust a male salesperson more.

Are they right? Will you get a better deal from a woman?

The truth is, you probably won't come out any better financially—she is, after all, still a salesperson, probably working on commission, and her aim is to go for as much profit as she can. But you may well come out better psychologically, and that can count for a lot. A woman is less likely to be condescending to other women and more likely to be sensitive to women's concerns. At least, in principle.

➡ **"Sometimes I wonder if we don't expect too much from other women. As though we hold them to higher standards than men. It's like waiting till a woman comes up for nomination to start asking questions about nanny taxes. Sometimes I think we hold women *too* accountable."**

—Nurse, Washington

➡ **"I don't know about dealing with a woman. There was this woman in one dealership who was even sleazier, because she tried to cozy up to me, like it was some special woman-to-woman thing."**

➡ **"I came across one too, and she played exactly the same game as the guys."**

➡ **"At least she didn't call you Honey or anything, did she?"**

➡ **"No, worse than that—she cozied up to my husband!"**

—Pennsylvania group

The Elegant Grovel

Unless you are into diamonds and emeralds, a car is the second most expensive purchase you ever make. (The first, of course, is a home.) What I demand when making such an expensive purchase is what I call "the elegant grovel."

This is what I want dealers and automakers to understand:

I am going to spend a large amount of money at your dealership. In return for that large amount of money, I expect—and this shouldn't even require saying—a perfect product. I expect *zero* problems with the car.

Second, I expect to be treated like a princess, whether I'm spending ten thousand dollars or fifty thousand. Kindly understand that if I make $25,000 a year, ten thousand dollars is to me what fifty thousand dollars is to someone making $125,000. If I went to a department store and spent ten thousand dollars, the salespeople would be fawning on me. I expect you to do the same.

No, you don't have to kiss my feet (though you may if you ask very nicely). But you do have to demonstrate appreciation of the fact that I'm there.

I expect you to bring me coffee, not to leave me waiting or sitting. I expect you to expedite matters as much as possible. I expect you to make this a good experience—no, make that more than good, make that a pleasure. I certainly expect you to appreciate the fact that I am about to spend a considerable portion of my annual income in your dealership. And I absolutely will not tolerate any last-minute add-ons to the negotiated price.

All this involves courtesy and respect, of course. It involves the common kind of courtesy and respect that strangers in line for a movie accord each other—*plus* the infinitely larger amount of courtesy and respect that should come from the fact that you presumably want my business.

If there is any doubt in any dealer's mind as to how successful the elegant grovel can be, they should go visit a Lexus or Infiniti dealership, where it's done so well that it is all elegance and no grovel. Or a Saturn dealership, where it takes the form of a celebration—a kind of family atmosphere that congratulates you on having the means and the wisdom to choose one of these cars.

As Saturn has proved, it's not a matter of courtesy and respect for wealth, but of courtesy and respect for the customer. It is also a basic principle of good retail business practice. And if any customer finds a dealership wanting in this respect, dealers should know that she will exercise her rights, walk out, and go elsewhere.

The Five Basic Principles of Dealing with Dealers

1. Negotiate.
2. Be polite but firm.
3. Never say how much you can afford per month.
4. Do your research.
5. Remember, you can always *walk out.*

Not Dealing with Dealers

Unless you're buying a used car privately, it's hard to get away from dealers altogether. But there are now ways to avoid the hassle of dealing with dealers—to deal with them, that is, without having to negotiate the deal.

One-Price Selling

In 1990, someone began something absolutely revolutionary in the car-selling biz. They were told it couldn't work. They were told they were crazy.

They weren't.

The someone in question was Saturn, a semi-autonomous division of General Motors operating in Tennessee, at a healthy distance from GM's Detroit bureaucracy.

And the something absolutely revolutionary was exactly what so many car buyers had been demanding for so long: cars with one price. No negotiating, no dickering, no bargaining, no haggling. Just one price for each model. The same price for everyone. Everywhere in the country.

The cars were still sold through dealerships, but those dealerships were hand-picked, and their salespeople were paid by salary, not by commission.

You and I could have predicted quite easily what happened, though it took Detroit by surprise: Customers responded with enthusiasm. Saturns were by no means great cars. They were, and still are, economy cars, sold at reasonable prices with reasonable quality. Yet within a couple of years, Saturn claimed its place up at the top of the J. D. Power customer-satisfaction lists along with the luxury nameplates of Lexus and Infiniti (both of which, take note, also had the ability to hand-pick their dealers).

Saturn's dealers were just as satisfied. They were making up to $1,000 a car, because Saturn was selling to them at a far larger discount than is usually given on economy cars. Soon, Saturn dealerships were selling more cars per dealership than anyone else.

Impressed by Saturn's success, other automakers have been trying to persuade individual dealers to adopt one-price selling on certain models, otherwise known as the *no-dicker sticker*. And it looks as if more and more dealers are going for it, in particular those dealerships owned by the sons and grandsons of the founders, who want to change the snake-oil image and like the idea of what one called "honorable profits."

By the end of 1994, almost a third of American dealers (excluding Saturn dealers) were selling at least one model at a fixed price. These models are often cars with popular option packages. The major advantage for dealers is increased consumer trust, with higher sales, as well as more trade for their service departments, which is where dealers make two-thirds of their overall profit. The major fear: that other dealers in town will undercut them.

On a fixed-price deal, you will probably pay a little more than you would if you negotiated well at another dealership. But you may consider this money well spent since it means you avoid the time and hassle of the usual bump and grind.

Saturn's success led to yet another innovation: one-price models, also known as *value-pricing*. These are different versions of the same model, offered at one set price. Ford, for instance, was having trouble selling the station-wagon version of the Escort, so it offered value-pricing on that model line: the same price no matter whether the car was a sedan, a coupe, or a wagon. Since the wagon was otherwise the most expensive of the three, it was clearly the best deal, so Ford sold many more wagons.

Buyer's Agents and Brokers

Despite the successful customer-oriented approach of Saturn, Infiniti, and Lexus, the "dealership experience" is still so often so bad that a new breed of middlemen has come into being: buyer's agents and brokers.

Both will find the model you want and negotiate the final price of the car for you. With a buyer's agent, the only time you see a dealer (aside, of course, from test-driving the car) is when you go to pick it up. With a broker, once you've test-driven the cars you're considering, you never even have to see a dealer again.

Every woman in the groups who used a broker or a buyer's agent was extremely satisfied. All bought through brokers and agents who had been recommended by friends or acquaintances.

What's the difference between an agent and a broker?

Brokers are generally paid by the dealers. In effect, they take a cut of the sale, as well as a service fee from the client. Clearly this is a situation that is open to abuse, which is why brokers are illegal in some states. Make sure any broker you go to has a good reputation—don't just pick one out of the phone book. Usually the broker actually buys the car, then resells it immediately to you.

Buyer's agents receive a fee up front, which may be $300

to $500 depending on how much consulting you want to do as to what car to buy. They then go and negotiate for you. While brokers have an interest in which car you buy—the more expensive the car, the more they get—a buyer's agent's only interest is in getting the car you want at a good price. The cost of the car makes no difference, since the agent gets a flat fee. Moreover, a buyer's agent never takes possession of the car and accepts no money from the dealer.

Is it worth the fee? It usually is. Generally, a good buyer's agent can get the car for you well below your best negotiating effort. Ashley Knapp, head of the largest nationwide buyer's agency, AutoAdvisor (800/326-1976), which guarantees the lowest price in any area of the country, says that more than half the cars he negotiates come in *below* dealer's invoice.

With both agents and brokers, the more time you have, and the more specific you are about which car you want, the higher the chance of your being pleased with their service. If you want a car within two or three days, your choices will be more limited, and the price higher. If you can wait two or three weeks, you'll have more choice and a better price.

Like one-price selling, the increasing influence of buyer's agents and brokers is slowly changing ideas about how to sell cars. Some credit unions are now acting as brokers through their own buying services. And more and more dealers are warming to the idea: While they see a lower profit on each car, this is more than made up for by a higher volume of sales, and by increased business for their service departments.

Could this lead to a complete rethinking of dealer attitudes—an end to the old bump and grind?

I'd sure like to think so, but don't hold your breath.

Doing It Privately

Brokers and agents deal only in new cars, though some, like AutoAdvisor, will negotiate for a trade-in on your old car if you insist. Don't insist.

Best advice: If you can sell your old car yourself, you should. You will always get a better price that way.

In 1993, used-car sales exceeded new-car sales for the first time ever. With so many great used cars coming off leases, relatively new and in good condition, the used-car lots of dealerships are looking better and better. But that still means playing the negotiating game, so many people simply prefer to buy directly from the owners through newspaper or news-sheet advertisements.

Of course the price of privately sold cars is still open to negotiation, but at least both parties are speaking the same language, and there are no high-pressure tactics.

First, whether you're buying or selling a used car, check its value in one of the current blue books or in *Edmund's Used Car Prices*, or ask your bank or credit union to look it up for you, including all the options.

The wholesale value is what you would like to buy for; the retail value is what you would like to sell for. In both cases, you'll probably settle for somewhere in between, unless the car has particularly high or low mileage or is in particularly good or bad condition.

Local snapshot-filled trade news sheets tend to have more motivated readers, since they have to pay a dollar or two to buy the publication. But ads in your local newspaper also work fine.

A word of caution: If you are single and have placed an ad to sell your car, always say "we" rather than "I" when talking to a stranger on the phone. Is this really necessary? Probably not, but it doesn't hurt to play it safe.

And *always*, if you're buying a used car privately, get it

checked out by a trusted mechanic or an independent evaluation service, who can tell you if the car is in good condition and if it's worth the price being asked. Get this done even if you're buying from a friend, because if the car's not in great shape, that friendship is not going to last much longer if you buy it.

In many states AAA has a list of recommended mechanics, all of whom can do evaluations. You can also check under Automobile Diagnostic Services in the Yellow Pages, but in that case, make sure that the mechanics are certified by the National Institute for Automotive Service Excellence.

And one last word:

Get the car checked out *before* you buy it. This may sound obvious, but it's amazing how people get around to doing it only after they've already bought the car, and then get a nasty shock when they find out what shape the car is really in—and what the repair bill is going to be. Chances are the car is in great shape, but this is your money, so don't take chances: Make sure.

To Lease or Not to Lease

You know the ads: The car you've always wanted for $199 a month, nothing down? One of those pinch-me-I-must-be-dreaming ads. Sounds too good to be true. And once you read the small print, you might find out that it is. Or you might have found a great deal.

Leasing came into being a few years ago as another way for dealers to move metal. The automotive market was in a slump at the time, so the automakers' marketing departments got creative. By now, just over a fifth of all cars are leased, and over a third of all luxury cars.

This is how it works.

When you lease a car, the leasing company—usually a finance arm of the automaker—actually owns it, but it is registered in your name. You are responsible for *all* registration fees, insurance, maintenance, and repairs. This is not a rental car. It is, to all intents and purposes, yours for the duration of the lease.

Leases usually last two to four years. Most are for three years. And lease payments are generally about two-thirds of the average payment on a car-purchase loan.

That sounds great. But remember that dealers love leasing: They make a lot of money that way.

The Advantages

There are some great advantages to leasing.

- ✓ **Since you only have the car for three years, it's under warranty all the time you have it.**
- ✓ **You can indeed have a fancier car for however much you can afford per month.**
- ✓ **You don't have to worry about long-term maintenance or resale value.**

This is what the salesperson will tell you about leasing a car:

"It's a great way to get more car for your money! Just think, for the same price—for the money you're going to spend each month anyway—you can have a compact car instead of a subcompact" (or a Miata instead of a Civic, or a Rolls-Royce instead of a Mercedes, etc.).

In a way, this is true. When you lease, your monthly payments are based not on the car's initial value but on how much it's expected to depreciate while you're using it. Over three years, that depreciation would probably be about half the car's sticker price. So instead of making payments based on the full price of the car minus a down payment, you're making payments on only about half the sticker price.

This means that the monthly payment on a lease is often about two-thirds of the monthly payment on a car-purchase loan.

But of course there's a catch . . .

The Disadvantages

The dealer is omitting just one little detail: At the end of the lease, the car is not yours.

Leasing is like paying rent instead of owning a house. You may spend more on mortgage payments, but the house is yours, you build equity in it (that is, ownership value), and when you sell it, you keep whatever's left over after you've paid off what remains of the mortgage. (If you've already paid off the mortgage, of course, you keep it all.) Moreover, while your rent is not tax-deductible, the interest on your mortgage payments is. So the real cost of owning a home is usually less, in the long run, than the cost of renting.

The same is true with cars. Leasing a car is basically a fancy way of renting it—for a longer time than regular car rentals, with all the financial responsibilities associated with ownership falling on you instead of on the rental company.

This means that leasing is cheaper than buying only when you take the monthly payment into consideration. The *overall* cost is higher. Why? Because when you buy a new car, you own a car that's still worth several thousand dollars once the payments are all made; in leasing, you own nothing.

And there is one serious disadvantage to leasing that no dealer will ever mention:

If you change your mind about a car you've bought, or if your financial situation changes and you can't afford to keep it any longer, you can sell it. Albeit at a loss, but you can simply put it on the market. You can't do that with a leased car. You are locked into that lease for the full term—responsible for every one of the 24, 36, or 48 payments whether you use the car or not. You can opt for early termination, but you'll get hammered: It will cost thousands of dollars in penalties and outstanding payments.

It's best to regard a lease as you would signing up with the military: You're in for the duration.

Some Northeast states are working on legislation to permit termination of leases after half the payments have been made, but even then, there will still be some penalty to pay. Most leases also allow you to transfer the lease to someone else, but in that case, you are still held responsible for all payments, even if someone else is making them.

In 1994 Chrysler initiated an experiment in some areas with a six-month grace period: Lease the car, and if after six months you're not satisfied, you can terminate the lease without penalties. Whether this works, of course, depends on how many six-month-old cars Chrysler gets back. But when an automaker bets on customer satisfaction that way, you know something's going right.

The Tax Angle

For many, the decision on whether to lease or buy a car depends not on the monthly payments but on their tax situation. This is why so many company cars are leased, and so many luxury cars. If you use your car primarily for work, talk to your accountant. If you don't have an accountant, don't even think about leasing a car.

You may find that you can deduct a large part of the cost of leasing a car, while deductions on a car you own are strictly limited to the IRS's minimal idea of depreciation (the amount your car loses in value for every year of ownership). If you can indeed deduct part of the lease cost, then the total cost of leasing may be about the same as the total cost of buying, except that you'll be able to have a new car every two or three years.

Leasing Lingo

Leasing has its own lingo, and you need to make sure you understand it in order to negotiate a good lease. *Never* sign a lease without making sure you understand everything in it.

These are the main terms you'll come across.

Residual The estimated market value of the car at the end of the lease, or the resale value. The higher the residual, the less the monthly payments will be. Residuals on a three-year lease are usually just over 50% of the sticker price. You can check residual prices in *The Automotive Lease Guide* at your library or your bank.

Excess mileage charge Most leases are written on the basis of your racking up 15,000 miles a year. Some companies will give a discount if you sign for 10,000 or 12,000 miles a year, but this may be asking for trouble. If you run over the mileage limit, they charge you for every excess mile. Heavily. Fifteen thousand miles a year is a reasonable outside estimate for most people, but for some, it's not. If you drive a lot, leasing is not for you.

Security deposit This is usually the same amount as the first month's payment, and counts as the last month's payment.

Subvented leases A fancy word for "subsidized." Great deals, *if* you can still find them. Automakers who are experiencing slow sales on a particular model may offer leases at very attractive rates. What happens then is that the whole package is subsidized by the automaker, through its own "captive" finance company—General Motors Acceptance Corporation, Ford Motor Credit, Mazda American Credit, and so on. This can be done by setting high residual prices, or low interest rates. But automakers are now beginning to back off heavily subvented leases, and in any case, it's often difficult, if not impossible, to tell to what extent a lease has been subvented.

Capitalized (cap) cost This is the starting point of any lease. It's the negotiated purchase price: the cost of the car on which you're taking a lease. Compare it to dealer's invoice prices just as you would with a car you were purchasing, and negotiate the cap cost just as you would a regular purchase price. In fact, unless the dealer has advertised a great deal on a lease, **don't even say you intend to lease**

rather than buy until you've settled on a purchase price.

Then say you want to lease the car based on the agreed purchase price as the cap cost. Since your monthly payment is based on the difference between the residual and the cap cost, you obviously want a *high residual* and a *low cap cost*, so that the difference is as small as possible.

If a dealer refuses to tell you the cap cost on an advertised lease rate, walk.

And if you're making a *cap cost reduction*—lease-speak for a down payment or a trade-in allowance—subtract it from the cap cost. This is generally not worth it, though. A lease with no money down is a better deal. And you're better off selling your old car yourself.

Figuring the monthly payment Get out your trusty pocket calculator. (Remember, you should never go within a hundred yards of a dealership without one.) Add any applicable state sales tax (yes, you pay sales tax on a lease) to the cap cost. Subtract the residual from the result, which gives you what's known as *the principal.* Now take the *annual percentage rate* (APR), use the table on page 61 to figure out your monthly payment per thousand dollars of the principal, multiply by however many thousand dollars apply in your case, and voilà, you get your monthly lease payment. Or rather, you get a ballpark figure. Because don't forget, you're dealing with dealers, so nothing is simple. That's why there's the:

Lease rate Instead of a simple APR, the dealer uses something called a lease rate or a *money factor*, which tends to have lots of zeroes, like .00375. Aaargh! You see what I mean—it gets arcane. The only purpose that I can see to using a lease rate instead of a straight APR is to hide the true APR from the customer. So here's how to uncover it.

Ask for the lease rate. (If the dealer won't tell you this number, you know what to do: That's right, walk.) Multiply the lease rate by 2400 to find the true annual percentage rate.

(God bless trusty little pocket calculators.) Five seconds will tell you that .00375 translates into 9%.

Now compare the APR to what your bank or credit union is offering. If the dealer's is higher, negotiate it down, or walk away.

When negotiating a lease, don't forget to keep on negotiating once you've got the cap cost settled. You have three elements that can all be negotiated:

1. **The cap cost (as low as you can get it)**
2. **The residual (as high as you can get it)**
3. **The lease rate (as low as you can get it)**

Gap protection Suppose you lease a car, and it's totaled by a drunken driver. Your insurance covers the cash value of the car. But the finance company treats the car's nonexistence as an early termination and charges a huge penalty. This is the "gap." Captive finance companies generally offer gap insurance free, as part of the deal. Other lease companies may charge $100 to $200. Don't pay more.

Open-end lease Not a good idea. "Open-end" means that if the car's actual value at the end of the lease term is less than the residual (which was an estimate, remember), you're responsible for the difference.

Closed-end lease You are free and clear at the end of the lease term. And you still have the option of buying the car at the residual price, though if the residual has been artificially inflated in order to make the monthly lease payments more attractive, you probably won't want to. As the end of the lease approaches, compare the residual with the wholesale price in the used-car price guides; if the residual is lower, buy the car—you can always turn around and sell it instantly at a profit. If the residual is at or near the retail value, it's time to part ways with no regrets.

Wear and tear Sign a contract only if "normal wear and

tear" is spelled out. Dings in the doors, chipped paint around the grille, modest tire wear should all be considered normal wear and tear. There are heavy penalties for abnormal wear and tear, so don't treat a leased car like a weekend rental.

Note: The fact that you've leased a car from one dealer or automaker does not mean that you have to go back there at the end of the lease. Any dealer will buy a car off-lease—that is, pay off the residual to the leasing company—because of the demand for good used cars, and because that gives the dealer the opportunity to make a double profit, both on the car you turn in and on the car you buy or lease next.

The To-Lease-or-Not-to-Lease Checklist

___ You have Jaguar tastes but a Honda budget.

___ You want a new car every two or three years.

___ You don't mind monthly payments from here to eternity.

___ You don't drive more than 15,000 miles a year.

___ You don't hanker after pride of ownership.

___ You use your car primarily for business.

___ You have an accountant.

Lease only if you've checked all or most of these. If you find yourself in doubt, you're better off buying.

Used-Car Leasing

As leasing has increased, so too has the number of cars coming off lease: in 1995 alone, 1.5 million. Since they've been driven for only two or three years, the vast majority of these cars are in excellent condition. Which means that there'll be better choices than ever before on used-car lots, including the option of leasing a used car instead of buying it.

All the terms of leasing new cars apply to used-car leases too. But to sweeten the deal—and of course to move the cars as leasing grows and more and more cars come off lease—automakers have begun to offer excellent terms on re-leased cars. These include extended warranties, as well as factory-backed inspection and, if necessary, reconditioning. Ford has been the most aggressive of the automakers in promoting used-car leases, but other automakers are rapidly getting into the action.

Prediction: Used-car leasing will be the most rapid-growth sector of the car market in the next few years.

3.

On the Road

Drive, She Said

➡ **"You know what's so great about driving? It's that you can't do anything else. You can't read, you can't write, you can't watch TV, you have to be where you are, in that moment. So it becomes like your own time, your own place."**

—Consultant, British Columbia

A pronouncement:

I am sick and tired of the boring old assumption by automakers and salespeople that women don't like to drive. Where do these people live? Don't they know any women? Aren't they married to one or two?

Of course women like to drive:

Nearly 60% (59.4%) say they like driving a lot.

Another third (31.6%) say they like driving somewhat.

6% say they like it only a little.

A mere 3% say they don't like driving at all.

In fact, many women who don't particularly care about cars one way or the other, love driving. It's not which car that matters; it's the driving itself.

➡ **"I don't think of myself as a person who loves cars, but in fact I guess I do like them more than I think because I love to drive. I take a lot of trips and I always rent a car and take lots of maps, and I love just bombing out into the countryside, going really fast, just that feel of being in a car and driving."**

➡ **"The same with me. Driving has always been tremendously important to me. The car itself has been less important."**

—California group

Just as infuriating as the notion that women don't like driving is the one that we don't drive well. Women merely use cars for transportation, in this view of the world, while men are real *drivers*.

Such a view, of course, is a male problem, not a female one. Women certainly don't buy into it.

47.8% say they drive better than the men in their lives

36.3% say they drive the same

Only 15.9% say they drive worse

In a *New York Times* column called "He Drives Me Crazy," writer Molly Haskell broached "the taboo subject of the driving-impaired husband," also known as "the HLD syndrome" (husband-lousy-driver syndrome).

"If the image of the lousy woman-driver has been advanced with such relish," she said, "it is to disguise a truth that goes against the very definition of manhood in a country in which driving and virility are synonymous." This truth, of course, is that women drive better.

Her husband drives more slowly than she does, with one hand waving in the air to make some conversational point and eyes everywhere but on the road. He has at least one "freak accident" a year (that is, it's never his fault, of course), including rear-ending a truck, sideswiping a parked car, and burning out the emergency brake by driving with it on.

The women in the focus groups clearly agreed with Haskell, and the record backs them up. It shows that in fact, women do drive better than men. Or at least, more safely.

The Insurance Institute for Highway Safety—the institution that ensures that we get lower insurance rates than men—says that across the board, fatality rates for women drivers are half those of men, and for women in their early twenties, only one-third.

"Men do more stupid things," says the Institute's vice-president, Chuck Hurley. "It's not so much motor skills we're talking about, as judgment skills. And women clearly have better judgment."

Leonard Evans, a General Motors research scientist, attributes the difference to a dangerous blend of machismo and alcohol, which often leads men, especially young men, to driving faster than they can handle, tailgating, and the kind of aggressive driving that leaves no margin for error.

But there's also a third factor: Women drive more with children in the car, and that drastically alters their willingness to take risks.

➡ **"Do you find that you drive more carefully when the kids are in the car?"**

➡ **"Absolutely. You're suddenly aware of how fragile life can be."**

—New York group

The Three Keys to Driving Well

The first key to driving well is **FOCUS.**
Any fool can drive a car: Start it, engage the gears, press

the gas, and steer. But to drive it well, on different kinds of roads and in all kinds of weather and traffic conditions, takes thought.

☞ A good driver is *thinking* all the time. Not about unpaid bills, or about work to be done, or about an argument, or an assignation: She's thinking about the road ahead.

☞ She's *looking* at the road ahead. Far ahead: at least a quarter mile down the road, and if she has a clear view, then farther. And she's also looking at the road behind, through the rearview mirror. On the highway, she's checking traffic in lanes on either side of her, using the side mirrors.

☞ She *knows*, at all times, where every other vehicle on the road is

And knowledge is the key to good driving

Not knowing is like driving blind. You place your faith entirely in the ability and good judgment of other drivers—who may not have either ability or good judgment.

☞ A good driver is all there, in mind as well as body. She's *not* putting on makeup. Or changing the music. Or talking on the phone. Or turning around to talk to someone in the back seat. In fact, she never takes her eyes off the road. That's why a well-designed car has distinctive knobs and buttons on the dashboard. That way, a driver can find what she wants— indicators, stereo controls, lights, heat controls, horn—without having to search for them.

They used to call this "being in the here and now," and it's a good thing to be, except that on the road, you have to be both in the here and now *and* in the immediate future.

138

The second key to driving well is **ANTICIPATION.**

Look and think far enough ahead, and you'll find that your driving improves immeasurably. You're ready to take a corner. Moving out into another lane is no problem because you know when you'll be able to do it. But most important, far fewer things will take you by surprise.

If you're thinking ahead, you'll be able to react in good time when a car suddenly pulls into another lane, or turns left without signaling, or turns left when he's signaled right.

Thinking ahead means both getting ready for what *you* want to do, and bearing in mind what anyone else *might* do. Remember: You may be as predictable as the best Swiss clock, but the other driver is not.

Anticipation involves predicting unpredictability. (Yes, I know this sounds like a Zen riddle. But it works.) It also involves leaving as little as possible to chance.

So if you are in a confusing situation on the road, always err on the side of caution. For instance:

☛ If it's unclear who goes first at a four-way stop sign, wave the other driver on unless you're waved on first.

☛ If a car is swerving from one lane to another, assume the driver is either drunk or mad, and don't take the risk of passing when he or she might swerve out at you. Slow down, take it easy.

☛ If a truck driver waves you on as you're approaching a blind corner or the top of a hill, don't go. *Always trust your own judgment, not somebody else's.*

Remember too that if you leave a safe distance between you and the vehicle ahead of you, you'll have more time to react. The rule of thumb is two seconds. That is, at least two seconds between the time the rear bumper of the vehicle ahead passes a stationary object such as a post, and the time you pass it. (At night or on the freeway, this should be three seconds, and in rain or on ice, four.)

The third key to driving well is **JUDGMENT.**

Not daring. Judgment.

Every race driver I know tells me this. And nobody's more daring than they are. So if it works for them, it'll work for all of us.

Judgment means making a realistic assessment of what's happening on the road. Do you really have time and room to pass that car on that back road, or will it be a tight squeeze? Is there really room to turn into traffic from your driveway right now, or are you relying on oncoming traffic braking? Have you really left enough room between you and the truck ahead of you, or if he brakes suddenly will you risk slamming into him?

(One simple rule for driving behind a truck—if you can't see its rearview mirrors, you're too close. Moreover, if you can't see its rearview mirrors, its driver can't see you.)

Good judgment means making a realistic assessment of both your own driving ability and traffic and road conditions. It means not doing anything that will scare you or your passengers or other drivers. It means behaving like an adult on the road.

About Passing

☛ I'll say it again: Don't rely on the judgment of others. Too often, they have none. It makes no sense to pull out to pass just because the car ahead of you has done so: You can't see the road ahead, and you have no idea what might be coming.

So forget piggybacking on others: You might be

hitching your life to that of a seventeen-year-old male suffering an overdose of testosterone and alcohol.

Unless you're sure the road ahead is clear, wait till the car ahead has pulled back in again, then check if it's clear to go.

☛ Step on the gas pedal! Don't baby your engine. If you have a manual shift, shift down and then step on the pedal. If you have an automatic, go down heavy on the gas to make it shift into a lower gear. The reason: Valuable seconds can transform a tight pass into an easy one.

If you're on the highway and using cruise control, use the gas pedal to go faster than your set speed. When you lift your foot after passing, the cruise control will automatically reestablish the speed you were at. Do not merely meander past at your set speed. Other traffic behind you may be going faster, and it's not only courteous to give them room quickly, it also makes sense: The last thing you want is to be tailgated by some speed-hungry idiot.

And of course, on a highway, always return to your previous lane. And signal for returning to your lane as well as for moving out to overtake.

☛ Always be prepared to abort a pass. Forget your ego: Better to slink back into place alive and well than brazen it out and realize too late you haven't got the room.

☛ Remember that overtaking uphill takes a lot longer than on a flat surface.

☛ Never, but *never*, even think of overtaking when you're approaching a blind turn or the top of a hill. No matter if you're behind a bicycle or a tractor or a giant snail. Stay there until you can see the road ahead.

About Cornering

It's not hard to avoid that rolling, lurching feeling as you round a tight corner. The main thing to remember: Don't brake in the corner.

Of course this does *not* mean don't brake at all. It means you should brake *before* you reach the corner. Then accelerate out of it.

You'll find you have far more control of the car this way, with less body roll and a firmer grip of the tires on the pavement. And you're far less likely to skid.

The same applies, by the way, to patches of wet leaves and to ice: Brake *before* you get there, not when you're there, so that you have maximum traction when you need it.

About Skids

You've probably heard it a hundred times: Always turn into the direction of the skid.

Fine, but what the heck does that *mean?*

Simple: A skid develops when the back end of your car swings out to one side. "The direction of the skid" means the direction of that back-end swing. So if the back end begins to swing out to the right, ease off the gas (do *not* do it suddenly, and do *not* jam on the brakes) and steer to the right.

The good news: You'll probably steer in the correct direction automatically. The hard thing to remember is to keep your foot *off* the brake pedal, since that goes against instinct.

It helps to look where you *want* to go, not where you *are* going. The hands respond to what the eyes see, so keep your eyes steady on the road.

If you catch the skid in time and have steered in the direction of the skid, good. But you also have to calibrate the amount of steering. Too much and you'll get a nasty counter-skid, with a sharp hook to it. So after the main correction in the direction of the skid, you may need another smaller one in the other direction. This one is not so automatic, so you'll need your wits about you.

The main thing: Stay cool, keep looking where you want to go, and remember that you *can* control the car, even in a skid.

About Braking

About braking? Am I crazy? You want to brake, you put your foot on the brake pedal, right?

Yes indeed, but you can use a few simple techniques to brake more quickly and safely.

Emergency Braking

About two-thirds of the way down the travel of the brake pedal, you'll find a spot where the brake becomes much harder. This is known as the threshold. Threshold of what? Of lock-up.

Lock-up is when the wheels lock—when you have so much braking pressure that the wheels literally stop turning. Sounds like a good idea, but it's not, because the car still has forward momentum. You then have a ton and half or two tons of steel careening forward, just sliding over the ground, with no control because, since the wheels aren't turning, you can't steer. This is not a good idea.

So the secret to good braking is to keep the car on the threshold of lock-up—just before that point where the wheels stop turning, so that you have maximum braking power while still keeping control of the car.

How? The old-fashioned way is to pump the brakes. It's a good idea, but not nearly as effective as simply learning where that threshold is on your car, and keeping your foot right there. If you feel the wheels locking, just lift your foot slightly—very slightly—but keep it on the brake pedal.

If you have antilock brakes (ABS), these will do this for you. All you have to do is stomp all the way down on the brake pedal and keep your foot firmly planted there.

Do *not* lift your foot at all in an emergency stop with ABS.

Why not?

Because then the antilock brakes will stop working. The ABS is controlled by a small computer that senses when the wheels are about to lock, and adjusts the brakes accordingly. If you lift your foot, the ABS can't work.

The ABS computer basically pumps the brakes, but far faster than any human being could possibly manage. When you keep your foot all the way down, the computer keeps the wheels at maximum braking action, which is just short of lockup. You can still steer the car, and you won't go veering off the road in all sorts of interesting but horrendous directions.

Saving the Brakes

There's one simple word for this: DON'T.

One Washington woman got a ticket because she was going too fast downhill. She was, she explained to the judge, only trying to save the brakes and produce less asbestos dust. The judge was not sympathetic.

First, forget saving your brakes. Trying to save wear on the brakes is like trying to save wear on your feet by not walking. They're there to be used. And they're not made of asbestos anymore. The brake pads do wear and do have to be replaced every now and then, but trying to delay that replacement is a false economy: your life or someone else's life for the sake of a few dollars.

Second, you can use the gears in manual shift to increase braking power. It's not really necessary, but guys love doing it and get impressed when you do it too. You simply slow down, shift to a lower gear, and use the brakes more lightly. The trick is to slow down enough before you shift to a lower gear so that the engine speed—the RPMs—meshes fairly smoothly with the speed of the lower gear. But remember: Braking power is *always* greater than gears for stopping.

About Winter Driving

One major rule for winter driving—in snow or on ice—and that is SLOW.

Okay, one other word too: CAUTIOUS.

Slippery surfaces mean that it will take you much longer to stop, and that you run a much greater risk of losing control of the car.

And it should be obvious that if you can't see where you're going, as in fog or a heavy rainstorm or snowstorm, you can't drive safely. So if your car does not have daytime running lights—low-power lights that turn on and off with the ignition, which have been mandatory on Canadian cars for some time but are only just being introduced on American cars—be sure to turn on your lights whenever it's drizzling, raining, foggy, or snowing. Even in the lightest rain.

On Icy Roads

☛ Give yourself more room than usual from the vehicle in front. Lots of room.

☛ Drive much more slowly than usual.

☛ Keep an eagle eye out for what other traffic is doing. Do not assume that because one car races by at 70 mph, it's safe to go 70. It's not. Watch for the back ends of other cars waving from side to side: You'll know there's ice on the ground there. And watch, of course, for other cars' brake lights, so that you'll have plenty of time to brake.

☛ Beware of wet leaves on the road in the fall. They can be as dangerous as black ice.

In Fog or Heavy Snow

☞ Get off the road as soon as you can. Do not stop by the side of the road, since other vehicles may not be able to see you. Take the earliest turnoff you can find.

☞ Open the side window a crack to prevent condensation, and keep the air flow directed toward the windshield to keep it clear.

☞ Do not follow another car's taillights. This may be one way to get through; it may also be one way to crash. First, you don't know if conditions aren't going to be worse up ahead. Second, you have no idea if the driver of the vehicle you're following knows what he or she is doing or is a complete fool. You may be the blind following the blind.

☞ If visibility is bad before you set out, don't start driving at all. Wait. Or don't go. Or stay over. Or pay for a motel: Your life is worth it.

☞ If you have a four-wheel-drive vehicle, like a sport-utility, do not think that all the above do not apply. They do. Four-wheel drive may give you an extra edge on slippery surfaces, but it won't replace common sense.

In Heavy Rain

☞ Follow the rules for bad visibility.

☞ Beware of hydroplaning. This happens when there is so much water under the wheels that the tires lose contact with the road. You're not driving anymore then: You're skiing on wheels. And you've lost contact with the road. If you do start to hydroplane, *ease* your foot off the gas pedal, steer very *gently*, and when you feel the tire gaining traction again, apply just a little power, very smoothly. Do *not* brake; since your wheels have no contact with the road, this will only send you into a skid.

Best way to avoid hydroplaning: Watch the road surface carefully. Steer clear of large, deep puddles. And above all, reduce your speed.

About Drinking

You don't need me to say this about drinking and driving, but I'll say it anyhow:

DON'T!

Over one-half of all traffic accidents are due to drinking. That means, in the United States alone, between twenty and twenty-five thousand deaths a year.

It's easy enough to say you can manage to get home. If nothing untoward happens—no child dashes into the road, nobody turns left when they're signaling right, no floppy-eared dog suddenly appears in the headlights—you may indeed make it without injury to yourself or others. But if something happens that needs quick reaction, an amazingly small amount of alcohol can double or triple your reaction time. When you're at the wheel of a vehicle going 60 mph, say, a one-second delay uses thirty whole yards of road. Even an extra split second can mean ten yards that will make the difference between hitting someone and stopping in time. Between, literally, life and death.

It's been said before, but it's still worth saying again: A vehicle can be a lethal weapon when that much steel hits a

➤ "I know what stops me driving when I've been drinking is that if I drove drunk and hit somebody, I couldn't live with that. With knowing that I'd done that. You need to know, if you do hit somebody, that at least you did everything right, did all you could to avoid it."

➤ "Having children makes a big difference."

➤ "Right. You think what if something happened to you? What about the kids?"

—Pennsylvania group

pedestrian or another car. So, once again, please, if not for your own sake, then for the sake of others: When you drink, don't drive.

About Long-Distance Driving

☛ DO stop every couple of hours, get out, and walk around. Stretch some. Jog a bit, perhaps. Get the blood moving again, and oxygen flowing to your brain. If you're driving with a companion, make a driver change every couple of hours.

☛ DON'T be macho. You don't have to get cross-country in three days. You don't have to try to impress friends by telling them how quickly you got there. (If your friends are impressed by this sort of thing, consider a change of friends.)

☛ DO stop driving when you feel tired. Pull into a rest stop, lock the doors, and take a nap. If it's late, check into a motel.

☛ DON'T take pills to stay awake. If they're illegal ones, they'll send you into la-la land and make you dangerous on the road. If they're legal, over-the-counter ones, large doses of caffeine can make you even drowsier.

☛ DO listen to the sound system. Music's good, but not the soothing kind. Talk is better. Can't stand talk radio? Either rent books on tape or borrow them from your library. The number for the best books on tape rental outfit—called, surprise, Books on Tape— is 800/626-3333.

☛ DON'T eat junk food on the road. Make sure you have fruit juice, fresh or dried fruit, nuts, and sandwiches in the car with you; it's hard to find good

148

food on the interstates. Driving long distances is more wearing on the body than you might imagine. Your body needs good fuel.

☞ DO drive with the ventilation set for fresh air and with one window open a crack. If you have a moonroof, open that a crack too. It will be slightly noisier, but the fresh air is worth it. Stale air makes you drowsy.

About Kids in Cars

☞ ALWAYS use child seats for infants and young children. The backseat is the safest place for them. Built-in child seats are best but rarely available. Make sure that any child seat you buy has easily adjustable straps. Use cushions to raise the height of children too big for child seats, so that they can see easily out the windows: This helps prevent car sickness and provides a better fit for the seat belts.

☞ Make a ten-minute rest stop every two hours. Bring along Frisbees or jump ropes or anything the kids (and you) can play with to get the blood moving and stretch cramped muscles.

☞ Have pillows and a car blanket in the car.

☞ Keep prepackaged moist towelettes in the car, and a roll of paper towels.

☞ Create a good store of games, especially ones that require the kids to look out: counting horses, for example, or out-of-state licenses, or things beginning with A, B, C, and so on.

☞ Make sure you have tapes or CDs that the kids know and like.

- ☞ Bring along a good supply of some sweet but healthy snack that won't end up squished all over the seats. Any dried fruits, for instance.

- ☞ And of course, toilet paper.

- ☞ If it's a long trip, and the kids are old enough, assign them map-reading duties. Make them feel they're part of the trip, not just passive passengers.

- ☞ If an argument develops, as inevitably happens sooner or later if you have two or more kids in one car, don't try to resolve it while driving. Pull over, stop the car, *then* turn around and deal with whatever it is. Not even a Supermom can drive and resolve arguments at the same time.

About the First Thousand Miles

This is the break-in period for a new car. I know dealers say you don't need to break in a new car anymore, but they're the guys who get to fix it and charge you for the pleasure. If you want your car to have a long and healthy life, treating the first thousand miles as a break-in period is still a very good idea.

Breaking in your car is rather like breaking in a horse: Don't baby it. Exercise the engine. Don't drive long stretches at a constant speed; vary the speed every ten miles or so. You don't have to go slow, and highway speeds are fine. Drive the car at different rev speeds (2,500, 3,000, 3,500, 4,000 on your tachometer) for five minutes or so at a stretch, switching between high and low revs by switching gears. Don't be leery of high revs—unless it's over the redline, the car is built to work with them. It really is like working all the muscles on your body. And just as you would if you were in an intense workout at the gym, don't accelerate or brake suddenly unless you really have to.

Get an oil change after the first thousand miles. I know the owner's manuals don't mention this one, but the oil will have absorbed any loose metal filings or dust from the manufacturing process, and you want them out of your engine. From then on, drive as you normally would.

About Accidents

Nearly half of the women in the groups—49.6%—had been in at least one accident. Of these:

20.6% had been rear-ended by someone else.

17.5% rear-ended someone.

7.9% were hit by someone going through a stoplight or sign.

9.5% hit someone else by going through a stoplight or sign.

14.3% lost control on ice or in snow or rain.

21.2% totaled a car, either through their own fault or someone else's.

Of all these accidents, 47.6% were the driver's fault, and 52.4% were not.

The Accident Checklist

If you've just been in an accident, no matter how minor, you may be quite shaken. Though most accidents are relatively minor and do not involve serious injury, they're still very unsettling. This checklist can see you through, and possibly save you a lot of hassle later with insurance claims, even for a minor fender-bender.

1. First check if anyone is *hurt*. If anyone is injured, get someone else to call an ambulance.

2. Turn on your emergency *flashers*, then set up flares so that oncoming traffic can see and avoid you. Get someone to direct the traffic away from you if you can. The last thing you want is for your accident to cause another one.

3. Ask someone to call the *police*.

4. Try *not* to move the cars or sweep up broken glass and debris. The police can verify what happened only if nothing has been moved. Sometimes traffic conditions will mean you do have to move the car; in that case, go to step 6 first.

5. Write down all the following *information* if the accident involves another car:
   • Other drivers' license numbers
   • Vehicle license numbers of all vehicles involved
   • Year, make, and model of all vehicles, and their VINs (vehicle identification numbers)
   • Other drivers' insurance carriers
   • Names and numbers of drivers, passengers, and any witnesses

6. Make *notes* of weather and road conditions, and diagram the accident on paper: Draw the direction of travel of the vehicles involved, and the angle and point of impact.

7. If the police arrive (often only if there's an injury), make sure you write down the names and *badge numbers* of the officers.

8. Get someone to call a *tow truck* if your vehicle is so badly damaged you can't drive it.

9. Don't claim *responsibility* for the accident. Even if you think you're at fault at the time, you may not be

once the full picture is known. Be as honest and cooperative as possible when describing the accident to the police, but don't say it was your fault. The police will come to their own conclusions.

10. Be sure to get the *file number* of the police report.

The Five Oddest Accidents

✗ "I hit a hearse in a funeral procession; it was very embarrassing."

✗ "I collided with a runaway U-Haul trailer."

✗ "It was a Corvair accident: The car just went out of control."

✗ "I was attacked by an out-of-control car in mountain snow."

✗ "I ran over a Miata."

The Angriest Accident

✗ "A drunk driver ran a red light and totaled my new candy-apple-red Celica GTS."

The Security Issue

➡ **"I love that I can lock all the doors with one button."**

➡ **"Keyless entry is wonderful, I adore it."**

➡ **"What I like is walking toward the car with the remote control in my hand, knowing that if anything happens I can press the alarm button and the car will start flashing and honking, like it's coming to my defense!"**

—Washington group

Security is a major issue for most women living in urban areas. Personal security, that is, in the car.

There is a world of difference between paranoia and reasonable security. A lot of businesses out there see women's concerns about security as the perfect opportunity to make money; they prey on our fears in order to sell assorted alarms and devices. I call these people paranoia-mongerers, and I don't have to tell you what I think of them.

Still, the security issue won't go away if we just try to ignore it. So as my mother always said, "Better safe than sorry." Of course, she wasn't talking about cars. But the principle still applies.

Here are ten things you can do to enhance your security in a car without spending any money at all.

1. Always drive with your doors locked. With central locking on all newer models now—all the door locks can be controlled from a switch by the driver's seat—this is simple. Lock the doors immediately after you get into the car, before putting on your seat belt and starting the ignition.

2. Always be aware of what's happening around you on the road. This, of course, is part of good driving in any case.

3. Do you need me to tell you not to park on dark, unpeopled streets at night? (And if you park during the day but don't expect to be back until after dark, take that into account.)

4. Never leave anything remotely stealable lying around in open view inside the car. I've lost a lot of sunglasses and cassette tapes this way—and had to pay for a lot of new windows. In fact, never leave anything at all that you don't want stolen anywhere in the car, even in the trunk.

5. Never feel embarrassed to ask a coworker, a friend, or an employee at the mall or the supermarket to walk you to your car.

6. Always have your keys or your remote control out and ready before you reach your car. Fumbling in your purse beside the car leaves you vulnerable. In an emergency, the keys can also be bunched in your fist, with the sharp ends sticking out between your fingers, and used as a weapon.

7. Lock the car whenever you leave it, even if you know you'll only be away for a minute: when you go to pay for the gas at a gas station, for example.

8. When parking, if something makes you nervous—not enough light, somebody lurking—trust your

instincts, and drive away. There's always somewhere else to park. Consider well-lighted parking garages with attendants: Your security is worth the expense.

9. If you suspect you're being followed by another car, drive around the block. If the car is still there, head for the nearest police station or to a full-service gas station, where you can call the police. Do *not* head home.

10. Never drive with an almost-empty gas tank. Make a practice of filling it up when it's half or a third empty, so that you don't have to stop for fuel at night in an area where you feel uncomfortable.

Locking Up

➡ **"Keyless entry is great when you have the kids with you. You just press the button and the car is open. You don't have to fumble around. Then you bundle everyone in, lock the doors, and then get them buckled up. That's why minivans are so great—you can move around inside them."**

—Homemaker, New York

Locks are the first line of defense in a car, just as they are in a home. If you lock the door to your home, then you should lock the door to your car too—when you're in it as well as when you're not.

Some cars have automatic locks that lock either when the engine is started or when the car reaches five miles an hour, and stay locked until you switch off the engine. A good idea, though you might not want them to unlock the moment you switch the engine off. (See page 74.)

The best keyless entry systems give you two choices on how to unlock the car: Press the button once to open the driver's door only, and twice to open all the doors. If your car unlocks all the doors every time, you might want to get the dealer or an automotive electronics technician to reprogram it for you, so that it opens the driver's door only. This will cost money, but it's worth it.

Cellular Phones

Many of the women in the focus groups either had or were considering buying cellular phones as security devices. If you can afford the phone and the service, it's a good idea: You don't have to find a call box if your car breaks down, you don't have to ask a stranger to call for help, and you don't have to pull off the highway to find a call box in an unfamiliar neighborhood if you're running late or lost. You can call for help quickly and easily. (But check when you get the phone what numbers to call—the emergency number is not necessarily 911 in the cellular system.)

If you do want a cellular phone, decide if you want a car phone (also known as a *mobile cellular*), which is permanently installed in the car, or a *portable cellular* phone, which you can take with you when you get out of the car. If you use a lot of different cars—company cars or rental cars—you may prefer a portable, many of which are now small and light enough to carry around in your purse.

There is one major problem with cellular phones in cars, however, and that's driving safety. Cellular phones are rarely used for emergency calls, for the simple reason that emergencies are rare. The vast majority of cellular phone calls are business or personal calls.

So what's wrong with that? Well, someone talking on the phone usually has one hand off the wheel, holding the phone. If she's dialing as she's driving, she's not even looking at the road. If you've ever driven behind someone talking on the phone, receiver clamped to ear and attention somewhere else entirely, you'll know what I mean. That person is driving poorly.

The best—and of course more expensive—cellular phones avoid the worst of this problem. They're voice-activated or hands-free; you preprogram the numbers you're most likely to call, press one button to dial, then talk without holding the receiver. Some even respond to your voice ordering up a number to be called.

➡ "Half the women I know, their husbands have bought them car phones: for birthday presents, for Christmas presents, for Mother's Day presents. Always for security."

➡ "It's the latest 'in' gift for women."

➡ "Tell my boyfriend that. I want one because if I break down by myself in the middle of the road at night, what do I do? With a car phone I can just call Triple A, lock the doors, and wait."

➡ "I do have one, and I bought it myself. I use it mainly to say I'm going to be late or to pick up messages. I've never used it in an emergency, but it's good to know it's there if I ever do need it."

—California group

A second caution on cellular phones: They invite more break-ins, which gives antenna-less portable phones the edge over mobile phones. Make sure you put the phone away before parking the car. If it's a portable, take it with you.

And a third caution: Be aware that there are no cell sites for these phones in many remote areas. If you're planning to travel out of cellular reach and still want the communications capability, you might think about getting a Citizen's Band radio, on which Channel 9 is kept free for emergency use.

Self-Defense

When you've heard one report too many about crime on the local evening news, it's easy to start thinking of carrying weapons. Guns are the first to come to mind, and though none of the women in the focus groups carried a gun, a few had considered it. Personally, I wouldn't want one, though I understand women who do.

But guns and cars really do not mix. First, it's illegal in many states to carry a concealed handgun in your car. Second, if you insist despite the law, and your car is broken into, you'll have contributed yet another gun to the vast underground armory. And third, if you have children, a gun in your car is asking for very bad trouble indeed.

An alternative is pepper spray, which seems to have replaced Mace as the purse weapon of choice, partly because Mace is illegal in most states, and partly because pepper sprays work just as well, yet are safer. If you do carry pepper spray, make sure it's within easy reach, and make sure it works—outdoors, with the nozzle pointed away from you and the wind behind you. But once more, if you have children, don't even *think* of carrying it. Either it will be so well locked away that you won't be able to get to it in an emergency, or it will be within easy reach of the kids as well as you. Again: bad trouble.

Your best weapons are still foresight, alertness, and keeping your wits about you.

Alarms

Does anyone pay any attention at all to car alarms anymore? The sirens and honking horns of car alarms have become part of the aural nightlife of every American city, and a major nuisance, whether they've been set off by accident or by a break-in.

Still, I'd say better to have an alarm than not. That little red light on the dash may help deter more amateur break-ins (a pro can disable most alarms in a few seconds) as well as joyriders. Many cars now come with manufacturer-fitted alarms. You can also have an alarm installed at any auto-electronics shop. Make sure you know how your alarm works—read the owner's manual—so that your neighbors don't come to hate you because the alarm goes on every time you open the door.

Some keyless locking systems now have personal alarms on the keyring remote control. Press a button as you walk toward your car, and the car's lights start flashing, and its horn or siren starts going off. There's still the question of whether anyone will pay any attention, but the surprise of it may be enough to put an attacker off his guard for a moment, giving you time to get away.

The best thing about car alarm systems is that most of them also disable the ignition, so though your car may be broken into, it's less likely to get stolen. I say only "less likely" because a professional auto theft ring will simply drive up a flatbed truck, load the car they want onto it, and take off.

The Insurance Institute for Highway Safety keeps tabs on which cars are the most stolen. Their theft rates are included in many of the comparative pricing reports (see "Tire-kickers for Hire," page 61), or you can check them with your insurance agent.

Other Antitheft Devices

Your car may be broken into for several reasons: A thief may be looking for anything that can be sold for drug money, or he may want a car to take joyriding, or he may be looking to steal the whole car so that it can be broken up and sold as parts.

Different antitheft devices address different reasons for theft. Some don't even aim to stop your car being broken into; they aim to stop it being driven away. These, in addition to the ignition-disabling devices built into all factory-installed alarm systems, range from the simple, like the metal bar-lock for the wheel marketed as the Club, to the high tech: devices that disable the car after it's been driven a few feet.

All will foil some amateurs, but not most pros. One of the neatest is the Mul-T-Lock transmission lock, which locks around the gearshift in any car with a floor-mounted shifter, whether manual or automatic. It has the advantage of being a visible theft deterrent, like the Club, and simple to use, unlike the rather unwieldy Club, which can be removed by any thief equipped with a can of Freon.

One ingenious device is a removable steering wheel. But it's one of those ideas that's too clever for its own good. After all, can you really imagine yourself walking into a restaurant with your steering wheel hung over your arm?

Devices providing a kind of passive defense against theft focus on the radio, which is what the majority of thieves—the ones out for quick money—are after.

Many radios now have special codes that won't allow them to work anywhere except in your car. That sounds clever, but the thief may find that out only after he's stolen it. There is a little notice on these radios saying that they won't work anywhere else, but it's questionable how many thieves either can or will bother to read.

Perhaps the most effective antitheft device for radios is

the Benzi box—a simple frame that your mechanic installs around your radio, allowing you to pull it out and take it with you when you leave the car. While nobody walks into a restaurant with a steering wheel dangling from her arm, quite a few people do walk in carrying their radios. But remember to take the radio every time: No self-respecting thief can resist the sight of a Benzi box with the radio in it.

Many people simply put the radio under a seat or in the trunk, but this is not a great idea, since you have no idea who may be watching as you do this.

Any auto parts store will have quite an array of antitheft alarms and devices. But be aware that salesmen will prey on your fears. Don't expect full protection. And resist buying fuzzy dice while you're there.

Secure Driving

➡ "I try not to drive at night at all."

➡ "I think that's overdoing it, but I will drive home with the fuel-empty light on because I don't want to stop at a convenience store, where you're all alone at the gas pumps. And I'm thinking 'Okay, now do I want to risk running out of gas or do I want to risk a gun in my back?' "

➡ "I won't even stop at red lights at night. I'll yield and make sure nobody's coming, but I'm not going to sit there by myself and wait."

➡ "Right. When I get gas at night, I'm poised to run if I have to. And I'll also run red lights if I'm coming home alone at night."

➡ "I'll go to a full-service station if I need gas at night. I know it's more expensive but it's safer."

—Texas group

The secret to secure driving, as to safe driving, is alertness. And trusting your instincts. (And *not* allowing your gas tank to run so low that the fuel-empty light comes on.)

Several women in large-city focus groups said they regularly go through red lights when they're driving home alone at night. They pause first, check nothing's coming, then go. But unless you have specific reason to feel that you're being followed or threatened, this isn't a great idea. It's not only illegal, it's also dangerous. You may think nobody's coming, but so does the guy barreling along at eighty in order to make the green light on his side.

If you do feel threatened, however—someone approaching your car in a way that looks like trouble, for instance—it makes sense not to just sit there and wait for the trouble to happen. But do you really have to go through the red light? A quick turn right on red is just as effective in getting you out of any potential trouble. Especially if you honk your horn as you drive: That way, you attract attention, which is the last thing a would-be attacker wants.

Carjackings are relatively rare, but they do happen. If someone comes up to you in a parking lot, says he wants your car, and has a knife or a gun to back up his request, let the nice man have the car. Even if it's a Rolls-Royce.

The same goes, of course, for demands for your purse.

Don't argue. Unless you're a seventh-degree black belt in karate, just hand over the keys.

There've been some well-publicized cases of carjackers intentionally rear-ending another car so that the owner will pull over to the side of the road and get out to check the damage. If you are rear-ended and have any reason to be suspicious, trust your instincts. Don't stop, but drive on to a full-service gas station where you can call for help, or better yet, a police station. Get the other car's license-plate number if you can, or at least note as much as you can of its type, make, model, and color. Report all this to the police. And remember to get a police file number for your insurance.

Favorite news item: **When a thief tried to steal a Detroit woman's car as she was leaving it to go pay for gas, she grabbed the Club and used it as . . . a club, beating him over the head. Her six-year-old was in the car. The thief was hospitalized, and then charged.**

Safety Questions

Several questions about safety came up repeatedly during the focus groups. Since you may have the same questions, here are the ones most asked, and my answers.

Belts and Bags

Question: **Do I really need to wear a seat belt if I have an airbag?**

Answer: **Yes. Absolutely.**

For a time, I had one of those cars with motorized seat belts: Close the door, and the shoulder belt wrapped itself into place. I had no great objection to it—in fact I was rather fond of it—but every one of my passengers hated it, especially when I insisted that they do up the lap belt too.

"Why doesn't this car have airbags?" said one. "Then we wouldn't need seat belts."

"Wrong," I said.

Dead wrong.

Seat belts are the main line of defense against injury in

an accident. Airbags, called supplementary restraint systems (SRS) in the auto biz, are precisely that: supplements to seat belts. Certainly they help save lives. But just as certainly, they don't take the place of seat belts. They can't.

Here's why.

The purpose of both seat belts and airbags is to keep you from moving inside the car in an accident. The less you move, the less the chance of serious injury, which often results from being thrown around inside the car or, worse, from being thrown out of it.

A wheel- or dashboard-mounted airbag will explode only if there is a sudden impact to the front of the car, or within fifteen degrees of dead front. But most accidents are not frontal. You can be hit from the side and the rear as well as the front. And many accidents aren't even the result of an impact at all: Spins and rollovers, for instance, are often single-car accidents—the result of loss of control, not of a collision. In such situations, a seat belt is your most valuable asset.

In research in the early 1990s, General Motors found that while airbags alone will save you from serious injury or death in 21% of serious accidents, seat belts alone will do the job in precisely twice as many cases: 42%. Seat belts *plus* an airbag are the most effective of all, preventing serious injury or death 47% of the time.

By seat belt, I mean a three-point belt. That is, it's anchored at three points: above your left shoulder, on the floor on your left, and on the floor on your right. Basically, you're wearing two belts: a shoulder belt and a lap belt. Most three-point systems combine the two belts into one. Motorized belts like the one I had are only shoulder belts; the lap belt still has to be buckled manually.

If you do have a motorized belt, buckling the lap belt is vital. In an accident, you can slide forward under a shoulder belt—it's called "submarining"—unless your lap belt is fastened.

Why was my passenger so confused about bags and belts? To some extent, the federal government is responsible. Back in the mid-eighties, the government decided there had to be some form of "passive restraint system" in all passenger cars. That is, some kind of safety system that would work automatically. The reason was that at that time, under half of all American wore their seat belts. At least this way, the government reasoned, the number of people wearing belts would rise, and those who still refused would be protected by airbags.

Their intentions were good. The results were not so good. Airbags were still so expensive that they were placed only in luxury cars, and automakers installed automatic belts instead. The worst of these stretched out from the door and practically defied you to figure out how to get into the car. Motorized ones sometimes threatened to strangle you if you opened the door with the engine running. Others stretched from the top of the door to the floor in such a way that anyone trying to get into the back of a coupe had to literally clamber over them to get in.

By now, nearly all new cars have airbags. (In fact, the law mandates dual front-seat airbags in all cars by 1998.) That is wonderful news. But not if it means we think we don't need seat belts anymore.

I confess I was quite casual about seat belt use until I got into a formula race car on a track. My instructor told me to do up the five-point harness—two belts over my shoulders, one from the floor either side of me, and one between my legs—so tight that it hurt. "Believe me," he said, "once you're on the track, you won't notice." He was right. And I gained a new respect for belts. If race drivers put so much stress on them, I reasoned, maybe I should too.

Since then, I never drive any distance at all, not even a hundred yards, without my seat belt fastened. This isn't because of any law. It's a simple matter of self-preservation. And of self-respect. Driving well also means driving responsibly. And if I can't be responsible to myself, I certainly won't be responsible on the road.

Four examples of how well seat belts work come from women who were wearing them at the time of an accident. None of them had airbags in her car. And none was injured any more seriously than minor cuts and bruises.

➡ "I took a corner too fast and I lost control; the car went skidding off the road and the next thing I knew, it was rolling over, and went skidding on forward on its roof. I remember thinking 'So this is how it happens.' I was amazed when it stopped and I was still alive. I unbuckled the seat belt and squirmed out the side window, and discovered that though I was badly shaken, I only had two small cuts. The car was totaled."

➡ "I was sideswiped in an intersection by a car running a stoplight. He slammed right into the side of my car and sent me spinning into a wall. I walked away from the car, but it was a write-off."

➡ "I was on the highway in my little convertible when the truck ahead of me braked suddenly to avoid colliding with a car that had come full speed from the on-ramp without looking. The truck swerved and his back end hit my front fender and sent me into a spin. I remember how strange it felt to realize I was moving backward on the highway. The car was damaged, but I was okay."

➡ "I hit black ice when I was driving some friends home one night, and the car went off the road and straight into a tree. Nobody was injured, but the car was badly damaged. So was the tree."

Pregnancy and Belts

Q.: Do I have to wear a seat belt when I'm pregnant?

A.: Yes. Definitely.

It always surprises me when pregnant women tell me they don't wear seat belts because the belts are uncomfortable. It seems to me that when you're pregnant, you should be even more concerned about safety.

The problem is that seat belts, as currently designed, don't take pregnancy into account. The reason why is clear: The men who design cars never get pregnant. When General Motors finally began to use a "pregnant" crash dummy in 1994, the news was treated as an occasion for sophomoric humor by those automobile magazines that even thought it important enough to report.

Adjustable lap and shoulder belts will be mandatory on all new passenger vehicles as of 1998. Clearly we can expect some improvement in seat belt design in the near future, possibly even a belt designed especially for pregnant women. In the meantime, however, enlarged breasts and belly demand some adjustment.

For the breasts: If your shoulder belt is not adjustable, you can buy a small contraption at any auto-parts store that will hold the shoulder belt back to the height that's comfortable for you. It's basically no more than a hook, but it does the job, and it's easy to install.

For the belly: Place the lap portion of the belt under your belly rather than around or over it.

And please note: The American College of Obstetrics and Gynecology *strongly recommends* that all pregnant women wear seat belts.

On the Road

167

Airbag Injuries

Q.: Is it true that airbags can cause injuries?

A.: Yes. But this doesn't mean they're not safe.

Airbags are not feather pillows. True, they cushion the impact on a driver's or passenger's body, but "cushion" is not quite the right word. These are, literally, exploding bags. They're there to prevent serious injury, especially head and chest injury. To do that, they must inflate quickly. In milliseconds, or less time than it takes to blink. That means they have to explode with force.

This is why airbags make a loud popping noise when they go off, though in an accident, you probably won't even notice it. And the force of the impact of the airbag against your face can cause a number of minor injuries such as abrasions and bruises.

But then, as I've noted before, if the choice is the intensive care unit or a quick patch-up with ointment and a BandAid, which would you go for? The undeniable fact is that there are 24% fewer driver deaths in front and front-angle crashes of cars with airbags.

In earlier airbags, the hot gas that inflates the airbags (harmless nitrogen) also caused mild burns, but automakers have solved this problem by changing the position of the air vents that deflate the bag. Also, many people report a slight burning smell after an airbag deployment. Don't worry about this: There is no chance of fire from the airbag. The smell is from the chemical reaction that inflates the bag, and the "smoke" that some report is the talc in which the bag was packed.

Your driving position also makes a big difference. In most cases of injury from exploding airbags, the driver was sitting too close to the steering wheel. What is too close? Ideally, if you stretch out your arms, your wrists should touch the top rim of the steering wheel. If you're closer than that, you're too close. And if you can't see without being that close, that probably means you need either a new prescription for your contact lenses or a height-adjustable seat or a pillow to sit on.

Moreover, most of those drivers injured by airbags were not wearing seat belts at the time of the accident. Seat belts help hold you back against the seat, lessening the chances of overviolent contact with a deploying airbag.

Side Impact

Q.: How am I protected in a side impact?

A.: Your seat belt is still your main line of defense.

Volvo introduced side airbags in 1994—small bags that emerge from the outside edge of the front seats. But though they're a great idea, side bags are still in the early stages of development. To work well, they have to be much quicker than frontal bags, because the distance between the door and your body is far shorter than the distance between the front of the car and your body. In other words, impact happens far quicker.

For the time being, most automakers are focusing more on improving side-impact technology by reinforcing the doors, using both steel beams and special impact-absorbing "honeycomb" materials inside the door. New laws mandate protective door beams in all cars built from 1997 on, though many automakers began installing them far earlier.

None of this, however, makes the seat belt any less important. The impact of collision will still throw you around inside the car unless you're wearing a belt.

Child Seats

Q.: How do I know if I'm using the child seat correctly?

A.: Use the following checklist of the American Academy of Pediatrics for a seat with a three-point or five-point harness.

Always use properly belted child seats. They lower the number of children's deaths in auto accidents by 71%, and injuries requiring hospitalization by 67%. The checklist:

__ **1.**   Is the seat facing the right way?

Infants up to one year old and/or 20 pounds should face the rear of the car, since their necks and spines can't support the violent forward lurch of impact. The backseat is the safest place for them. *Never* place a rear-facing infant carrier in a car's front seat if that seat has a passenger airbag, since an inflated airbag could injure the infant by driving it into the back of the seat.

Toddlers should always be in the backseat, and can face forward. Seat belts alone can be used when the child is about four years old, depending on size, though the use of booster seats until the child is about 60 pounds is a good idea.

__ **2.**   Is the angle of the seat correct?

Rear-facing infant seats should be at a 45-degree angle; forward-facing seats should be upright.

__ **3.**   Is the belt routed correctly?

Double-check on this in the manual that comes with the seat you buy, since different kinds of seats have different paths for the belt.

____ **4.** Is the seat firmly anchored?

It's extremely important to check this. Follow the installation instructions exactly. When the child seat is in place, the seat belt should not give or expand when the seat is pulled or rocked hard.

____ **5.** Are the harness straps positioned correctly?

Again, follow the installation instructions exactly. Some child seats can be used facing either forward or backward (convertible seats). When the seat faces the rear, the straps should come from slots below the child's shoulders. When the seat faces forward, they should come from the highest slot. Make sure the straps are snug, and use the harness clip to tie them together. In a built-in child seat, be sure to use a metal locking clip to hold the shoulder and lap belts together if the car has a continuous-loop belt.

Antilock Brakes

Q.: Do antilock brakes really work?

A.: Yes, superbly.

Antilock brakes (ABS) mean that you can stop in an emergency quickly and safely, without skidding. Without ABS, if you stomp all the way down on the brake pedal—the natural reaction in an emergency—the brake pads clutch the wheel so tightly that they stop it turning altogether. But the car still has forward momentum, so what happens is that you just skid along over the road with no steering ability because your tires have lost traction; what stops the car is more likely to be a tree or another car than the brakes.

With ABS, the natural reaction—stomping on the brakes—is the correct one. Put your foot to the floor and keep it there. A small computer will sense when the wheels are about to lock and feather the brake pads at that point so that the wheels remain just the right side of locking up—that is, with maximum braking power and maximum control.

In an emergency stop with ABS, *you must keep your foot all the way down on the brake pedal* or the ABS system will stop working. If you feel the pedal vibrating under your foot, that's fine: it means the system is doing its job. To my mind, ABS is the single most important safety advance on passenger cars in the past twenty years, more important even than airbags. An airbag can help you survive an accident; antilock brakes can help you *avoid* it.

4.

Fun in Cars

Sex, Looks, and Automobiles

79% of women have had sex in a car.

Ten responses to "Have you ever had sex in a car?"

"What do you mean by sex?"

"Kind of."

"Of course."

"Yes!!!"

"Yes, carefully!"

"Can't remember."

"About a hundred years ago."

"Last night!"

"Only because it was a Ferrari."

"Only because it was a VW Bug."

Is there really such a thing as a sexy car? Fully 90% of the women in the focus groups said there most definitely is. But not all sexiness is the same.

➡ **"There's really two kinds of sexy: There's nasty-sexy and there's classy-sexy. The Mercedes SL is classy sexy. A Corvette is nasty sexy."**

—Sales manager, Oregon

Most men go for the nasty-sexy—or at least they feel duty-bound to do so, certainly in front of other men. They'll cite a litany of Ferraris, Lamborghinis, Bugattis, and other hard-to-handle supercars with sharp, aggressive angles and the kind of horsepower that will lose you your driving license.

Women, as we all know, are far more subtle about sex, and far more aware that sex is a state of mind.

The Sexiest Makes

32.7%	Jaguar
13.1%	Porsche
10.3%	Mercedes
5.6%	Ferrari
2.8%	Corvette

➡ **"Sexy means the freedom involved with a car, the liberating quality of a car. It's something you can feel about yourself. Another person can make me feel sexy, but when you're alone in your car, if it's the right car, the car itself can make you feel that way."**

—Engineer, New York

What is "the right car"? So far as women are concerned, it's far and away a Jaguar. Some go for old ones, others for new. But whether we're talking a vintage E-type or a brand-new XJS, you might say that women have something of a fixation on Jags. They outrank second-runner Porsches by more than two to one.

The rest of the field was spread over a wide range of cars: expensive, sporty, convertible, vintage, or all of the above. But in case anyone thinks women go only for the upscale, it's reassuring to know that two women did name "old Volvos" as the sexiest car.

Why Jaguars? The word "sensuous" kept coming up, as in: "They're so sensuous," or "Long and lean and sensuous," or "Sensuous and glossy."

Clearly, if women bought cars for sex, Jaguar would be the biggest-selling make in America. But of course, we don't. Between sex and ownership, as between sex and marriage, pragmatism intervenes. The cars we think sexiest are not necessarily the ones we most want to own (much as the men we think sexiest are not necessarily the ones we'd marry).

Women also know that while feeling sexy in a car is one thing, attracting sexual attention in one is something else. The Jaguar is a good choice, because unless you're driving the most expensive, convertible model, you probably won't attract too much attention in it. Not all such attention is welcome.

The Makes Women Most Want to Own

14.8%	Jaguar
12.5%	Mercedes
7.0%	Saab
7.0%	Jeep Cherokee
4.7%	Lexus

➡ **"When I drive my mother's Honda Prelude instead of my station wagon, I get more looks, and more flirtatious driving behavior."**

➡ **"And that can be threatening sometimes, that kind of behavior."**

➡ **"Yes, like a friend of mine's parents had this Jeep Wrangler, and the guys were all over us, two girls in a Jeep. But whenever we were in her car, this big old American boat, we never had any trouble at all."**

—Washington group

Young men in sharp-looking sports cars often think of them as "girl magnets." Let them have their illusions. But many women are finding out that when they drive the same cars, the cars do indeed become man magnets.

While some women hate this kind of attention, others find it amusing, if also puzzling.

➡ **"My son left his bright red Trans Am with me when he went to Europe for three months, and what happened was amazing. When I drive my old Mercedes, men** don't drive up alongside me at stoplights and give me these looks. . . . It's never happened to me before and it hasn't happened since."

—Homemaker, British Columbia

➡ "I bought a '66 Mustang convertible brand new and I still have it to this day, and if you ever want a car to attract men, I guarantee you it is not a new sports car, but a '66 Mustang!"

—Interior designer, California

➡ "I had my very first climax in a car."

➡ "What car?"

➡ "It was a '62 Chevy Impala."

➡ "There's going to be a run on '62 Impalas."

—Texas group

A word of warning, however: A car that seems to exert a magnetic effect on men will have the same effect on the highway patrol, with somewhat different results. A bright red sports car is to a patrolman what a red flag is to a bull. It's a sure way to get the laser and radar guns going, which is why you see so many Porsches being driven sedately along on the inside lane. Maybe it's a good idea to keep that old beige Volvo after all . . .

➡ "We kept trying to have sex in the back of my Volkswagen Bug. There must be ways to do it, I know there are ways. . . ."

➡ "There are: double-jointed hips."

—Pennsylvania group

Fast Women

➡ "I once had a '72 green Ford Granada named Bessie with an eight-cylinder engine and it could go fast. I got it up to 125. . . ."

➡ "What happens if you go as fast as it will go? Does the car blow up? Does it stop?"

➡ "You find yourself making strange noises, rather like a rodeo cowboy. Once you top it out, the car just doesn't accelerate anymore."

➡ "But doesn't it shake a lot?"

➡ "Well, yes, it vibrates a lot at that speed. So do you."

➡ "This is like confessing to sexual experience!"

—Texas group

Women are not supposed to be interested in speed. That's the general opinion. Insurance rates reflect that, so maybe I shouldn't really be writing this section. It might be letting an expensive cat out of the bag. Still, here goes.

It's true that speed is a top priority to only a minority, but still a sizable one—over a quarter of the women in the focus groups. Yet that doesn't mean that other women are indifferent to it: Far fewer say that speed is unimportant to them. Here's how it breaks down.

20% say speed is very important.

49% say it's somewhat important.

17% say it's not so important.

14% say it's unimportant.

This means that the majority—nearly 70%—say speed is either very important or somewhat important.

What women enjoy about speed is very much the same as what men enjoy about it: the excitement and the challenge of it, the test of nerves and ability, and the pure sensation of it.

The average top speed of women in the groups was 97 mph.

For the majority, their top speed was a one-time affair: something tried once out of curiosity or on a dare, usually as a teenager. Having children, many women noted, makes them far more responsible drivers, even when the children aren't in the car. Perhaps this is one reason "everybody knows" that women drive slower than men. Or do they?

42% drive faster than the men in their lives, 28% drive the same speed, and 30% drive slower.

So the old saw about women being slower drivers just isn't true. And neither, it turns out, is the one about women thinking that slow driving is necessarily better driving.

Of those who say they drive better than men, 51% say they drive faster, 18% slower, and 31% more or less the same speed.

Of those who say they drive worse, 41% say they drive faster, 53% slower, and 6% more or less the same speed.

With driving as with everything else, making generalizations about women is something men do at their own risk. Women know better. And often drive better. And faster.

Ticket Jeopardy

It should probably come as no surprise that the majority of women in the groups—about two-thirds—have had speeding tickets, though the vast majority of tickets were not, as one woman put it, "really worthwhile tickets."

➡ "If I got a ticket going all out at 120, that would be a ticket that had earned its keep, so to speak. But I always get them for going 35 in a 30-mile zone, stuff like that."

—Teacher, Washington

➡ "I just have this innocent look, and I really am convinced all the time that I truly *am* innocent, and it works, I've never gotten a ticket."

➡ "I must have a really guilty look because I'm always getting tickets."

—Pennsylvania group

The good news is that it *is* still possible to talk your way out of one. And as long as the Highway Patrol resists going fifty-fifty male and female, being a woman certainly helps.

The most popular way to get out of a ticket, by far, is . . . yes, tears.

The second way, short of tears, is to act pathetic. Real pathetic.

The third is more of a surprise: Bring a wedding into it! Cops get sentimental too.

The fourth way is to be lost, or at least to act as if you're lost.

The fifth is to be in dire need of the bathroom, or at least say you are.

And the other ways. . . . Well, the table tells all. You could almost feel sorry for the Highway Patrol.

Almost.

10 Ways Women Get Out of Tickets

POPULARITY	METHOD	WHAT SHE DID/SAID
#1	Tears	I just started crying. It was a really bad time in my life, so it was easy. I was just totally distraught.
#2	Being pathetic	It was late at night, I was wearing my nerdy glasses, and I said I was a woman alone just trying to get home. He asked where I worked, and I looked really sad and downtrodden and said, "I don't work, sir, I'm just a mother doing the best I can."
#3	Wedding	It was a week before my wedding and I was an emotional mess and when he pulled me over I started gushing tears. I said we were on our way to a wedding.
#4	Being lost	I said, "I'm so sorry, officer, but I have no idea where I am or how to get where I'm going. Can you help me?" I was following a friend's car because I didn't know the way, so when I got stopped I said, "Look what you've done! Now I'm absolutely lost!"
#5	Bathroom	I looked really embarrassed and said, "I'm so sorry, Officer, but I have to go to the bathroom real bad." I said my period had just begun and I was trying to get to a rest stop to find a tampon.
#6	Kids' tears	My kids were in the back and he saw them both with tears in their eyes.
#7	Name-dropping	When I was working on the Mardi Gras, the chairman's name worked like magic.
#8	Being pregnant	It was the week before I went into bed rest with the twins, and I was humongous, the wheel pushing into my stomach, and when I leaned over to get the papers out of the glove box I got stuck.
#9	Bare flesh	I was wearing a swimsuit. I think he was too embarrassed to give me a ticket.
#10	Jail	I was going to the prison to teach a class, and when he asked where I was going, I said, "To jail."

WHAT HE DID/SAID	DRAWBACKS
"Just watch your speed in the future."	They have to be real tears.
calmed her down.	Again, real tears only
"Do you think you could slow down a bit?"	Contact lenses won't cut it.
"Okay, it's just a warning."	Needs that "mad housewife" edge.
"I'm giving you a wedding present"—and let her go.	None. Good emotional outlet.
"I don't want to spoil the day for you."	Needs a gift on the backseat.
gave her directions and a warning.	Could have given directions and a ticket.
He apologized.	Make sure no maps are visible.
"Go, go!"	None. "It always works."
He went bright red.	Don't try this on women cops.
"Okay, not this time."	Kids may not cooperate.
chatted about Mardi Gras.	Can backfire.*
"It's all right, don't bother. Forget it. Go!"	Need to be very pregnant.
"Just watch your speed, ma'am."	Could be cold in winter.
laughed, said, "It's not that bad," and let her go.	You may not pass Go.

*The same woman was stopped taking a local TV anchorman to a Mardi Gras meeting. She said she had him in the car. The patrolman looked in, said "I don't know him," and wrote the ticket. "The anchorman was livid!"

I once asked a champion race driver how many speeding tickets he'd had.

"None," he replied.

I was, to put it mildly, surprised. "How come?" I asked, expecting tales of admiring speed cops asking for his autograph.

"I always leave early," he said.

This is the single best piece of advice I've ever had on how to avoid speeding tickets. Those who yearn for speed are best advised to do as I now do, or at least try: save it for the track. (See the next section, "Track Time.") Now that tickets have become a major source of revenue, and cops far quicker on the trigger of "instant-on" radar guns, the joy of speed isn't worth the hassle of being caught, let alone the meteoric rise in your insurance rates once you have a ticket on your record.

But what about *radar detectors?*

Well, I used them for years, and now don't bother any longer. They're wonderful little gadgets, and wonderfully expensive too. But they're illegal in six states, and seventeen more states are considering making them illegal.

They do indeed work most of the time, but only if you drive on the constant alert for signals, which makes fast driving so exhausting that it stops being fun. Moreover, "instant-on" radar and photo radar are almost foolproof if the officer positions himself well, just over the brow of a hill, for instance, or just beyond a turn. And many officers have gone back to the simple method of following you at some distance with their lights off, simply clocking your speed on their speedometers. I speak, believe me, from experience.

Since most of us get tickets when we're in a hurry, my race driver friend's advice has to be worth a lot more than the most sophisticated radar detector: Arrange things so you don't have to be in a hurry. Leave earlier. Usually it's only a matter of five or ten minutes.

Many people use *cruise control* to limit their speed. That's a fine idea, but be aware that when you have the car on cruise control, it's easy to be lulled into inattention, because of that feeling that the car is driving itself. Your foot is off the gas pedal, and the gas pedal is your foot's guide to where the brake pedal is. So it may take up to a full second longer to get your foot on the brake pedal when you're using cruise control. By all means use it, but cautiously. Remember, it's still *you* driving the car, not the cruise control.

Track Time

Guys love racing. Most of the time, mind you, they don't know what they're watching: I've been to races where I asked people hanging over the fences who was in the lead, and they had no idea.

The truth is that women aren't immune to the thrill of the race either.

Over a third (35.3%) have had fantasies of driving a race car.

Of these, 55% won the race. But this doesn't mean that the other 45% lost. They simply said that winning wasn't the point of the fantasy, but the experience itself.

If you do enjoy speed, here's the perfect outlet for it: an advanced-driving or a competition-driving course. These take place on racetracks all over the United States. Some are in small race cars, some in sporty sedans, some in your own car, whatever it is.

The competition courses may be more dramatic, but the advanced-driving courses, with the instructor beside you in the passenger seat, are by far the more useful. There is nothing better to boost your confidence and ability as a driver than spending a morning on a skidpad, learning how to produce a skid and then how to control it, or driving into an accident simulation setup and coming through it with skill and aplomb.

Yes, it's scary.

➡ **SUGGESTION:** "Why can't automakers offer advanced driving courses to customers who buy sports cars or powerful cars. In fact, to anybody who's interested? Porsche does it, but nobody else does. I'd really like to know how to get the most out of my Lexus. It's made so well; I want to know how to drive it as well as it's made."

—Stockbroker, Texas

Yes, it's exhilarating.

Yes, you should do it.

The courses are pricey, but I don't know a single woman who's taken one and not raved about it. Or learned a lot from it—about driving, and about herself. As one woman put it, "Once I knew I could handle myself on the racetrack, I knew I could handle anything."

Three advanced driving schools offer courses nationwide.

The Skip Barber Racing School This is where I learned both advanced and competition driving, with superb instructors. The school provides two main courses:

1. **One- and two-day advanced driving courses, teaching techniques of safety and performance driving in Dodge Vipers, Stealths, and Stratus sedans.**

2. **Three-day competition course, teaching you how to drive a small open-wheel formula race car (Formula Ford) on the track. Half-day introductory courses also available.**

The Barber courses are held at over twenty locations in the United States, but if you're in the Northeast, go for the scenic home track, Connecticut's Lime Rock Park. The school can be reached at P.O. Box 1629, Lakeville CT 06039 (Tel: 800/221-1131).

The Bob Bondurant School of High Performance Driving This school uses Ford Mustangs, Ford Probes, or Formula Fords in several courses.

1. **Two- or three-day high-performance driving.**

2. **Four-day Grand Prix road-racing.**

3. **One-day highway survival training, including an accident-avoidance simulator.**

4. **Two-day teenage defensive driving.**

The school has its own purpose-built training center at its Arizona headquarters, with a road track designed by Bondurant himself, but offers courses elsewhere in the country too. Headquarters are at 20000 South Maricopa Road, Gate 3, Chandler AZ 85226 (Tel: 800/842-7223).

TrackTime Performance Driving Schools Beginner, intermediate, and advanced two-day courses—in your own car—are offered at fourteen tracks around the country. There are flexible instruction schedules depending on driver's ability and interest.

TrackTime is headquartered at 4600-A Middle Drive, Youngstown, OH 44505 (Tel: 216/759-1868).

More localized schools with excellent reputations include the following.

In California

The Russell Racing School boasts the most beautiful location of any school: the Laguna Seca Raceway in Monterey. Their basic three-day racing course is called Techniques of Racing, and uses Formula Fords, but they also offer a one-day street-survival course in Mitsubishi Galants. (Write to: 1023 Monterey Highway, Salinas, CA 93908. Tel: 408/372-7223.)

In Colorado

The Jean-Paul Luc/Bridgestone Winter Driving School in Steamboat Springs offers half-day, one-day, and two-day courses. This is the place that teaches ambulance drivers, police officers, and firefighters winter-driving techniques, using a snow- and ice-covered one-mile road track. (Write to P.O. Box 774167, Steamboat Springs, CO 80477. Tel: 303/879-6104)

Go 4 It Services, based near Boulder, offers a number of courses: ten-hour basic, intermediate, and advanced street-driving courses, two- or three-day high-performance and road-racing courses at four Colorado race tracks, ten-

➡ "The high-performance driving school was the most memorable thing that's ever happened to me in a car. It was the first time I went 150 mph—it's an unbelievable feeling to know you're going that fast. If you think about it too long, it makes you really nervous. But then later I realized that it wasn't the sheer speed of it that was so impressive, but the sense of control. It was just an incredible discovery of a refinement of control that I'd never thought possible."

—Lawyer,
Texas

hour winter-driving courses, and a one-on-one "supercourse" lasting from half a day to as long as you want. (Write to: 713 Grant Avenue, Louisville, CO 80027, Tel: 303/666-4113.)

On the East Coast

Car Guys. Why they call it Car Guys when one of the joint owners is a woman I don't know, but it's a school with a difference—not a racing school at all, but car-control clinics, offered in several locations from Pennsylvania to Georgia. Excellent feature: You bring your own car and learn in it. Clinics begin with a tech inspection. A one-day defensive driving course and a two-day on-track course are offered. (Write to: P.O. Box 21275, Roanoke, VA 24018. Tel: 800/800-4897.)

In Georgia

The Road Atlanta Driver Training Center offers one- and two-day advanced driving schools in a variety of Nissans (NSXs, 240SXs, Stanzas, Sentras), as well as one-, two- and three-day racing schools in Nissan NSXs, all on a 2.5-mile road course. (Write to: 5300 Winder Highway, Braselton, GA 30517. Tel: 404/967-6143.)

In Ohio

The Mid-Ohio School offers several courses, all at the Mid-Ohio Sports Car Course in Lexington, Ohio, in either your own car, or Honda Civics or Accords. It offers one-day high-performance, one-day advanced driving, one-day teen driving, and half-day car-control clinics.

(Write to: 94 North High Street, #50, Dublin, OH 43017. Tel: 614/793-4609.)

In Pennsylvania

The Bertil Roos Grand Prix Racing School offers a two-day advanced highway-driving course in Volvo 850s, and half-day, one-day, and three-day racing courses in small For-

➡ "Whatever I drive, I drive it really fast. When I get in the car and go to the city, it's sort of like 'How fast can I make it from A to B?' I'm a very safe driver, I don't take chances, but I love to get the pedal down to the metal. It's exciting."

➡ "I agree. I'm always trying to shave a minute off my time. I don't know why. It makes getting there more fun. I often feel that in a former life I must have been a race car driver."

—California group

188

mula 2000 race cars at Pocono Raceway as well as oval-track time at the Nazareth Speedway. (Write to: P.O. Box 221, Blakeslee, PA 18610. Tel: 800/722-3669.)

Racy Language

Aerodynamics: A lot of racing talk is airplane talk, and at speeds over 200 mph, you can understand why. Put your hand out the window of your car at 50 mph and you'll see how much drag there is on it, caused by the speed with which you're cutting through the air. Imagine that times four or more, and you can see that a race car has a lot of air to cut through. Thus the swoopy shapes, the big winged tails, also known as spoilers, the air dams in front: Race cars are designed to cut through air, much like airplanes.

Dive: When you apply the brakes hard and quickly, the balance of the car shifts. It goes down low on the front wheels—it dives down onto them. You might not notice it in your car at 30 mph, but in a race car at speed, it alters the whole handling of the car.

Drafting: You see this a lot in stock-car racing. One car follows another so closely that sometimes they are literally bumper to bumper. Why? Because doing so works to the aerodynamic advantage of both cars. The lead car relieves the second car from having to cut through the air, so that the second car saves energy for when it might be needed. But both cars go faster together than either one would solo, since the second car relieves the lead one from air pressure on its back end. (The air streams over both cars as if they were one.) Do *not* try this on the road.

Dropping the clutch: Used to be much favored in drag-racing until hotrods went automatic. You put your foot down on the clutch, disengaging it, keep your foot there as you rev the car up real high, then take your foot off the clutch (thus reengaging it, or dropping the clutch disc into place). The car will shoot forward. This is good for a real showy tire-screeching quick start, and is thus still practiced on the streets by macho types.

Flags: Track workers hang out different flags to warn of hazards as well as to start and stop the race. Green is start, yellow means caution, red means stop. Black is a sign to a particular driver to "pull into the pits for consultation," usually because of a breach of rules. A white flag means the lead car is entering the last lap, and the black-and-white checkered flag is, of course, the finish sign.

Grid: The starting lineup for a race. Positions are determined by qualifying trials.

Ground effect: More aerodynamic talk stolen from airplanes. The bottom of the car creates a low-pressure air cushion between the car and the ground that helps hold it on the track at high speeds.

Line: Every track has its own racing line, which is the quickest way around the track. This is not the same as the shortest way round the track, which would be the inside of the track. (Holding a car on the inside at 235 mph would be impossible.) The quickest way may be very wide on a certain corner and very close to the inside on the next one.

Methanol: IndyCars run on this (Formula One and other race cars run on gasoline.) Usually it is an alcohol distilled from wood, but it can also be made synthetically. It needs less oxygen to burn than gasoline and, unlike gasoline, can be doused with water if it catches fire. The drawback: Methanol fires have no visible flame.

Oval track: A track in an oval shape, or sometimes a "tri-oval," which is an oval with one side pushed up into a peak. These tracks are often called speedways, and are banked up to 33 degrees at the turns.

Pace car: The car that leads the field of race cars around the track until the flag drops for the start of the race, and that comes back onto the track whenever there's a yellow caution flag. Nobody can pass the pace car or anyone else while the pace car is on the track, and everyone has to keep to the pace car's (relatively) slow pace. Automakers love when one of their cars is chosen as the pace car, because it's tons of free publicity, and the car gains testosterone glamour from the association with racing.

Pits: This is where the cars are serviced. Each car has its own area at the pit stop and its own crew of mechanics, who can refuel a car, change all four wheels, and have the car moving again in as little as seven seconds flat.

Pole position: The position on the grid that goes to the qualifier with the fastest time. It's the inside position in the first row.

Redline: Taking a car all the way up to the rev limit in any gear. Most passenger cars have an automatic cutoff at the redline—the fuel-injection system cuts back fuel—but race cars don't, so the race driver looks at the tachometer more than the speedometer to judge engine performance.

Road track: A curving asymmetrical track, as opposed to an oval, usually anywhere from one and a half to four miles long. It's more fun to drive than an oval track but harder to watch. On an oval you can see the whole track from the grandstand; on a road track you can see only part of the course.

Slicks: Racing tires are called slicks because, well, that's what they are—smooth, with no tread, so that the maximum amount of rubber grips the pavement. (Do *not* let your tires get to this state.) In rain, the pit crews will put on rain tires, which do have some tread; otherwise the cars would be slewing around all over the track.

Squat: The opposite of dive. When you accelerate hard, the weight of the car shifts to the rear wheels, and the car actually squats, lifting the front end higher. Again, you won't notice it in a passenger car (at least, you shouldn't), but in a race car, it changes the handling dramatically.

Telemetry: The latest high-tech wrinkle in Formula One and IndyCar racing. Not only does the driver stay in contact with the pits via radio, but the car stays in contact too. Computers on the car monitor fuel, oils, engine pressure, and temperature, constantly readjusting and calibrating the car's performance and sending their findings back to the pits.

Threshold braking: The most effective way to brake short of antilock brakes. The driver holds the brake pedal about two-thirds of the way down, so that the car teeters just the right side of the wheels locking up. Developed in racing, threshold braking means that the driver spends less time on the brake and more on the gas—a clear advantage on the track.

Wings: Racing is clearly obsessed with trying to get cars to fly. The wings are the huge panels mounted high at the back and low at the front of Formula Ones and IndyCars. These are designed to create "downforce"—that is, to get air to press down on top of them, pushing the car downward so that it holds the pavement better.

Racy Types

There are so many auto races that the names can get confusing. So here's a quick guide to the main types of racing, just so's you'll know who's driving what, where, and how.

CART (Championship Auto Racing Teams): This is the *IndyCar* series, run mainly on oval courses by those cars that look like a cross between a dragonfly and a dinosaur. IndyCars are rear-wheel-drive single-seater open-wheel race cars (that is, the wheels are exposed). They weigh 1,550 pounds, have 3-liter turbocharged engines, and develop up to 700 or 800 horsepower. Fifteen of the sixteen races are run under the CART IndyCar banner; the sixteenth is the famous Indy 500 (500 miles, not laps), which is sanctioned by the U.S. Auto Club.

FORMULA ONE: Also known as *Grand Prix* racing, is run mainly on road courses by factory-sponsored teams. The cars look very similar to IndyCars, but unlike IndyCars, they are not turbocharged. They have 3.5-liter engines and weigh 1,100 pounds. This is where the automakers claim they refine technology, but the truth is they're just having very expensive fun. Most famous race: the Grand Prix of Monaco.

SPORTS CAR racing: This is divided into professional and amateur wings. The pros have the prettiest cars on any track, swoopy sculpted things called *GTP* cars (Grand Touring Prototype—the touring is in the title because they have roofs and are therefore dubbed touring cars). Teams are factory-sponsored: more expensive fun. The FIA—Federation Internationale de l'Automobile—is the main sanctioning body for sports-car racing internationally (it also sanctions all Formula One races), while in the States, IMSA—the International Motor Sports Association—is the main sanctioning body. The best-known race is the 24-hour Le Mans.

Amateur sports-car racing is sanctioned in the United States by the SCCA (Sports Car Club of America) and is open to anyone with an SCCA license, obtainable by taking the advanced racing courses offered by most of the schools listed in the "Track Time" section.

NASCAR (National Association of Stock Car Auto Racing): Stock-car racing, though these cars are only remotely connected to showroom stock. A Chevy Lumina stock car, for instance, may look rather like a Lumina on steroids, but all its components—the engine, the fiberglass body, the suspension, even the wheels—are absolutely different. NASCAR races are mainly on oval tracks, and the most famous is the 24 hours of Daytona.

There *is* such a thing as showroom-stock racing, and that's part of the SCCA amateur racing circuit, where rules will allow only the most minimal safety alterations to a showroom car.

NHRA (National Hot Rod Association): *Drag-racing,* where cars compete in pairs, and the competition is not directly against each other but against the clock, over a straight quarter-mile stretch from a standing start. There's lots of noise and vibration at the starting line as they rev them up and spin the wheels, and there are parachutes at the finish to slow them down.

Slick and Silly Car Gifts

There's a weird and wonderful array of auto-related toys, gidgets, and "accessories" out there, in auto-accessory stores, in chains like Wal-Mart and Kmart, in "design" stores like The Sharper Image, and by mail and phone order. So for Christmas, birthdays, or just for the heck of it, here are fifteen of the most fun ones.

1. A car-karma candle: Called the Lucky Automobile Karma candle, it comes in a glass jar with an invocation on the back, including: "Ensure my way is paved with abundant free parking spaces. . . . Grant divine guidance so that I may never be lost. . . . And may I always be provided with open gas stations on my side of the road." From Everyday Icons (206/726-5980).

2. Car cologne: If you can't afford that Jag you covet, try Jaguar cologne instead. It's a men's fragrance. Wear it yourself to feel sexy, or persuade a man you feel sexy about to wear it. Comes in a green bottle—British racing green, of course—with a wooden top and the leaping jaguar on the front. At any good department store.

3. Giant windshield wipers: In electric Day-Glo colors plus gold and silver, they look great on pickups and sport-utes (and pretty bad on anything else).

4. Ultrasonic deer whistles: Deer can hear them, you can't. A great idea, since a collision with a deer is much like a collision with a truck. But be cautioned that sound doesn't travel around curves. You can get fancy chrome-plated ones from Hammacher Schlemmer or cheap and equally effective plastic ones at any truck stop.

5. Outrageous seat covers: I hanker after zebra-striped ones, but there's something to be said for Flasher Fur covers, bright pink and flagrantly fake.

6. Wooden-bead seats: Cab drivers swear by them, but if, like me, you have a bony back, avoid them. At Hammacher Schlemmer, they call them "car seat ventilating massagers" and charge triple what they charge for the same thing at Wal-Mart.

7. Coffee on the move: You've stopped smoking, but go ahead, use the lighter anyway (it's sometimes marked as an electrical outlet nowadays) and plug in an espresso coffee maker (pricey ones from Beverly Hills Motoring Accessories, at 800/421-4513, or ones for one-sixth the price at Wal-Mart).

8. Toy cars: How to get a great deal on a sixties Caddy or a Ferrari: Get it in miniature form. You can pick up small cheap ones at variety and kids' stores, or order die-cast replicas from companies such as Exoticar Model Co. (1/18-scale models of everything from old Vettes to the latest dream cars) (800/348-9159).

9. Solar-powered ventilator: So there are no solar cars in the near future, but meanwhile at least you can cool off your car—and you—with this solar-powered

gidget, which pulls hot, still air from a parked car. It slips over the upper edge of a closed side window, and needs no wires or batteries.

10. Bad-girl driving gloves: Pick them up at—where else?—any Harley-Davidson store. Black leather cut off at the fingers, a Velcro strap at the back of the wrist, and holes for the knuckles. Vroom!

11. A fancy steering wheel: You can simply wrap a fake leather strip around the wheel—actually, you have to stitch it on, but the needle and thick thread come with it, and it looks great for just a few dollars. Or if Publisher's Clearing House have come knocking on your door, you can change the whole steering wheel and get a fancy one in African mahogany with gold-plated spokes. From Beverly Hills Motoring Accessories, of course.

12. Driving shoes: A gift for your feet, or someone else's—and for road safety. These are soft moccasins with pebbled soles to prevent your foot slipping on the pedal. Just keep them in the car and slip into them before you start up: They're safer and more comfortable than high heels, and cost anywhere from $35 to $170 depending on where you shop.

13. Aromatherapy for your car: The Drive Alert air freshener plugs in to the lighter outlet and wafts an invigorating mix of peppermint, juniper, rosemary, and basil. Pricier (about $20) but much better than those weird-smelling little fir-tree cutouts favored by cab drivers.

14. One of the neatest radar detectors around: the tiny, cordless Solo from Cincinnati Microwave (800/433-3487)

and . . .

15. You knew it was coming: fuzzy dice! Get 'em big or small, red or black or white or lime green, with hearts or diamonds or whatever you fancy. Dangle them for silly fun. You can even get dice-shaped valve-stem caps for your tires (but alas, not fuzzy ones).

And here's one to avoid: the car bra.

No kidding: Those black leathery things you see over the front fenders of some flashy cars are called bras. That's probably why the male owners buy them. (They're most likely the ones who still call their cars "she" as well.) The bras don't provide any support; they're supposed to protect the paint from chips made by small stones thrown up from the road. Of course the paint is chip-resistant anyway, so you know they're there just for show.

➡ **"Our car's first Valentine's Day gift: pink dice with hearts."**

——**Massage therapist, Pennsylvania**

➡ **"They're cool: I have them hanging from the lamp in my bedroom."**

——**Office clerk, Washington**

The Diciest Gift

Women don't go for fuzzy dice. The overwhelming majority said they were either tacky or dumb (or stupid, or silly). But the truth is in the details.

Ten Things Women Say About Fuzzy Dice

"Jerk indicator"

"My ex just got them for his truck"

"Dicey subject"

"Anti-intellectual pro-conformist icons"

"Fuzzy memories from the fifties"

"They make me giggle"

"Macho insecurity"

"Ye gods!"

"No way!"

"Urk."

5.

Neat Machines: How Cars Work

Awe of Engines

Once we lose our awe of the engine, we can stop think-ing of it as a mysterious alien object sent to plague and perplex the female race and see it for what it is: an ingenious system for making cars move.

In fact, the male race is equally plagued by the mysteries of motion. Men just hide their perplexity better. Yet the idea persists that mechanical ability is somehow related to the genes.

➡ **"Men like machines. Women just use them."**

➡ **"I think it's more than that. I think there really are boy genes and girl genes. I have these two therapist friends, very politically correct, and yet before their son could even speak, he was making all sorts of car noises. He could downshift, rev up, squeal to a halt. I've never known a girl do that."**

➡ **"They don't. I tried to get mine to do that and all she wanted to do was hang on to fabric."**

—**California group**

It's not really a matter of genes, of course. It's something in our upbringing—an accumulation of subtle and not-so-subtle cues and expectations—that makes women leery of machines, leaving us willing to use them but just as willing to throw up our hands in professed ignorance if they break down.

Men have been raised to be more at home in the world of objects. Women are still too often raised to expect men to fix things for them. I was raised that way too. It was only when I worked one summer as a mechanic's apprentice that I even thought of taking things apart and seeing how they worked.

For the first time in my life, I felt capable with things. Not just cars, but all sorts of appliances. I knew I could get inside them and see if I could fix them. If I couldn't, there was nothing lost. If I could—and most of the time I could, because it was something minor like a loose wire—I gained not only financially, but also in my sense of self. I was capable. In control.

There aren't many women in the top echelons of the auto biz—nine out of 290 executives, or 3.1%, including not a single division head, let alone a CEO, chairperson, or president. But most of the small group who have risen as far as the glass ceiling of the oh-so-male world of Detroit are the daughters of men who worked in the business. They grew up with the talk, never learned to be afraid of engines, and so didn't fall into the it's-a-boy's-thing way of thinking.

Few of us were so lucky. When I first started writing about cars, one of the things that most infuriated me was the lack of a clear explanation, in comprehensible language, of how a car works.

"Read the repair manual," I was advised, but the repair manuals were written for mechanics and made no sense unless you already knew what they were talking about.

"There must be a clear description somewhere of how a car works," I kept saying.

There wasn't.

So there is now, starting on the next page.

➡ "When I got divorced, I decided I had to learn how to change the oil. So a friend taught me how, and I was amazed at how easy it was."

➡ "And you've changed your own oil ever since?"

➡ "No, I pay my $14.95 and they do it in a few minutes. But I know that I can do it if I need to. What was important was to prove that I *could* do it."

—Pennsylvania group

A Guided Tour of the Engine

Seven years ago, when I wanted to find out how cars work, I felt like a kid trying to find out about sex: Nobody was giving me straight answers. Every book I looked at was either too technical or too sketchy. Nobody was telling me exactly what went where and what it did.

Here's the big secret: How cars work is really quite simple. (You didn't really think all those mechanics out there were rocket scientists, did you?)

I know lots of guys are going around moaning that cars are getting so complicated that the age of shade-tree mechanics is past. But even on modern cars with electronic fuel injection and computer monitors, the same basic principles apply as on a Model-T Ford.

This section, then, is a guided tour of the engine.

If, like me seven years ago, you are vaguely aware that the various engine parts exist but have no firm idea as to just what they are or what they do, this section will explain it all clearly. So the next time your mechanic mutters something about the valves or the timing belt, or a motorhead male friend starts with the torque talk, you'll have an idea what they're talking about.

Let's get one thing straight right away:

A car is a very neat piece of machinery, a logical matter of cause and effect, all put together to make one main thing happen—that is, to make the wheels turn.

Everything in an engine is connected, just like in that old song "The hipbone's connected to the thighbone." All you have to do is figure out the sequence.

It helps to think of a car as a much simplified version of a human body. If the wheels are the feet, how do we get them to move?

First, of course, the body has to be alive. It needs air and food. No problem.

The car's food is *gasoline*. It eats the stuff, burning it for energy, much as the human body digests food, then eliminates the waste matter at the rear end in the form of what are politely called emissions.

And the *air?* The air for your lungs is air for the car too: to be precise, fifteen parts of it mixed with every part of gas. You thought your car ran on gasoline? No, the truth is it runs mainly on air mixed with gasoline vapor. The air is sucked in through the air intake manifold, which is that daunting silvery piece of metal like fused pipes or a giant's fingers right at the top of the engine.

So far so good. But first we need a heartbeat. When the car's turned off, there is no heartbeat. The trick is to create one—rather a God-like task every time you turn on the engine.

Here's how you do it in a modern car with electronic ignition and fuel injection (EFI).

When you turn the ignition switch one notch, you contact the BATTERY. The battery wakes up the ELECTRONIC CONTROL UNIT, a computer that turns on the fuel pump and gets the fuel injectors ready to start delivering fuel.

Now turn the ignition switch another notch and power flows from the battery to the STARTER. The starter is the piece that actually cranks the engine. It turns the CRANK-SHAFT, which is the driving force of the whole engine.

You know those old pictures of chauffeurs cranking a car from the front? The starter in your car is doing the same thing, but it uses electricity to do it instead of musclepower. A far better idea, unless of course you can afford a chauffeur.

The crankshaft lies just beneath the pistons, which act like pedals on a bicycle to keep the crankshaft turning once the starter has given it the first few turns.

The PISTONS are the heart of the engine. But they work a lot faster than the human heart, which is a very relaxed organ by comparison. Each one is encased in a CYLINDER and moves up and down inside the cylinder.

What makes each piston move up and down? The explosive force from a very small, very gentle, very controlled fire inside it. The fuel for this fire is provided by the FUEL INJECTORS, one for each cylinder. The fuel-injection system bypasses the need for an old-fashioned carburetor—a mechanical device for mixing fuel and air. It provides up to 15% more power, and helps create a cleaner burn.

The spark for the fire is provided by the SPARK PLUGS, one for each cylinder.

The spark plugs have two small electrodes at the bottom, with a gap between them. When electrical current from the battery jumps the gap, you get a spark.

This spark ignites the fuel-air mixture in an area at the top of the cylinder known as the combustion chamber; the force of the combustion then pushes the piston inside the cylinder down against the crankshaft; the crankshaft turns; the piston comes up again for more.

Logic says you need only two strokes of the piston to make this happen, one up and one down—just like lungs inhaling and exhaling. And indeed, some engines are two-stroke engines. But in fact an extra up-and-down movement between inhaling and exhaling works better—it burns more of the fuel mixture for more power and less waste—so modern engines have refined the action into a four-stroke one.

Spark Plug

The Piston's Four-Stroke Act

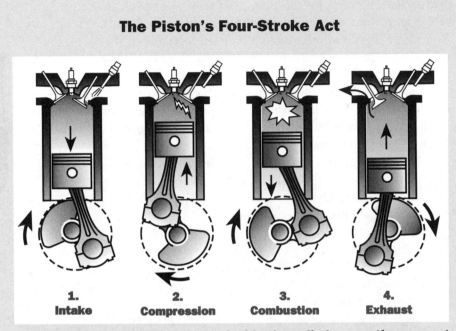

1. **Intake**
2. **Compression**
3. **Combustion**
4. **Exhaust**

Stroke 1. The piston moves down inside the cylinder as a tiny amount of gasoline is sprayed to the *intake valves* by the fuel injector, while air is forced in via the *air-intake manifold.* The intake valves, together with the exhaust valves (usually two of each for each cylinder), lift up and down to open and close. They're connected to a sculpted rotating rod called a *camshaft,* or cam for short. As the cam rotates, it lifts and closes the valves in sequence. The cam may be a single rod or a double one, which allows for faster operation.

Stroke 2. The valves close, sealing the cylinder so that as the piston pushes up, it compresses the fuel-and-air mixture in the combustion chamber above it. As the piston reaches the top of the cylinder, the spark plug sends a small spark into the combustion chamber.

Stroke 3. The spark ignites the fuel-and-air mixture, creating a small, controlled explosion that forces the piston down again.

Stroke 4. The piston moves up once more, forcing the exhaust gases from the explosion out of the exhaust or outlet valves.

Why all this pumping up and down?

Each piston has a CONNECTING ROD at the bottom, and each connecting rod is attached to the crankshaft. Getting the crankshaft to turn is the be-all and end-all of the pistons.

In fact, the crankshaft is not so much a shaft or a rod as a series of linked pedals, one for each cylinder. Each is at a different height because the pistons are operating on different time schedules. Linking them is a series of beautifully sculpted lobes that also act as balance weights.

Here's a drawing of a crankshaft. You can see what I mean about sculpture.

Think of a human on a bike. Her legs pushing down on the pedals are like two pistons: She's cranking the bike. Now imagine if she had four, six, eight, even twelve legs instead of two, and you can see that the more pistons, the more force created to turn the crankshaft.

But the speed of the engine is literally inhuman. At 3,000 rpm, say (that's REVOLUTIONS PER MINUTE, and the revolutions in question are those of the crankshaft), each spark plug fires twenty-five times a second, and the pistons each do their four-stroke act—up and down twice—*fifty times a second.* That, to put it mildly, is fast.

At most auto shows, you can find at least one cut-away moving model of an engine showing the pistons pumping up and down, turning the crankshaft. It's one good reason to go to auto shows. But the models show everything in slow motion. Very slow motion. If they showed it in real time, you'd see nothing but a complete blur, and you'd have no inkling of the finely timed rapid sequence—so fine that not even a hummingbird could figure it out.

Now here's an ingenious wrinkle: The crankshaft is connected to the camshaft (that's the one that lifts and closes the valves at the top of the cylinders) by a belt or, in some cars, a chain. This runs on pulleys attached to the ends of the two shafts. It is called the TIMING BELT (or timing chain), because once the engine gets going, the crankshaft *drives* the camshaft, so that they're working together in perfect harmony. (See "All Those Belts" on page 220).

Great! We have heartbeat. The valves are lifting and closing, the pistons are pumping up and down, and as a result, we have motion—the crankshaft is turning. Now, only one little problem: How does the motion of the crankshaft get to the wheels?

Answer: Through a series of connections: gears, shafts, and joints, much like simplified human joints.

The rotating crankshaft is connected to a flywheel, which sits up against the CLUTCH. The clutch is an ornate disc that literally clutches at the flywheel—a big disclike wheel that stores the rotation energy of the crankshaft. When you engage the clutch, you force it forward so that it clutches the flywheel, transferring the rotation onward. When you disengage it, you pull the two pieces apart, so that although the crankshaft is still turning, it's turning in a kind of vacuum, and its motion is not transferred onward.

The far side of the clutch is the TRANSMISSION, or gearbox. This is a series of interlocking GEARS that tame and refine the raw power of the crankshaft's rotation, then "transmit" that power to the wheels.

Gears are really quite simple. Imagine a gear with thirty teeth meshing with a gear with fifteen teeth. Each time the smaller fifteen-toothed gear does a complete revolution, the larger thirty-toothed one will have done only half a revolution. So it will make any shaft connected to it move at half the speed. Put a series of four or five gears of various sizes in a gearbox, moving in and out of mesh with others as you move the shift stick, and you have a pretty sophisticated system to change rotation speed.

In an AUTOMATIC TRANSMISSION, something called a torque converter does this for you automatically, without a clutch. It uses a hydraulically driven system of friction bands and plates to pull the different gears into and out of action. This is why the oil called TRANSMISSION FLUID is so important in an automatic transmission.

The fluid's pressure is controlled by a transmission pump, which reacts to changes in engine speed. It works harder when the engine goes faster, thus raising the hydraulic pressure and prompting a gear change. At low speed, you have lower pressure, so only the lower gears respond; as speed increases, so does the pressure, and higher gears come into play.

Whether the transmission is manual or automatic, the crankshaft enters the gearbox turning at the same speed as the engine, while the gears make the shaft emerging the other side of the gearbox—the DRIVESHAFT—turn at a different speed, depending on which gear is engaged. Neat, huh?

Why are the gears necessary?

Because they take the raw force of the crankshaft and transform it into the kind of power you want in any specific driving situation. This is the secret behind what techies call GEAR RATIOS.

Low gears make the driveshaft turn slower than the crankshaft, say once for every four crankshaft revolutions (which is what they mean by a gear ratio of 4 to 1). All the power of the engine is channeled into fewer turns, giving you more propulsion force, or TORQUE. In high gear, the ratio can drop to about 1 to 1, which means that the crankshaft and the driveshaft are turning at the same speed; this way,

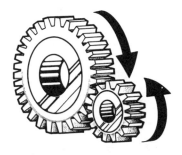

Gears

the wheels turn much faster, but you have less torque, or ability to accelerate. That's fine; generally you're in high gear when you're cruising along; you have momentum on your side, so you need far less power to keep the car moving.

How to Talk Engines

Engine Placement

The engine can be at the front or at the rear of the car. Nearly all cars are now *front-engined,* though there are a few mid-engined supercars (with the engine right behind the driver's seat, where it makes enough noise to deafen you to normal conversation for days). Porsche is the only major automaker still devoted to *rear-engined* cars (of which the VW Beetle is probably the most famous).

Most compact and midsize front-engined cars now have the engine placed sideways, or transversely. This is known in the biz as an "east-west engine" (though it can also go west-east).

Drive Wheels

Most cars are driven by two wheels—that is, power from the engine is transferred to only two wheels, while the other two come along for the ride. Modern compact and midsize cars are generally *front-wheel-drive* as well as front-engined. Most sports cars and larger cars are *rear-wheel drive.* Front-wheel drive is a more efficient design and improves traction on slippery surfaces since all the weight of the car is up front, over the drive wheels. *All-wheel drive* sends power as necessary to all four wheels, as in most Subarus and the higher-level sport-utilities. Other sport-utilities and some pickups are *four-wheel drive,* meaning that they work most of the time in two-wheel drive but can be shifted into four-wheel drive if necessary.

Cylinder Arrangement

Engines usually have anywhere from four to twelve cylinders (though more are possible, as are less—I once had, and loved, a Citroen 2CV, a car with only two). These cylinders can be arranged in different patterns in the engine block, usually either *in-line,* meaning in a row, or *V-shaped,* in a V formation.

The most common arrangements in today's cars are:

- I-4 (or in-line four): four cylinders in a straight row.
- V-6: six cylinders in a V shape, three on each side.

Engine Size

This seems arcane but isn't: The number of cylinders, you see, is not the size of the engine. You may have six small cylinders that have less displacement than four big ones. The *displacement* is the total volume in all the cylinders when the pistons are at their lowest point. This used to be measured in cubic inches but is now generally measured in liters. The bigger the cylinder, the more fuel and air mixture it will hold, and thus the more downforce it will exert when that mixture is ignited.

C-V (Constant Velocity) Joint

Okay, so the raw power of the engine has been refined. Where does it go now?

In front-wheel-drive cars, the power is directed to the front wheels. And since the wheels must be able to move up and down in order to ride smoothly over uneven road surfaces, flex is provided by constant-velocity joints, or C-V JOINTS, which act much like the joints in your knee and ankle. In fact, they look like big knuckles.

Between the transmission and the wheels is the DIFFERENTIAL, another set of gears that does indeed differentiate power, allowing more power to go to one wheel than the other in a corner. Why? Because as you corner, the outside wheel needs to turn a lot faster than the inside one, since it has more distance to travel.

In front-wheel-drive cars, the transmission and differential are combined into a TRANSAXLE, with no need for a separate driveshaft. In rear-wheel-drive cars, where the rear wheels push the car from the back, the driveshaft extends underneath the car from the transmission to the rear wheels, using universal joints—U-JOINTS—instead of C-V joints. Here it enters a center differential that changes the direction of the power 90 degrees and sends it along a metal shaft called the AXLE to the rear drive wheels.

All this—the engine to the wheels—is called the DRIVETRAIN or the POWERTRAIN.

And we now have propulsion.

Now that we're in motion, some form of control would be a good idea.

Acceleration would be useful, and that comes via the THROTTLE, which increases the amount of fuel in the fuel-air mixture, so that the explosion in the combustion chamber is more powerful and the car goes faster. This is why they talk about "opening up the throttle" when you step on the gas pedal; you are literally opening it up, because that's what the gas pedal does.

Steering is another excellent form of control. One form of steering linkage connects your steering column to a rack on the other side of the fire wall (that's the wall between you and the engine compartment). The rack is a flat piece of toothed metal, like an open gear. At the end of the steering column is a pinion, which is a small gear. Pinion meets rack, and the two mesh. When you turn the steering wheel, the pinion turns and moves the entire rack to the left or the right. Thus the term RACK-AND-PINION STEERING. Other forms of steering linkage use a WORM GEAR (so called because it does indeed look rather like a metal worm) and a lever to do the job.

The rack or lever is connected to bars called TIE RODS, and these are what actually pull or push the wheel in the direction you want.

BALL JOINTS on the steering linkage allow the front wheels to move like a door hinge. Other joints at the end of the tie rods are called, with stunning logic, TIE-ROD ENDS.

It can take quite a bit of pushing and pulling on the steering wheel to get all this stuff to move, so POWER STEERING uses hydraulic pressure to supplement human musclepower. A power-steering pump boosts the pressure, easing the effort of turning the wheel. Add a computer control unit to this and you get SPEED-SENSITIVE STEERING, which eases turning effort at low speeds—parking, say—but fades at higher speeds where you need more "road feel."

So we can move forward and we can turn corners. Now we might also need to stop.

Most cars today have DISC BRAKES on at least the front wheels. These are quite simple. You know the way bicycle brakes use a caliper—a two-pronged device rather like a clamshell that clamps down either side of the wheel. Disc brakes work similarly, except that they're hydraulic. This means that when you step on the brake, brake-fluid pressure builds to close the caliper. This is why you have a MASTER BRAKE CYLINDER under the hood, with feed lines or tubes leading to the brakes.

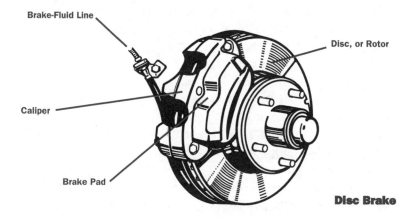

Brake-Fluid Line

Disc, or Rotor

Caliper

Brake Pad

Disc Brake

The disc is just that: a large disc or rotor inside the wheel assembly. The brake caliper has two pads inside it—the BRAKE PADS—and when it closes, these squeeze the disc on either side, slowing it down.

Most modern cars have POWER BRAKES, or power-assisted brakes. The power assist doesn't boost the brakes themselves but the brake pedal, making it easier to press by using a power booster between the pedal and the master brake cylinder.

DRUM BRAKES are used mainly on rear wheels nowadays. A hydraulic cylinder inside a round, hollow drum on the back of the wheel pushes two BRAKE SHOES, or linings, against the inside of the drum. Like brake pads, brake shoes are made of asbestos in older cars, and of metal and synthetic blends in newer cars.

As the brakes are used, the linings of the pads and shoes gradually wear away. This is normal. Do *not* try to save your brake pads. They're made to wear. And to be replaced. Many cars now have wear indicators on the brake pads: When there's not much padding left, a vibrating reed comes in contact with the spinning rotor and makes a shrieking noise you can't ignore. And shouldn't.

All new cars now have DUAL BRAKING systems, which is why the master brake-fluid cylinder is divided into two. This means that one half works separately from the other, so that if you lose your brakes, perhaps because of a clog in a brake line, you lose only half your brakes. Usually, if you lose your front brakes, you still have your rear brakes, and vice versa. An even safer way to do it, pioneered by Saab, Volvo, and Mercedes, is to split the brake system diagonally, so that one front and one rear brake will always be working. This is particularly valuable since it ensures you always have at least some braking force on the front wheels, which take more of the weight of the car in braking than the rear ones.

What about the EMERGENCY BRAKE? That's actually a misnomer. The emergency brake won't do you much good in an emergency. It used to be called a parking brake, and that's a far better name for it. It's a simple mechanical cable, manually operated, usually attached to the rear wheels, and always to be used when you park. An effective parking brake will not let you drive off unless you disengage it first; if you can drive your car with the parking brake on, you need to get it tightened.

Now an awkward question: What happens to the gasoline we've been burning to get the car to move?

Like the human body, cars produce waste. We eat food, absorb the good stuff, and eliminate the rest. So does a car.

When gasoline burns, it creates not only energy but also waste products—the exhaust—including harmful ones such as hydrocarbons, nitrous oxides, and sulfuric acid. These are the infamous EMISSIONS, now subject to increasingly tough laws designed to drastically reduce air pollution from automotive tailpipes.

Remember that the waste gases from the combustion in the cylinders are vented through the exhaust valves. The gases then pass through the EXHAUST MANIFOLD, which combines the separate pipes emerging from each cylinder into one, and leads into the exhaust pipe, which at the rear of the car becomes the tail pipe.

Underneath the car, in the exhaust pipe, a pollution control device called a CATALYTIC CONVERTER chemically stimulates the decomposition of most of the exhaust into carbon dioxide and water. And near the end, on the tail pipe, a MUFFLER controls the noise of the venting gases. (Anyone who's ever had a hole in her exhaust knows how loud they can be.)

Catalytic converters ensure that cars pollute far less than they used to. They're still not squeaky clean, and never will be unless electric cars take the place of gasoline ones. (See page 285.) But the converter, combined with more efficient modern engines (that is, engines that burn a higher percentage of the fuel-air mixture and thus produce more power for their size as well as less waste), helps ensure that a gasoline engine is now 90% cleaner than twenty years ago.

Now you know most of how a car works. Just a few more details and the mysteries of motion will no longer be so mysterious.

The SUSPENSION system is what protects you from all the slings and arrows of outrageous road surfaces: bumps, potholes, and so on. It cushions your ride and keeps the car from swaying and lurching all over the place on sharp turns. Think of it as a really high-tech sneaker, one that absorbs a lot of shock yet gives your foot and ankle good support.

The suspension is a system of interlinked bars, dampers, and springs attached to the lower frame of the car. The SPRINGS may be flexible leaf springs, made of several thin layers of metal, which have more give than one thick bar. Or they may be coil springs, which look like old-fashioned bed springs. Near the wheels, there are often STABILIZER BARS, which keep your ride stable even when one wheel is higher than another over uneven ground. All of these are attached to the frame with rubber BUSHINGS—small supports on which they sit—and these allow for more flexing and absorb some of the vibration.

I didn't really "get" the whole idea of the suspension until the Infiniti Q45 came out, with a very refined suspension system. They were so proud of their creation at Infiniti that they made a moving model to be displayed at auto shows—just the tires and the suspension, with the rest of the car taken away. When I came across it at the Detroit Auto Show, I was fascinated. I stood there for half an hour watching metal bend and flex as the tires were shoved up and down by a simulated rough road. I know this sounds weird, but it was beautiful.

The main task of absorbing road vibration and bumps falls to the SHOCK ABSORBERS, or shocks for short. These are close to each wheel, and cut down on vertical jolting by gentling the up-and-down motion of the springs. Like so many things about cars, the name is misleading. (That's one of the things that can happen when men design cars.) It's the springs that absorb the shock, or the jolting, and the shocks that then dampen the springing. A newer kind of shock called a MACPHERSON STRUT is now often used instead of regular shocks: It combines springs and shocks in one unit, taking up less room, and makes for better handling.

Cooling is another of those full-picture details. With all that heat being generated by the engine (the fuel mixture burns at about 4,500 degrees Fahrenheit, which is plenty hot enough to melt metal), you can see that a cooling system might be a good idea. In fact, the COOLING SYSTEM works well enough to keep the engine running at about 275 degrees Fahrenheit, which for an engine is rather like a comfortable 70 degrees Fahrenheit for us.

The cooling used to be done with water. Now it's done by a mix of water and ethylene glycol—basically the same mixture as antifreeze—and this mix is called the COOLANT.

The coolant keeps the engine from overheating, and from freezing up in frigid weather. It is pumped through a series of small passageways tunneling around and through the engine. The heat of the engine is transferred to the coolant, which by then needs cooling off itself, so on it goes to the RADIATOR. This literally radiates the heat away. (That's why radiators are made of all those little fins, so that there's plenty of metal to absorb the heat, and lots of surface for air to flow over it and dissipate the heat.) And where does the air come from? From a FAN, much like the one you use to cool off when you don't have air-conditioning, except faster. Fans run electrically nowadays rather than off a fan belt, which explains that disconcerting whirring noise under the hood after you shut off the engine in some cars—the fan is still doing its cooling work.

This whole cooling process starts when the engine temperature gets up to about 180 to 200 degrees. It is switched on by a THERMOSTAT, which is simply a temperature-sensitive valve between the engine and the radiator.

Now here's an extra trick of the engine-cooling system: It's also the heating system for the car. Since you have all that hot water down there under the hood, why not simply siphon some of it off and route it to a smaller radiator under the dashboard, with its own electric fan to blow the heated air into the passenger compartment. A couple of hoses in strategic places, and you have your HEATER. As my grandmother used to say, waste not, want not.

OIL is also part of the cooling system—usually about five quarts of the stuff, not much more than the amount of blood in the human body. The oil serves a double purpose. First, it lubricates. You know how much easier your hand slides over your arm when you put lotion on it. Well, the oil is the body lotion. It forms a microscopically thin protective film between moving metal parts so that they don't scrape against each other. That's why it also helps cool the engine: When metal grates against metal, you get a lot of friction, and therefore heat (and breakdown). So the oil keeps everything running smoothly.

The oil is sucked up out of the OIL PAN (aka the sump) by an oil pump, which pushes it through the engine. An OIL FILTER is necessary because the tolerances (the distance between metal parts, such as the piston and the cylinder) are so minute that the tiniest dirt particles can act like abrasives, wearing away the metal surfaces. They can also, of course, impede the flow of oil, much like blood clots.

One more full-picture detail, and the picture will be complete. That's ELECTRICITY.

I once picked up a textbook on electricity to find the following first sentence: "Nobody really knows what electricity is." Oddly, I found this very reassuring.

A mechanic I worked with as an apprentice hated the electrical system; he called the electrical wires "spaghetti" and insisted that I read all the wiring diagrams. Which turned out to be rather like reading a route map.

You already know the starting point of the main route, which is the BATTERY. This stores enough electric current to get the car started, sending voltage to the fuel injection system, to the starter, and to the spark plugs.

But you need a high-voltage current to get those plugs to spark, and the battery generates only 12 volts. So close to the spark plugs, there's a series of IGNITION COILS, one for each plug, which use magnets (honest!) to transform the 12 volts coming in from the battery to a magnificent 50,000 volts going out to the spark plugs. The coils are more efficient than old-fashioned distributors, and are the essential element in what's known as DIS, or "distributorless ignition systems," though some cars still have coils *and* a distributor.

As you know, the spark plugs are fired at first by electrical power from the battery. But once the car is running, the ALTERNATOR takes over. This is a small generator producing AC, or alternating current—thus its name. It is powered by the engine itself—specifically by the crankshaft, to which it's attached by the alternator belt.

Once the engine is running, the alternator provides current to the whole ignition system. It also recharges the battery, which powers the wipers, lights, sound system, demister, and other electrical gidgets like power windows and seats. The battery and the alternator thus have a nice little reciprocal relationship going, helping each other out as needed.

The finishing touches to the electrical system are the FUSES, which break the circuit of electrical current if a wire gets too hot: It's much better for a small, cheap fuse to blow than for something expensive like your radio.

All Those Belts

One end of your engine has an ingenious system of pulleys linked by rubber belts or by chains. You'll often find a large molded protective plastic shield over the top and bottom of these belts, but if you peer down to the side of a transverse engine, and at the front of a frontal engine, you can see them.

The main pulley is at the end of the crankshaft. This is the center point of the whole belt-and-pulley system, since everything else runs off the revolving power of the crankshaft.

The *timing belt* links the crankshaft to the camshaft, which controls the lifting and closing of the intake and exhaust valves at the tops of the cylinders. This way, the speed of the crankshaft and the speed of the fuel-ignition system are perfectly synchronized. Thus the belt's name.

The timing belt also passes over the pulley for the coolant pump, thus powering the cooling system. That's neat, because the faster the engine works, the hotter it will get, so the more cooling it needs.

The *alternator belt* runs from the crankshaft pulley to the alternator, which generates electricity. This used to be called the fan belt, because it also powered the radiator fan, but most radiator fans are now electrical.

The *accessory belt* runs off the crankshaft pulley to the power steering pump and air-conditioning compressor.

In some engines, these three belts are combined into one, which is then called the *serpentine belt* (because it snakes over and under all the pulleys). Others may have two belts: the *drive belt* (combining timing and alternator) and the accessory belt.

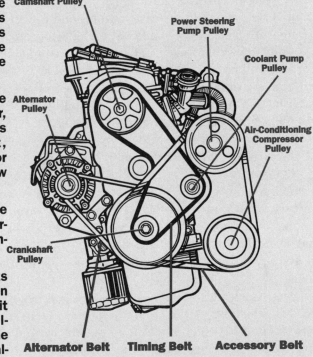

Camshaft Pulley

Power Steering Pump Pulley

Coolant Pump Pulley

Alternator Pulley

Air-Conditioning Compressor Pulley

Crankshaft Pulley

Alternator Belt   Timing Belt   Accessory Belt

The fuse box is a useful thing to get acquainted with. In New York City once, I drove into a parking garage to find an attendant hacking with a hammer at the battery of a brand-new luxury car. He was trying to disconnect the battery to stop the horn, which had been triggered accidentally by the alarm system and wouldn't stop. It apparently hadn't occurred to him that a wrench would be a more suitable tool than a hammer.

"Why don't you just disconnect the fuse for the horn?" I asked.

"Fuse?" he said.

So I leaned in, opened the fuse box, and started pulling fuses—pulling one and replacing it when the horn kept going, then trying the next, and so on until about the fourth or fifth fuse I tried, I got the right one.

There was blessed silence.

The attendant was staring at me as if I'd solved some arcane theorem that had stumped mathematicians for centuries.

It was a simple matter of common sense and a basic acquaintance with how cars work, but girl, it felt good.

I'd like to say I parked free in reward for my mechanical brilliance, but this was still New York: I paid.

Three Good Reasons for Knowing How Your Car Works

1. You know what the mechanic's doing when you take the car in for service.

2. You can find your way around the engine in case of emergency.

3. It's empowering.

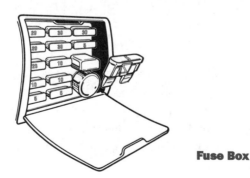

Fuse Box

Neat Machines: How Cars Work

Tender Loving Care

Okay, it doesn't have to be tender. It doesn't even have to be loving. But yes, you do have to care for your car—just a little. The most minimal maintenance goes a long way, while none at all is asking for trouble.

Your best friend when it comes to maintenance—your bible, in fact—is the *owner's manual*. It continually surprises me how few drivers ever read the manual. They might look up something in it—if they can't find a light switch, for instance—but hardly anyone, female or male, reads it all the way through.

Confession: Neither did I until I started writing about cars. Then I had to. When you're test-driving a different car practically every week, you start groping for the basic switches and controls unless you've checked them out first. But I found there was far more in the manual than which switch did what. It turned out to be an excellent introduction to a car, and I got into the habit of reading the manual before I even drove a car. The good ones are written quite clearly, in more or less plain English. And most of them nowadays are good.

Every owner's manual will tell you what grade of gasoline to use, what oil, and what tire pressure. If it's a good one, it will include an annotated drawing of your engine compartment, with the main elements identified. It will show you what all the gauges and buttons and levers are, how the locks work, how to use the cruise control, how to set the clock, even how to use the sound system. (Some are so complex nowadays that you do need to consult the manual.) Some will even explain AM and FM. (Don't worry, I won't.)

A good one will show you the fuse box and what each fuse is for, where and how to connect jumper cables to a dead battery, and how to change a tire. It will also—and this is very important—give you a *maintenance schedule*. Generally, you can take it that the manual errs on the side of caution, so don't worry if you go one or two thousand miles over the stipulated mileage for any particular service check. The manual is a guide, not a military regime.

➤ *SUGGESTION:* "Why can't rental-car companies have a copy of the owner's manual in every car? You arrive at night, you get into a car you've never driven before, and you can't find the lights, or you drive into a filling station and you can't figure how to open the gas cap. I understand that people would take them if they just left them lying in the glove box, so why not laminate each page and chain them to a point inside the glove box?"

—Lawyer, Texas

I am a great advocate of doing routine under-the-hood checks of oil and other fluids, and in this section I'll explain how. It's easy, it only takes a couple of minutes, and it can save you a lot of time, expense, and trouble down the line.

In principle, I think doing basic maintenance such as oil changes yourself is a good idea, and I'll explain how to do this too. In practice, however, who has the time? Changing the oil and the oil filter is simple enough, as you'll see, but it can also be a dirty job; most women, like most men, prefer to pay $15 or $20 and let someone else do it. That's what I do.

Still, *knowing* how to do it yourself is empowering.

223

➡ **"I change my oil myself because it makes me feel independent. When I lived in Alaska, I changed to snow tires myself for the same reason."**

—Teacher, Pennsylvania

➡ **"I did all my own work on the car until I was about thirty. It was a point of pride to say "I can do that." Now I don't want to: It's easier to call somebody and have them take care of it."**

—Realtor, Oregon

➡ **"Knowing how to change the oil makes me feel competent, and there's pride in that. You don't have to do it, but it's nice to know how. And it makes me feel like I'm giving my car something back."**

—Florist, New York

First things first: opening the **hood.** It can be really embarrassing to go to open the hood of your own car and find yourself flummoxed. I know: It's happened to me with rental cars.

Pull the hood-release latch, which is often down to the left of the driver's legs underneath the dash. This unlocks the hood and opens it a fraction. But it's still latched by a safety catch. The tricky bit can be figuring out the safety catch. Slip your fingers under the front of the hood and reach around for it (or crouch down and look). You'll find a small lever coming out of the latch. You either press, push, or lift this lever (check your owner's manual for which way it goes—and don't ask why they don't just make a standard latch that's the same on all cars), and presto, it's open!

Now prop up the hood with the support rod (it lies across the front, pulls up from the left, and hooks into the underside of the hood) and you're ready.

224

"Ready for what?" I'd have growled seven years ago.

I found it immensely frustrating to lift up the hood and have no idea what I was looking at. In fact, it was almost humiliating. Most people consider me extremely intelligent, but the moment that hood went up, I felt like the world's biggest idiot.

What I wanted was an annotated photo of what I was looking at. And there wasn't one. I could find technical drawings galore, but not a simple under-the-hood guide to an engine.

So here's one on the following pages. Everything you can see in this engine, you'll be able to see on your own. It may not be in the same place—all engines are different, like all faces, and a lot depends on whether the engine is transverse or frontal—but believe me, it will be there.

This engine belongs to a 1994 Dodge Neon. It's an in-line four-cylinder transverse engine with a single overhead camshaft. I chose this one because it's that rare thing, a clear photo of an engine, and because it's easier to look around with a single-overhead cam than with a double one. (That's when you find a big shiny box on top with DOHC stamped on it in large lettering.)

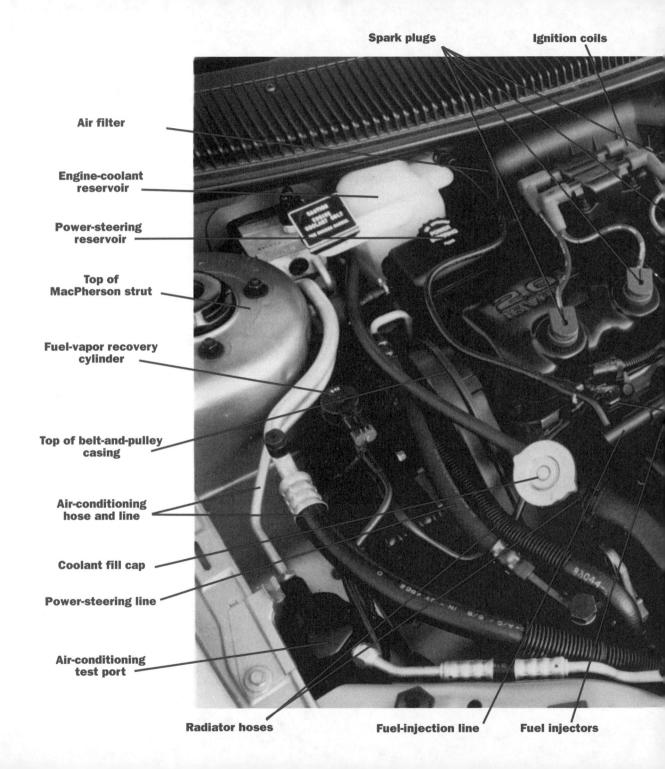

Spark plugs

Ignition coils

Air filter

Engine-coolant reservoir

Power-steering reservoir

Top of MacPherson strut

Fuel-vapor recovery cylinder

Top of belt-and-pulley casing

Air-conditioning hose and line

Coolant fill cap

Power-steering line

Air-conditioning test port

Fuel injectors

Radiator hoses

Fuel-injection line

Fuel injectors

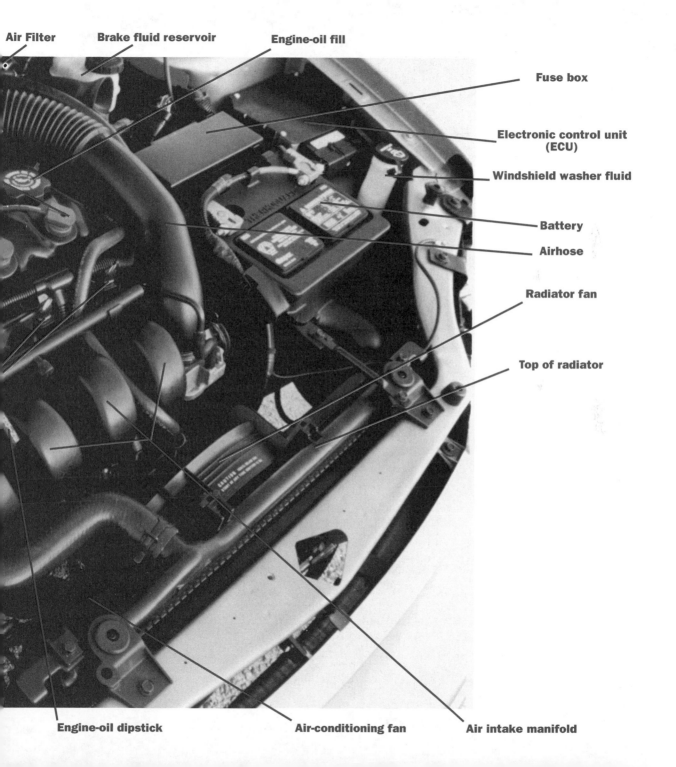

Air Filter

Brake fluid reservoir

Engine-oil fill

Fuse box

Electronic control unit (ECU)

Windshield washer fluid

Battery

Airhose

Radiator fan

Top of radiator

Engine-oil dipstick

Air-conditioning fan

Air intake manifold

Checking the Fluids

This is a simple six-point check of various fluid levels (only five if you have a manual shift), to be done at least once a month. You can trust someone else to do it for you, but since it's your car, and you're driving it, wouldn't you rather do it yourself and make sure everything's in order?

1. Check the Oil when the engine has been shut off for a few minutes. Make sure the car is parked on level ground. Pull up the dipstick, wipe it off with a clean rag or paper towel (always good to have a roll of paper towels in the car), and then insert it again, pushing it all the way in. Now take it out again, and there will be oil just at the end of it. (The oil is from the oilpan, which is where it sits when it's not running through the engine.)

Check the color of the oil—it should be honey-colored and runny. If it's dark and gooey, you need an oil change, whatever your owner's manual says.

Now check the level of the oil against the markings on the dipstick. Most dipsticks have two lines, one marked Full, the other Low. The oil level should be between the two. If you're near or at low, add half a quart, then recheck. If it's still low, add the other half of the quart. Never overfill with oil: Too much is as bad as too little, since it creates high pressure that can blow out gaskets.

Most cars hold five quarts of oil in all, and you should never need to add more than a quart at a time; if you do, you have a leak. See if there's a small puddle of oil on the ground beneath the car, or oil glistening on some visible part of the engine. If there is, a visit to the mechanic is in order.

Your owner's manual will tell you what kind of oil to use.

It may recommend two different weights of oil, depending on the temperature range you expect to be driving in. In most passenger cars, go for lighter oil like 5W-30 in cold weather, and for a heavier oil like 10W-30 in warmer or hot weather. Lighter oils are also called multigrade oils because they can be used over a wide temperature range.

2. Check the Brake Fluid This is usually in a small plastic box or bottle up near the firewall on the driver's side of the car. This is the stuff that gets pushed down into your brake lines when you step on the brakes. You definitely want enough of this.

As with engine oil, there are different kinds of brake fluid, so it's important to check your owner's manual for the right kind.

It should be at the maximum level, which will be marked. It does drop as you rack up the miles, so make sure to check it regularly. And refill carefully: This stuff is murder on car paint.

3. Check the Coolant by checking the levels in the coolant reservoir against the marks on the side. The coolant reservoir is often toward the front fender on the driver's side. It's especially important to check this if you're going into cold weather, since the coolant includes antifreeze. If you do need more coolant, just flip the lid of the coolant reservoir and add. Do *not* touch the coolant fill cap: That's used only when changing the coolant, and is safest to leave to your mechanic.

One major caution: Coolant has a sweet smell, a pretty blue color, and a sweet taste, yet is deadly to kids, pets, and the environment. So keep bottles of coolant securely stored, and clean up all spills.

4. Check the Windshield Washer Fluid. There's a float in the plastic reservoir bottle indicating the level. If you have no special washer fluid on hand and you're really low, plain water will do so long as the outside temperature is well above freezing. If it's cold, of course, only use special washer fluid, since this contains a solvent that won't freeze.

5. Check the Transmission Fluid if you have an automatic shift. It's best to check this after driving for about thirty minutes. Put the car in Park on a level surface, set the brake, leave the engine idling, and with the engine still idling, pull out the transmission dipstick, wipe it clean, put it back, and pull it out again. Check your owner's manual for how to read this dipstick, since the markings differ from car to car, and for the right type of fluid for your car. Transmission fluid is a clear pinkish oil. If it looks or smells burned, it needs to be changed by a mechanic.

6. Check the Power Steering Fluid. The reservoir for this is generally down toward the front fender, while the dipstick is usually attached to the inside of the cap of the power steering pump. With the engine idling, unscrew the cap and wipe the dipstick clean with a paper towel; then reinsert it, take it out again, and inspect the level. It should be between High and Low.

Remember, on all these checks, make sure you don't overfill. Full or High means full or high. Fuller or higher will hinder rather than help.

And that's it! You've checked the fluids.

But while you've got your nose under the hood . . .

Take a look around. With the ignition off, the keys out, parking brake set, and the engine cool, of course. Don't be afraid to touch anything: If the engine can withstand pot-holes and winter highways, it's certainly not going to come apart under your fingers.

Check the *hoses* and their connections (the flexible metal clamps around the ends of the hoses). These hoses carry coolant to and from various parts of the engine. Make sure that they're well connected. (It's amazing how they can come loose.) Usually a turn or two of a screw with a screw-driver is enough to get the clamps nice and firmly attached again. If there's a leak, you'll see little spots on the metal parts near the hose. Also make sure the rubber is in good shape, not soft, spongy, or pitted, and with no bumps or bulges.

And check the *wires* too. Yes, the wires. Make sure they're attached properly. (Give them a slight wiggle. If they're loose, just tighten the connection with a screw-driver.) If you can see the metal of a wire showing through the insulation, or if the connection points look corroded or messy, see a mechanic straightaway.

One more quick check: the *terminals* of the battery. Make sure they're clean, not corroded, which may be a sign of a slow discharge.

By now you'll be feeling quite professional and probably enjoying it, closing the hood with the feeling of a job well done. But don't drive off just yet. First, check the *tire pressures* as the last of your routine checks. (See page 266 for how.)

Tune-up Time?

What exactly is a tune-up?

On modern cars, it doesn't exist.

Most cars built since 1975 have electronic fuel injection (EFI) instead of carburetors—mechanical devices for controlling the air-fuel mixture. Carburetors needed constant adjustment, or tuning, and this was known as a tune-up.

If your car has EFI and your mechanic tells you he'll do a

tune-up, you might have the wrong mechanic. More likely, it's a communication problem, and he's using an old-fashioned term for a new-fashioned process: a check and possible adjustment of the electronic ignition and fuel-delivery system, which needs to be done anywhere between 50,000 and 100,000 miles, depending on the car. Or he may simply mean a check of the spark plugs, which your owner's manual calls for anywhere between 30,000 and 100,000 miles, depending on the car. Simply ask what he means by a tune-up.

It was once fairly easy to check the spark plugs yourself: You simply pulled off the rubber covers (known as cable boots) and unscrewed the plugs. But in newer cars, you'll probably need a special ratchet for the job, and in cars with longer-lasting plugs, reaching some of them may be difficult. Which means, for most of us, let the mechanic do it. Still:

While only 12% of women have changed the spark plugs themselves, another 43% would like to know how.

If you're one of that 43%, insist on watching while the mechanic does the job.

Have a good look at the plugs he takes out. At the bottom, you'll see a small piece of metal emerging from the side and bending over the bottom, reaching as far as a pin in the center of the plug. These are the electrodes, and the gap between them is . . . the gap. Which is why mechanics talk about gapping the plugs.

Electrical current jumping the gap between the two electrodes is what creates the spark, but it needs the perfect-size gap to jump. So what the mechanic does is simply measure the gap. If it's too wide or too narrow, he'll push or pull on the side electrode to make the gap narrower or wider. That's all.

If the side electrode is worn away or burned, you need a new plug. Otherwise it just needs cleaning, gapping, and replacing.

Give Me Oil!

Engines want clean oil. They're fussy that way. The question is, how often should you change it (or have it changed)?

Most experts recommend every 3,000 miles or every three months, whichever comes first, though many owner's manuals now recommend every 7,500 miles or six months. General rules are tough to make since a lot depends on the car, the type of driving you do in it, the type of terrain, and the climate. Check your manual and your anxiety level, but do be aware that driving with dirty oil will shorten the life-span of your engine, and vice versa—driving with clean oil will lengthen its life.

Now, another confession: Though I know how to change the oil in my car, I never do it; it's just more convenient to take it to the repair shop and have it done in a few minutes for $15 or $20, including the oil and the filter (which should be replaced every second oil change, or with every oil change if you do a lot of stop-and-start in-town driving). But I do like knowing how. So do a lot of other women.

27% of women have changed the oil in their cars at least once, another 10% know how to do it, and yet another 21% would like to know how to do it.

So for those who'd like to know how, here goes.

First, you have to get under the car. For repair shops that's easy: They drive the car onto a hydraulic lift, press the button, and up it goes. Since the chances of your having a $10,000 hydraulic lift in your garage are slim, you won't be able to make the car go over you, so you'll have to go under the car. This is why you see all those guys with their legs sticking out from under the car on weekend afternoons. And this is why it's a dirty job.

So: Reach or wriggle under the engine. Staring you in the face, at the bottom of the oilpan, is the oil drain plug. Place a large basin under the oil drain plug, or very near it. Take a wrench and unscrew the plug until it's almost ready to come out. Oil will be dripping a bit at this point. Now get the basin under the plug if it's not already there, give the plug a last turn, and get your hand out of the way as quick as you can, otherwise you'll find dirty oil streaming all the way down your arm (which is what happened to me the first time I did it). Let all the oil drain into the basin.

Now simply replace the oil drain plug (make sure it's good and tight), get out from under the car, take five quarts of brand-new clean oil, open the oil filler cap, and use a funnel to pour the oil in. Replace the oil filler cap and you're done.

Well, not quite. You now have nearly five quarts of dirty oil in a basin. This is toxic waste, so you are *not* going to dump this on the ground. Instead, put it in a container with a secure cap—empty water, milk, or bleach bottles are good—and take it for recycling: Check with a local auto parts store for where to take it.

And changing the oil filter? Ah, that's a bit more of a job. It only involves unscrewing the old one, which is about the size of a tin can, and screwing in the new one. But nowadays you often need a special tool to reach the oil filter, because modern engines are so compact. And you also have to jack up the car and use jack stands, which are more stable than jacks, to take the weight. So unless you're in training as a mechanic, I'd say let the mechanic use his nice hydraulic lift and change the filter for you, along with the oil. And yes, do change the filter every time you change the oil: It doesn't need a lot of imagination to see what a dirty filter will do to clean oil.

Give Me Grease!

What's a lube job?

It's short for a lubrication job. Sounds kind of obscene,

but remember that oil and grease are your friends when it comes to cars.

Metal needs to be lubricated so that it can move smoothly, so a lube job involves packing grease into the many joints of a car's steering and suspension system with a grease gun. It used to be done along with the oil change.

The good news: Most modern cars rarely need lube jobs. They have neat little ball-shaped hard rubber boots over all the joints, and these boots hold the grease neatly in place. When you get an oil filter change, you should ask your mechanic to check the boots to make sure that none are torn or cracked; if that happens, dirt gets in, grease escapes, and you suddenly find that your car's steering is vibrating in the strangest way.

Most owner's manuals recommend inspecting the boots every couple of years or 30,000 miles, but since the mechanic is under there anyway, it doesn't hurt to take a look. I once drove a rental car with a cracked boot; the symptoms were first, shuddering, and then, getting gradually louder, the sound of rapidly revolving metal grinding against rapidly revolving metal. It was not pleasant.

Give Me Air!

The *air filter* makes sure you have nice clean air going into the combustion chambers of the cylinders. It's usually inside a large black plastic box on the driver's side, about halfway between the firewall and the front fender. You'll see big fat hoses leading into and out of it, and clamps around the side. This box is the air cleaner, and the filter sits inside it, at the top.

The air filter should be checked for dirt every six months (more often if there's a lot of dust around). The time-honored way to check for dirt is to hold the filter up to the light, but many new filters will show light when dirty, or no light when clean. So play it safe: check the maintenance schedule in your owner's manual, and abide by it.

Give Me Vision!

When I was learning to fly, my instructors kept drumming into me Principle Number One of air safety: See and be seen. It's Principle Number One of road safety too.

Seeing means being able to see out. It's easy to ignore your *windshield wipers* until they start blurring and streaking, by which time it's rather late since you're driving along and peering through the windshield as if you were half blind. (In fact, you *are* half blind in such a situation.) So clean the wiper blades regularly—just pull the wipers away from the glass and pass a damp rag along the rubber blades. You can use a mild detergent if you wish, but only a mild one.

While you're doing that, clean the *windshield* too. And the rear window. And the side windows. And the side *mirrors*. Even if the rest of the car is covered in dust, mud, grime, sand, or cat's-paw marks, always make sure all windows and mirrors are clean. Another use for that roll of paper towels you should always have in the car.

Your *lights* are also essential to seeing—and to being seen at night. So clean them too. Otherwise you'll be driving along in the dark wondering why it's so hard to see anything. And you're leaving yourself horribly vulnerable: If your lights are dirty, other drivers can't see you as well. In fact, they may see you too late to avoid a collision.

So I can't emphasize this enough: Always make sure your lights are clean, front *and* rear.

And always drive with your lights on when it's raining or snowing or foggy. In fact, it's a good idea to always drive with your lights on no matter what the weather. This does not use up your battery—remember, the electrical system works off the alternator once the car is running—and involves only the most minute increase in fuel consumption.

Canada has mandated *daytime running lights* for years. These run on low-voltage current to the headlights. They come on when you turn on the ignition, and go off when you switch it off. Research shows a drastic improvement in visibility, even in full sunlight, and many experts consider it only a matter of time until a similar mandate is established in the United States. Meanwhile, some American states mandate that drivers turn on their headlights in rain or snow, while General Motors started making daytime running lights standard on some of its 1995 models.

Give Me Current!

Your *battery* starts the car. If you want it to keep on starting the car every time you turn on the ignition, it's a good idea to give the battery a quick occasional check. Make sure the top is clean and dry. Make sure the terminals are clean and that the connections for the wires leading out of them are tight and secure. These may be coated with a bit of petroleum jelly or terminal grease. That's fine: They like that.

If the terminals look corroded (with a gritty or flaky whitish crust), you can clean them off with a paste of baking soda and water. Wear gloves and an apron to do this, or have your mechanic do it. You can also buy little red and green felt pads that look cute and fit over the terminal posts to stop any corrosion.

Batteries in cars built since the early seventies are maintenance free, so you don't have to open them up. In fact, please don't. Some batteries have neat little peepholes in the top: Look down inside them and if you see a blue or green spot on a dark background, your battery's doing fine; if you see just black, you're doing okay but not for much longer; if you see yellow or pale brown, you'll be lucky if it starts!

A battery should last a minimum of three years. Clearly, battery lifespan depends on how much stopping and starting you do—that is, how much demand you make on the battery to start the car—but so long as you're not in the habit of leaving the lights on, the best can last a good five years, and even as long as eight.

Give Me a Shine!

Have you ever noticed the number of men busy washing and polishing their cars on weekend afternoons?

Is it just another part of the guy thing, or are they onto something? After all, it's not going to run any better because it's clean—or is it?

No, don't worry, it isn't—with one important exception, and that's the brakes. Accumulated dust can wear into the brake linings, so an occasional hose-down of the wheel wells is a good idea.

Moreover, your car may well have a longer life if it's clean. Salt on winter roads in northern climes can really do nasty work on metal if you leave it on there, so a regular wash to hose the stuff off in winter is called for. And even though the finish on new cars is really good—far tougher than it ever was before—the chemicals in bird droppings and tree sap can work their way into even the best finish; if you want to keep up the resale value of your car—let alone have it look good—regular washing will help. And an occasional waxing too.

Most women do wash their cars fairly regularly.

Over half (51.5%) wash their car or get it washed once a month. Another 16% get it done every week—often at a filling station where an automatic wash comes free with a full tank of gas.

Others are more tolerant of dirt: Just over 29% get their car washed a vague two or three times a year. And 3% confessed to maybe once a year.

Automatic car washes are fine (except for convertibles and Rolls-Royces, which should never go near them—that's why you have chauffeurs). But they don't do nearly as good a job as you could yourself with some mild car detergent, a sponge, a bucket, a hose, and a soft old T-shirt or chamois leather. The automatic washes don't get into all the nooks and crannies, and they don't clean the wheels properly. They're good as a preliminary wash, especially when they come free or at a discount along with a purchase of gas; for a thorough wash, put the car through an automat first, then go over it yourself. You'll see what I mean about the automats.

And if you really treasure your car, you probably want to avoid automatic brush washes. Over the years, those brushes make millions of tiny score marks in the paint; these are invisible to the naked eye, but they will affect the sheen of the paint in the end, so look for brushless washes if you can.

Unless you're starting a car-detailing business or are totally obsessive, you really don't need separate cleaners for the seats, the dash, the tires, and so on. And as far as I'm concerned, one car detergent and one car wax is much like another (but then I feel the same way about kitchen cleansers).

There is one product out there that I find extraordinarily useful, however, and that's Rain-X. Wipe it on your windshield after you've cleaned it, and water just beads up and rolls off it. This gives you much better visibility in the rain, even with the best windshield wipers.

Whatever you do, *always* make sure, no matter what state of dirt or cleanliness the rest of the car is in, that all your windows, mirrors, and lights are clean. Clean the inside of your windshield too, since it tends to smear up. Cleanliness may be a matter of desire, taste, or protecting the value or long life of the car, but good vision is essential. See and be seen!

Surviving the Winter Wonderland

Read this and gloat, all ye who live south of the snowbelt. For all us poor sufferers who live north of it, AAA spokesman Jerry Cheske says that the greatest percentage of emergency road-service calls comes in sync with the first cold snap. So it's Girl Scout time: "Be prepared."

Here's a few words that may take a moan or two out of winter. Or at least a wheeze or two out of the battery.

This is what your *battery* faces when it gets cold: At 32 degrees Fahrenheit, it loses about 35% of its strength. At 0 degrees, it loses another 25%. That only leaves you with 40% of its normal charge. Moreover, that 40% has a lot more work to do than in summer: Oil thickens as it gets colder, which is why the engine is harder to crank. *And* you need higher voltage to ignite the fuel-air mixture.

So before you do anything else, check the battery. Check for corrosion. Check the cables and connections. Get the charging circuit checked if the car seems slow to start. And if it's an older car, check the *spark plugs* to see that they're clean and properly gapped.

On to the *oil*, which is thin and slippery when it's warm but can get as thick and sluggish as molasses in the cold. The heavier the weight of the oil, the thicker it gets. A lighter-weight oil—5W-30, for instance—stays more slippery, and many carmakers now recommend it for year-round use.

Antifreeze? In a newer car, the coolant includes ethylene glycol and corrosion inhibitors, which are in fact antifreeze, but older cars will need antifreeze added. (If you live south of the snow line, stop smirking: Antifreeze also helps prevent the radiator from boiling over in the heat.) You don't need to get the radiator flushed every year, but every two years or 25,000 miles (whichever comes earlier). Half and half is the ideal mix of antifreeze and water; use more antifreeze than that and you'll actually get less protection.

In really cold weather—we're talking below zero Fahrenheit here—add gas-line antifreeze to your gas tank. This will prevent an iced fuel line.

Brakes, of course, need to be checked: It takes far longer to stop in rain, on ice, or in snow—a little matter of less traction. And make sure your *tires* have a deep enough tread to wick away water, or you'll be in for a hydroplaning adventure you hadn't bargained for. (See "Four Rubber Patches," page 262.)

Snow tires have the deepest tread of all, but the deeper tread makes handling more unsteady—all that squishy rubber between you and the road—so you need to drive slower (which of course you should be doing in any case in snow). Studded snow tires can rip up road surfaces, which is why they're banned in several states. This used to leave you with the sole option of traction chains, but new studless snow tires are an impressive alternative, and can be driven on dry pavement as well as on ice and snow. Many drivers in the snowbelt keep two sets of tires and change them twice a year: snow tires on at the start of winter and off at the first sign of spring.

Also keep an eye on *tire pressure:* It decreases as the temperature plunges, one pound of pressure for every 10 degrees of temperature drop.

One item that too many overlook: the *windshield wipers.* Even the new artificial rubber compounds deteriorate quickly when it gets really cold. If your wipers are streaking and smearing now, they won't be up to the hard work of winter weather. Be a big spender and get new ones. The Car Care Council recommends special winter blades with flexible rubber boots to prevent them icing up.

And if it gets so cold that you need a can of de-icer for the door lock, take into account that it won't do you any good if it's inside the locked car. Carry it with you.

Above all, remember that, as AAA's Jerry Cheske puts it, "In winterizing your car, you've got to winterize your mind."

That means winter driving: less speed, more distance from the car ahead of you, cautious braking. True, it's less fun, but that way you'll be around to enjoy the summer, when you can put the antifreeze to its best use: preventing overheating.

Ten Snowbelt Essentials

1. A *window scraper*—a cheap and brilliant invention
2. Extra *windshield washer fluid*—you go through a lot of the stuff in winter
3. Spare *wiper blades*
4. A small folding *shovel*
5. A small bag of salt, sand, or *kitty litter* to scatter in front of the wheels of a parked car for traction.

And just in case you get really stuck:

6. A warm *blanket* or sleeping bag
7. *Boots* or galoshes
8. Extra *warm clothes* (down vest, ski mitts, skicap)
9. Bottled *water,* and a supply of dried frut and nuts
10. One-day supply of any regular *medication,* plus a few tampons

Note: These items, plus snow chains if you don't have snow tires on the car, are in addition to the regular all-year emergency kit detailed on page 250.

Help!

➡ **"Aren't cars a pain in the butt?"**

—Tom and Ray Magliozzi,
hosts of Public Radio's "Car Talk"

Rule number one about breakdowns is that there is never a right time for them to happen. They will always happen at the worst time. And though you wish the Magliozzi brothers were there to help you out, they're not. So who is?

Many automakers now offer *800-number roadside assistance*. These services began as the kind of extra benefit that kept luxury-car customers happy, but are now offered to many economy-car owners too. Sometimes they're free, but sometimes you pay an annual fee.

Most reports on these services are excellent, so if you have a new car and the maker offers this service, use it if you break down, if you lock your keys inside the car, or even if you have a flat tire.

Some programs pay for everything, sometimes even lodging if you're stuck, and an alternate car if yours has to be taken for repairs. Some pay for less: Check the small print, and if it says the automaker will "arrange" for a certain service, that service will be arranged for, all right, but you'll pay for it.

If you have a mechanical problem and also have a cellular phone, you can call the roadside assistance number and have technicians talk you through a check under the hood to see if the problem can be fixed without waiting for a mechanic to arrive. One woman was amazed at how this worked.

➡ **"Don't ask me what I did, because I have no idea. All I can tell you is that it worked. One moment the car was broken, and the next it was fixed, and I was gushing on the cellular phone telling the guy he was a genius, and he was telling me *I* was the genius!"**

—Accountant, Pennsylvania

If your car is not included under an 800-number roadside assistance service from the automaker, never fear—there's AAA.

You are, of course, a member of AAA (Automobile Association of America). If you're not, join. Now. Even if you have an 800 roadside assistance number. For $22 to $55 a year, depending on the state, AAA provides a lot of useful services, including car pricing and road maps as well as roadside assistance. Response times vary depending on where you are and the weather: If it's the first cold snap of the season, expect a longer wait, because all those people who didn't bother to prepare their cars for winter (see page 240) are calling for help.

The Three Troubleshooters

Once you've lost your awe of the engine as some mysterious foreign object, you'll find that you don't have to be a rocket scientist to figure out if something's wrong with your car.

Chances are, you might even be able to figure out *what's* wrong.

You have three basic troubleshooting tools, all free and easily available:

☞ **your eyes**

☞ **your ears**

☞ **your nose**

Your Eyes

Keep an eye out for warning lights that come on as you're driving, especially the temperature and oil pressure lights. These are alongside the speedometer, and are often the first sign of trouble.

Don't be alarmed when they come on briefly as you switch on the ignition. They're supposed to do this, along with the ABS and battery lights, so that you know that all the monitoring systems are working. If they don't come on when you switch on the ignition, there's a defect in your electrical circuit. And if one of them stays on, pay attention: It's telling you there's something wrong, so pull over, turn off the engine, and check to see if you can find the problem.

Some new cars with computerized diagnostic systems have lighted messages. I hate them, but some people love them. If your car has one of these systems, read your owner's manual to find out exactly what these tersely worded directives from your engine mean. "Service engine now," for instance, may mean it's time for an oil change, or it may mean "There's something wrong so please get me to a mechanic as soon as you possibly can." Don't ignore such messages. Just take the car to the mechanic, let him plug in his fancy diagnostic computer, and find out what's wrong.

And of course, keep an eye on the fuel gauge. *Never* let it go anywhere near empty. You don't have to be absentminded to forget to fill the tank, you just have to be busy. But a near-empty tank is a good way to find yourself stranded a few miles up the road.

Drips in the driveway. If you find oily patches under your car in the morning, you have a leak somewhere. The only exception: When you park your car and have had the air conditioning on, condensation will drip onto the ground under the car for a while after you've turned off the engine. It's easy to mistake for oil, but it's not, it's just water, and is normal. Oil drips are not normal (unless you're driving an old MG, which drips oil so much you might think it was normal).

Oil leaks may be due to a faulty seal or gasket, or to something as simple as a loosely tightened oil filter or oil-drain plug. Pale-yellow watery drips are from your cooling system and could indicate something as serious as a hole in the radiator or as simple as an old or loosely connected hose.

If you see steam or smoke coming from under the hood of the car, stop immediately and turn off the engine. Steam indicates overheating, probably because of a leak in the radiator or in a hose. Smoke can be from melted electrical-wire insulation, or from an oil leak that has sprayed oil over the hot engine; if the latter, the smoke should lessen and then stop once you've turned off the engine and the metal begins to cool down.

With steam, you know the car is overheating. Turn off the ignition, wait until everything's cooled down, then add coolant (or water if you have no coolant with you) to the coolant reservoir, being careful not to overfill. Check the hoses for leaks. Do not drive off immediately, but let the car idle for a while so that the cool water can run through the system.

With smoke, be every bit as cautious as you would with any fire. The good news is that engine fires are extremely rare in modern cars, and when they do occur, they are most likely to be the smoldering type rather than full flames. Still,

246

take no chances. Get out of the car quickly, and check under the hood only if you have a fire extinguisher to hand. (You should keep a small one in your emergency kit: see page 250.) Lean back from the engine compartment when you open the hood, determine the source of the smoke quickly, and spray with the fire extinguisher.

Your Ears

When you drive a car regularly, you get used to the sound of the engine, so detecting something unusual is not difficult. Still, it's easy to say "Oh, it's nothing, it'll pass." Don't ignore what you hear: It's a sign that something's wrong.

Squealing. If you hear squealing when you brake (aside from sudden emergency braking), your brakes are protesting and asking for attention. It may simply be that your brake pads or linings need replacement.

Hissing. The sound is that of escaping steam, and it means there's a leak in your radiator or in a hose.

Clunking. If you drive an automatic transmission, your transmission fluid may be low. Or one of the joints in your suspension system may be low on grease due to a cracked boot.

Flapping. This is usually a sign of a flat or stripped tire. Slow down, stop on the side of the road, and check.

Roaring. If you sound like a drag-racer, it's probably a damaged muffler or a hole in the exhaust pipe, especially if it's particularly loud when you accelerate.

Sputtering. This is also known as rough idling, and means that the engine is not getting enough fuel. Get the fuel system checked. It could be something as simple as a clogged fuel filter or worn spark plugs.

Grinding. If it comes as you shift gears, you need your gears checked. If it comes as you turn, a cracked boot over one of the steering-linkage joints has probably leaked grease.

Rattling. A rattle isn't always something wrong with the

car. In fact, it's amazing how simple a rattle can sometimes be. If it's coming from the dash, check your glove compartment. Any cassettes rattling around in there? Anything plastic or metallic bouncing around? Pad it with paper and see if you still have the rattle. If it's coming from the back, check the trunk and make sure nothing in there is rolling around.

Your Nose

You know the scenario: You're driving along and your passenger sniffs suspiciously and says, "What's that?" You're not passing a freshly fertilized field, there's no building on fire, and nobody's suffering from flatulence. So take it seriously.

Exhaust fumes. There's a leak in your exhaust system and the fumes are feeding into the car. Open all the windows, and get the problem checked out as soon as possible.

Gas fumes. There's probably a leak in the fuel line. Pull off the road and turn off the engine; you don't want to risk a fire. Call for roadside assistance.

Burning oil. You may well have an oil leak and the oil is spraying onto the hot engine. Turn off the engine, let it cool, and check the oil level on the dipstick. Look for signs of a leak. If necessary, add oil immediately, and take the car to your mechanic.

Burning rubber. This could be just a rubber hose that has come slightly loose and is lying against the hot engine. Check the rubber hoses and their connections. You might also have been driving with your parking brake half-on, which can produce a burning-rubber smell. Of course "burning rubber" is also a phrase for driving the heck out of a car—it's the smell of drag-racing, where they rev the car up high with the brakes full on before zooming off: The tires heat up and literally smoke. Do not do this with your car. Tires are expensive.

Burning plastic. This could be a sign that the electrical wiring has short-circuited. (The plastic is the insulating coating of the wires.) Pull off the road and shut off the engine immediately. Check under the hood only with extreme caution, and with a fire extinguisher handy.

Jump-Starting

If your car won't start, check the battery terminal connections first to make sure they're clean and securely connected. Try again. If you still get nothing, the problem may be a low battery. This can happen if you've left the lights on by mistake.

If your battery is empty (completely discharged), you can call AAA or an 800 roadside assistance service to come jump-start it. Or you can usually jump-start it yourself.

All you need is a pair of jumper cables and another car—a family member, a neighbor, or a kindly passer-by can provide that, unless you have the good fortune to be a dual car owner. The jumper cables simply take the juice from the battery of the second car and transfer a nice big jolt of it to yours.

Place the second car hood to hood with yours. Make sure the ignition in both cars is switched completely off. Now connect the ends of the red (positive) jumper cable to the positive terminal of each battery (that's the one with a plus sign on it) by simply clipping them on.

Next, the black (negative) jumper cable. Connect one end to the negative terminal of the second car (that's the terminal with a minus sign on it), and the other end to any clean unpainted metal (but not aluminum) surface in the engine compartment of your car, as far away from the battery as possible. Always do it this way, and in this order. This is important: random connections can cause a battery explosion. Check the instructions in your owner's manual too.

There may be a spark at this point, which is fine: That's the spark of life.

Now start the engine of the second car. Leave it running, and turn on the ignition of your car. Presto, it will start! Juice from the other car's battery is running through yours—and once your car has started, it gets its juice from the alternator, not from the battery, so you're fine.

Leave your engine running, and now disconnect the cables. Make sure you do it in this order: first, the black (negative) cable from your car; second, the black (negative) cable from the second car; third, the red (positive) cable from your car; fourth, the red (positive) cable from the second car.

If the battery was low because you left your lights on, it just needs recharging, and a good long drive will do that. But if it's low because it's old and you've been having problems starting the car, especially in cold weather, it's time to drive straight to the repair shop and get a new one.

Your Car's Emergency Kit

Every well turned out car should have the following items permanently stored in the trunk (along with a jack and a lug wrench, both of which should come with the car):

- A roll of paper towels
- An old cloth towel or T-shirt as a rag
- Two screwdrivers: a Phillips-head (with a cross in the tip) and a regular one
- An adjustable wrench and a pair of locking pliers
- Electrical tape (for a leaky hose)
- An empty one-gallon metal container with a tight cap (for gas if you run out)
- A quart of oil
- A small plastic funnel for the oil
- Jumper cables

- Flares
- A small flashlight
- A folding red reflector triangle
- A bottle of drinking water
- A small fire extinguisher
- A first-aid kit
- Pad and pencil
- Quarters (for emergency use in a pay phone)

Prepackaged emergency kits in nice little red plastic boxes are neat, but check the contents against the list here: The kits may contain most of these items, but they won't contain all of them, so check what you need to add.

Who Was That Masked Man?

Incredible as it may seem in the age of drive-by shootings and carjackings, old-fashioned chivalry is still alive and well on the American road.

Here are two stories of the stranger who appeared out of nowhere and disappeared back into nowhere having carried out his errand of mercy.

➡ **"We were in downtown Dallas late at night, not a good part of town, and I veered too close to the edge of a ramp and dropped a wheel off the edge. We were stuck. We set the flares, but we couldn't leave the car to go get help because all our stuff for the crafts show we were going to was in it, and we were afraid it would be stolen. Then this guy stops and asks what the trouble is. And we're really nervous. He's big and muscled and sort of threatening looking. But he says, 'We've got to get this car out of here for you,' and the next thing we know, he's lifting the rear of our car, all by himself. He sets it back on the ramp, gets back in** his car, and leaves us standing there open-mouthed before we can even say thank you."

—Jeweler, Oregon

➡ "My mother and I were on the highway and we ran out of gas. This guy stops and we're really afraid even to talk to him, but there's no way not to, so we tell him what the trouble is and he says he'll go to the next gas station, get some gas, and bring it back for us. He drives off and we're sure we've seen the last of him. Then twenty minutes later he's back with a gallon can of gas. He puts it in our tank, then follows us to make sure we get to the gas station, which was twelve miles down the road, so he'd driven an extra twenty-four miles just for us. Turns out he was in in the army in Germany and the same thing happened to him one time, and he vowed that he'd always stop and do the same for anyone else. He leaves and we go to pay, and that's when we find out he's already paid for a full tank of gas for us!"

—Student, Pennsylvania

Dealing with Mechanics

➡ "I felt like I was really at home in this town when I found a good mechanic. The ones I had before would look at me like I was crazy when I tried to tell them the car was making strange noises. This guy respects what I say and doesn't make me feel dumb. He relates to me as an equal. He explains everything, and the way he explains it, I can understand. I really appreciate that."

➡ "I agree: Until I found a good mechanic, I always felt vaguely skittish in cars. But with this guy, if I say there's a wobble in the steering, he doesn't look at me like it's me that's got the wobble. He says, 'Okay, let's find out what the problem is.' I've driven this car over 75,000 miles, and I think he's a large part of it."

—Texas group

A good mechanic can make all the difference.

So, unfortunately, can a bad one. Motor vehicle repairs are second only to motor vehicle sales in consumer complaints to state attorney-general offices throughout the country. Stories like the following explain why.

➡ "I had an engine fire, and I called the dealership where I have my car serviced, and the woman who answered said, 'There can't be a fire.' I was furious. It turned out they'd re-used the old gasket instead of putting in a new one when they'd checked the valves, so the oil was leaking out."

➡ "When we were checking out our car before a big trip, the mechanic said we needed new tires. 'I have four that are almost the right size,' he said. He put them on the car and we could only go in a straight line: They wouldn't turn because they were too big!"

—Pennsylvania group

You may have gathered that you don't have to be a rocket scientist to be a mechanic. But the best could well make pretty good rocket scientists if they wanted. They have a brilliant understanding of a car, sometimes almost intuitive. They also have the right tools, a clean shop, and respect for the customer.

There are as many superb mechanics as there are superb physicists, painters, or surgeons. In other words, they're a minority. Of the majority, some are really bad, but most are adequate. Think, though, if you'd go to a doctor you knew was only adequate. Your mechanic is the doctor to your car, so it makes sense to choose your mechanic with the same care you'd choose your doctor.

The Choice of Mechanic

Your first port of call when looking for a good mechanic is friends and coworkers. Who do they use? Who do they recommend? (Oddly, the answers to those two questions are not always the same: People sometimes use a mechanic who is close to their place of work rather than one they know is better but is farther away. I understand why they do this, but it's a false saving of time that they'll pay for in repairs farther down the road.)

The women in the focus groups spent quite a lot of time comparing notes about their mechanics. Some mechanics lost a lot of business in those groups. Others gained a lot. There was no doubt that the right ones lost and the right ones gained.

The most satisfied women by far were those who went to independent mechanics (not associated with a dealership or a chain). They felt they had a good relationship with their mechanic, and that the mechanic knew and respected both them and their cars. Some actually bought the same make of car again and again in order to stay with an independent mechanic who specialized in that make.

Visit any repair shop you're thinking of using, and check out the following.

Work conditions. You're not expecting an absolutely spotless place—cars, after all, are dirty creatures, as are the roads they run on—but you are expecting a neat one. If there are grease-covered tools lying around on the floor, for instance, that's a bad sign. A good mechanic respects his or her tools, never leaves them on the floor where people can slip up or trip on them, keeps them clean, and is careful to replace them neatly after any particular job.

Diplomas. Look for a "AAA-approved" sign, and for mechanics wearing ASE patches on their shirts or with an ASE diploma on the wall. (ASE stands for Automotive Service Excellence, and is determined by the National Institute for Automotive Service Excellence, which certifies the mechanic, not the shop.) Check what specialty each mechanic is certified in. The ideal shop is one where *all* the mechanics are ASE-certified.

Guarantee. Check if the shop provides a written guarantee of its work for at least thirty days.

Computer diagnostics. Since modern cars have so much

➡ **"We bought a lot of VWs because we had a good VW mechanic."**

➡ **"That makes sense: my mother has a Honda, and she says she'll never buy another kind of car because she says, 'It may sound silly, but they treat me respectfully when I come in.' "**

➡ **"That's the whole point: It's not silly."**

—California group

electronics in them, make sure any mechanic you deal with knows how to service and repair the electronics, and that the shop has the right diagnostic equipment. Look for certificates of in-house training programs run by the automaker.

Some repair shops offer services like a loaner car, a shuttle service to and from your place of work while the car is in the shop for the day, and free washing and vacuuming. All these services are very welcome, but don't let them decide you on which shop to use: Remember that you'll pay for them indirectly, in higher labor and parts costs on your repair bill.

It's generally better to go to a repair shop that specializes in your make of vehicle. Those who say they'll repair anything will probably repair nothing very well. AAA estimates that while in 1965, a mechanic needed to understand 5,000 pages of service manuals to service any car on the road, today that number would be 465,000 pages. Good repair shops specialize in certain makes or certain types of car. This means they have the spare parts within easy reach, keep up-to-date with new developments in that make or type of car, and have the right equipment to service it.

Before deciding on a repair shop, put in a call to your local Better Business Bureau and check if there have been any complaints about the place. (And of course, if a repair shop does shoddy, unnecessary, or outrageously expensive work, file a complaint with the Better Business Bureau. Often, the Bureau will be able to settle the matter between you and the repair shop, but even if it can't, you have helped warn others away.)

Many people take new cars to the dealerships where they bought them, at least until the warranty period is over. (And by that time, they're used to dealing with that shop, so they tend to stay with it.) In fact, *any* dealership of that make of car can do the warranty work, so you don't have to stick with the same one if you don't want to.

The advantage of the dealerships is that they usually have all the parts on hand or near at hand, as well as the

> ➡ **"A week after I had my car serviced it developed a problem and I took it back for repair. After he'd worked on it, I said, "How much do I owe you?" and he said, 'I'm not charging you for this—I just worked on this car last week!' "**
>
> **—Legal secretary, Oregon**

256

right diagnostic equipment for computer-controlled electronic systems. And good ones have a large enough staff to give your car to a specialist in whatever ails it, something a smaller shop may not be able to do.

The disadvantage: Since most dealerships have fairly large service departments, your repair order gets written up by a service writer, and you often have no control over who actually does the work on your car. Moreover, dealerships generally have higher overhead costs than independent mechanics, so charge more (remember too that this is where they make two-thirds of their profit), though on an oil and filter change, this may be a matter of just a few dollars. If you like dealing with them, or if warranty work needs to be done, stay with a dealer's repair shop.

But if the car or the problem is not covered by warranty and you don't like the dealer's shop, you might want to look for a good independent mechanic. One you can develop a relationship with.

Chains are another way to get your car serviced. For regular service, like oil and filter changes, they are generally cheap and quick, though the level of competence may vary widely. Beware of pressure to have extra work done that you may not need. And again, remember that there'll be no personal relationship between the mechanic who actually does the work and you or your car, and that a lot of relatively newly minted mechanics straight out of school are working in the chains (which is why they can offer such good prices—they pay lousy wages).

Consumer Reports tends to favor independent mechanics over dealerships, and dealerships over chains. Most women agree.

➡ **"I took my car in to have the exhaust pipe changed and a few days later the emergency brake went. It turned out it was burned through. I said it was because whoever had installed the new exhaust pipe had been careless with the oxyacetylene torch, but they said no, the one thing had nothing to do with the other, it was just coincidence, and insisted on charging me."**

—Student, Pennsylvania

Neat Machines: How Cars Work

Defining Noises

Sometimes you know something's wrong with the car because you can hear it, but you just can't explain the sound to your mechanic. You stand there trying to imitate the noise, and feel like an absolute fool. Here's a guide used by many better repair shops to help improve communication between owners and mechanics, and make diagnosis of the problem easier.

Boom	Rhythmic sound like a drum roll or distant thunder.
Buzz	Low-pitched sound, something like a bee.
Chatter	Rapidly repeating metallic sound.
Chuckle	Rapid noise that sounds like a stick against the spokes of a spinning bicycle wheel.
Chirp	High-pitched, rapidly repeating sound, birdlike.
Click	Light sound like a ballpoint pen being clicked.
Clunk/ Thump	Heavy metal-to-metal sound, like a thick hammer striking steel.
Grind	Abrasive sound, like a grinding wheel or sandpaper rubbing on wood.
Groan	Continuous, low-pitched humming sound.
Growl	Low, guttural sound, like a threatening dog.
Hiss	Continuous sound like air escaping a balloon.
Hum	Continuous sound like a wire humming in the wind.
Knock	Heavy, loud, repeating sound, like a knock at the door.
Ping	A higher-pitched knock.
Rattle	Sounds like something's loose, such as marbles rolling around in a can or a box.
Roar	Deep, prolonged sound like ocean waves or strong wind.
Rumble	Low, heavy, continuous sound, like thunder.
Squeak	High-pitched sound like you get when you rub clean glass.
Squeal	Continuous, high-pitched sound like a fingernail on a chalkboard.
Tap	Light hammering sound, like tapping a pencil on a tabletop. May be rhythmic or intermittent.
Whir/ Whine	High-pitched buzzing sound, like an electric motor or drill.
Whistle	Sharp, shrill sound, like wind passing through a small opening.

Six Ways to Protect Yourself

1. Never pay a repair bill without first making sure you *understand every item* and why that work or that part was necessary.

2. Always get a *written estimate* of repair work. Never allow further work to be done without your specific say-so. Do not leave it up to the shop, but insist that you be called before they do any more than the work you originally agreed to. Good shops will do this without being asked.

3. Always pay for mechanical work with a *credit card.* That way, you can refuse payment to the credit-card carrier if you believe you have been overcharged or if bad work was done. And of course, you earn frequent-flier miles or whatever other bonuses your credit-card company is offering.

4. Remember what you'd do with a doctor: If you're facing what sounds like an inflated repair bill, take the car elsewhere for a *second opinion.*

5. Most experts tell you to ask for any *used parts* that have been replaced to be saved and handed to you. In principle this is a good idea; in practice, how are you to know if these are from your car or not? A good mechanic will hand you the old parts without your asking. It's okay, you don't have to keep them: You can always just hand them back.

6. Don't fall for "Well, you'll have to have the brake pads changed in a few thousand miles in any case, so we might as well do that now" (or spark plugs replaced, or rotors ground, or muffler changed, or a new battery). Unless you are having trouble with the brakes, plugs, muffler, battery, or whatever, stick to the *maintenance schedule* in the owner's manual.

Women Mechanics

I once wrote a newspaper column in which I fantasized about opening up my own repair shop, employing only women mechanics. To my astonishment, I had a slew of letters from women mechanics around the country asking me to let them know when I opened shop: They'd move to New York, where I lived at the time, and work for me. The reason: All-male repair shops were loath to hire women mechanics. Which is incredibly dumb of them, because women—half the car owners in the country—would often prefer women mechanics.

44.5% of women in the focus groups said they'd trust a female mechanic more than a male one.

Nearly all the rest said either that it depended on the quality of the mechanic, not on the gender, or that they'd trust a man and a woman equally. Only two out of 150 said they'd trust a male mechanic more.

Fully 56% said they'd been treated unfairly by male mechanics because they were women.

Is this why so many women would prefer a woman mechanic? No, it's not.

Only 42% of those who said they'd prefer a woman felt that they'd been treated unfairly because of their gender.

Women are simply tired of being condescended to by male mechanics. Tired of being treated as though we are not responsible owners of our own cars. And tired of being taken for a ride.

Moreover, most women reckon that women mechanics didn't just fall into the field because they couldn't think of what else to do with their lives, and that any woman who has put up with the hassles and sometimes harassment of training in such a male-dominated field is going to be determined, committed, and good.

Right now, though, you'll have to look hard for a woman mechanic. As of 1994, only 5,000 out of 854,000 certified auto mechanics were women. But those who have found the financial backing to open up shop for themselves are doing very well indeed: Repair shops run by women report that anywhere from 40% to 70% of their customers are women (which also means that 30% to 60% are men), and they consistently report that they've been successful from day one.

Clearly, more and more people, women and men, are realizing what I discovered when I spent a summer working as a mechanic's apprentice: Car repair is a matter of brain, not brawn. The brawn is provided by all those hydraulic and power tools; that's why repair shops have them. The flamboyant muscles and the tattoos are just for decoration, same as the girlie calendars.

A note about those girlie calendars: You won't find them in women-run shops, of course, but why can they still be found in many male-run shops?

The culprits are repair-shop suppliers—tool companies, tire companies, oil companies, and so on—who pander to what they think of the male gender with a vast array of give-away pin-up calendars and mugs. Like too many dealers, they're living in some Paleolithic era. But since the mugs are thermal mugs, many mechanics do use them. And they tend to just pin the calendars on the wall and forget about them.

The absence of such pin-up girlies is a good sign. But their presence—unless there's a lot of them—is not necessarily a bad one. Use your judgment. Obviously if they're prominently displayed or if you find them offensive, go elsewhere. And tell the owner why.

Sign of progress: Snap-On, one of the major toolmakers, abandoned its traditional girlie calendar in 1995.

Four Rubber Patches: Your Tires

It always amazes me how easily people overlook tires. How cavalierly they say, "Oh, I can get another few thousand miles out of these," when their tires have next to no tread left on them.

Look at your car. How much of it is in contact with the road? The wheels, you say? No, not the wheels. Just a very small portion of them.

No matter what type of car you have, how large or how small, how powerful or wimpy, the fact is always this:

> **The only part of your car in contact with the road is four patches of rubber, each no larger than the span of your hand.**

These patches carry a lot of weight, both literally and figuratively. So of course you want the best contact with the road: You want tires that will grab the road, not slide over it.

Some tires do slide over it: These are tires with no tread, and they're called slicks. They're used for racing. You get lots of speed from them, and terrible handling in rain. If the tread on your tires is worn down, you're getting close to having slicks. Unless you're a race driver on a track, get them replaced quick.

The TREAD is the rubber surface of the tire. The patterns in it differ from make to make, but the purpose of them is to provide somewhere for water to go other than between the surface of the tire and the road. Once you get water between the surface of the tire and the road, you no longer have traction. That's bad. It's called hydroplaning. If you've ever skidded in rain or on ice, you know what that feels like. If you haven't, imagine a terrifying fairground ride.

The depth of the tread usually dictates the kind of tire. Performance tires, intended for high-performance cars in dry weather, have wider and shallower treads. Snow and mud tires have very deep ones. Most tires on new cars nowadays are ALL-SEASONS, which are ideal for most people in most conditions.

Just ten or fifteen years ago, all-seasons meant giving up performance or traction. But improvements in rubber technology (yes, there *is* such a thing as rubber technology!) mean that the new all-seasons are terrific. For the vast majority of us, they're definitely the way to go. If you live in a severe-winter area, however, you'll want even deeper treads, and that means snow tires for the winter months. Consider the new studless snow tires, such as Blizzaks, which give excellent performance both in snow and on dry pavement. (But remember, like all snow tires, they wear down much more quickly than regular tires, so swap them for regular tires as soon as the ice melts.)

Tires now have a built-in TREAD-WEAR INDICATOR—a smooth horizontal band across the tire that comes into view when the tread is worn down. When you see this, you *know* it's time to get the tires replaced.

Another way to check tread wear without waiting until the last moment: Insert a penny into the tread with Lincoln's head pointed down. If you can see the top of his head, get new tires.

You should get tires in pairs. In a front-wheel-drive car, make sure the new tires go on the front wheels, which get more wear, and the old pair on the rear wheels, unless all four of your tires are so worn that you need a full new set of four. Never use new tires on one side of the car only: You need even traction either side.

Do not, repeat, do *not* try to save money by driving on worn tires. Not unless you love danger.

How long should tires last? That depends on the kind of tire. The best tires, steel-belted RADIALS (yes, they do have steel belts inside) last more than twice as long as cheaper bias-ply tires and give you better handling, so though they're more expensive, they're well worth it. Good steel-belted radials should last 40,000 to 60,000 miles, sometimes more, depending on the type of driving you do and the road conditions. Certainly 50,000 miles is common with a good radial tire.

Decoding Your Tires

All tires are coded by type, and the code is embossed on the side of the tire in a series of mysterious numbers.

Decoding the most important part of the tire's numbers is less intimidating than it seems. You're likely to find something like this embossed on the sidewall of the tire:

P205/75R14 87S

Decoded, this means:

✔ **P is for Passenger car.**

✔ **205 is the tire width in millimeters.**

✔ **75 is the aspect ratio (ratio of height to width).**

✔ **R is for radial. (Most tires are now radials.)**

✔ **14 is the diameter of the wheel in inches. (Why this measurement is in inches while width is in millimeters is one of those mechanical mysteries that will be solved only when the male mind is fully understood.)**

✔ **87 is an arcane code indicating the maximum weight the tire can carry at its maximum rated speed.**

✔ **S is a speed rating, indicating the maximum speed the tire can stand. The common speed ratings are S for 112 mph, T for 118 mph, H for 130 mph, V for 149 mph, and Z for any higher than that.**

There's a whole pile more information on the side of the tire, but there's really no need to understand most of it unless you have a rubber fetish. Still, you should be aware of two more numbers on the sidewall: the tread-wear index and the maximum pressure.

The tread-wear index grades the tire's tread against a miserably treaded tire with a grade of 100. A tire with a 400 tread-wear index should last four times longer than a 100 one. A tread-wear index of 180 is low, while 500 is high.

The maximum pressure, or how much air pressure the tire can withstand, is given in *pounds per square inch* (psi). The pressure printed on the tire, however, really is the maximum. Use that and you'll be bouncing all over the place. For the *recommended pressure* for your car and tires, check your owner's manual. Or look for a small sticker on the edge of the driver's door (though it's sometimes on one of the other doors), which will tell you the automaker's recommended pressure for both front and back wheels.

Always make sure you replace your tires with the same type and size; *never* make do with smaller tires, and check with the dealer before trying larger ones. And always, of course, use all four tires the same size, and preferably the same make.

Checking the Pressure

The main cause of rapid tread wear is underinflation: not enough air pressure. This creates more wear and tear on the tire, and it reduces the car's performance by increasing drag. You'll get much longer life out of your tires if you check the pressure once a week. Once you know how, it only takes a minute.

Okay, so how do you do it?

Most of the women in the focus groups already knew this.

82% knew how to check air pressure, and 75.5% knew how to add more air or let air out.

In case you don't know, here's how.

First, you're better off getting your own pressure gauge than using one in a filling station, because those are notoriously unreliable. The pen-like ones aren't so great either. Get one of the round ones, which are slightly more expensive but easier to read and more accurate. You can get one at any auto parts store.

Second, check tire pressure only when the tires are cool (that is, when you have driven no more than two miles). If you've been driving for a while, or if it's very hot, the air inside the tires heats and expands. So for the most accurate reading, check in the early morning.

Third, it makes sense to do this at a filling station with a working air hose, so that if you need to add air, you have it at hand.

To do the check, remove the small screw cap from the tire's valve stem, which sticks out of each tire near the rim. Press the pressure gauge *firmly* against the valve stem. There'll be a short hiss as a little air escapes, and then the needle on your gauge will give you a reading.

If the pressure is too high, release some air by simply pressing the small pin inside the valve stem with the tip of your nail, or by altering the angle of the gauge against the valve stem. You'll hear the hiss of air escaping. Measure again, and see if you need to let more air out.

If you let too much out, don't worry. The air hose works the same way as your gauge: To add air, simply press the rounded end of the hose *firmly* over the valve stem for a few seconds. Then check with your gauge to see what the pressure is now.

Don't worry if it takes you a few tries: Nobody except a racepit mechanic gets it right immediately except by luck.

Checking your tires once a month is a good habit. And while you're about it, don't forget to check the spare tire too.

The spares are getting pretty weird these days. Don't panic if you check your spare and find that it's smaller than the regular tires. New cars often have special small temporary spares designed to last fifty miles or so—enough to get you to a repair shop. It's a good idea: They're smaller and lighter than regular tires, so you have less weight to carry and more room in the trunk. But be warned: These tires are *not* for normal driving. They're designed only to get you home or to a repair shop where you can get the flat tire repaired. If you have to put one on, do not drive over 50 mph. And drive with caution, because your car won't handle so well with one tire smaller than the others.

Changing a Tire

Your owner's manual should give clear instructions as to how to change a tire (yet another misnomer, since you're really changing the whole wheel).

In fact, most women know how.

57.5% have changed a tire themselves, while another 14.4% know how.

In case you're one of the lucky ones who's never needed

to figure it out but would like to know how, here's a 14-step guide, which includes a couple of wrinkles for using brain-power instead of brute force.

1. Make sure you're on level ground, and out of the way of traffic. Put your parking brake on and turn on the hazard flashers.

2. Remove the lug wrench, jack, and spare tire from the trunk.

3. Block the front and rear of the wheel diagonally opposite the tire being changed by placing stones, bricks, or large pieces of wood on either side of it.

4. Pry off the wheel cover with the sharp end of the lug wrench or with a screwdriver.

5. Loosen the lug nuts. These are the big nuts that hold the wheel in place. There are four or five of them, depending on the model of car. Your aim right now is just to loosen them up so that you can remove them by hand once you have the car jacked up. Since they've been put on by power tools, they'll be hard to budge at first. So use your legs and your weight instead of your hands and back.

   Insert the end of the wrench over the first lug nut so that the handle of the wrench sticks out parallel to the ground. Now simply stamp down firmly on the wrench, using the weight of your body. (This is called leverage, which is always a good thing to have.) Do this with each of the lugs.

   The whole process is much easier if you make sure you're applying pressure in the right direction. On most cars, you'll see the letter R or no letter at all on the lug nuts; this means they're right-threaded, and you should turn them counterclockwise to loosen them. If there is an L, the lugs are left-threaded, and you should turn them clockwise to loosen them. Your owner's manual will also tell you which way they go.

(Some cars come with wheel locks, in which case the key is generally either in the glove box or tied to the tire iron. Follow the instructions in the owner's manual for how to use them.)

6. Now, the jack. Make sure it's level on the ground—no small stones beneath it to throw it off balance. The owner's manual will tell you where the best jack positions are for your car. If you can't find them, place the jack under the side sill of the car, two or three inches in from the edge and about nine inches from the wheel.

7. Raise the jack. Some jacks are raised with up and down strokes, others with circular strokes. Your owner's manual will tell you which; so will simple trial and error. Raise the jack until it contacts the car frame, make sure it's touching solid steel, then continue raising it until the wheel is just off the ground. Don't raise it more than an inch or so off the ground: Wheels are heavy, so why make more work for your back when you take the old one off and put the new one on? This way, you can just slide them on and off.

8. Shake the car a little to make sure the jack is securely in place.

9. Unscrew the lug nuts competely, and put them somewhere secure. You don't want to get the spare on and then not be able to find the lug nuts.

10. The tire is now sitting on the exposed bolts. Simply ease it toward you. You'll know when it's clear: It's heavy. This is why you've raised it no more than one inch off the ground.

11. Lift the spare onto the wheel bolts. Push it all the way in.

12. Replace the lug nuts by hand, as tightly as you can.

   Important: Do not tighten the lugs in sequence, as on a clock, but in the following order:

   This ensures that the wheel sits as straight as possible.

13. Lower the jack, and once the car is resting on the ground again, use the lug wrench to tighten all the lugs as much as you can—in the order shown—again using your feet and your body weight for leverage.

14. Place the jack, lug wrench, and flat tire in the trunk, remove the blocks on the diagonally opposite wheel, and you're done!

Rotation Time

One way to make your tires last longer and ensure safer driving is to rotate your tires: Front tires go to the back, back tires to the front. (Many trucks still have bias-ply tires instead of the radial tires on most modern cars, in which case a crisscross rotation pattern is called for.) This means you get even wear on all the tires, since those on the drive wheels get more wear than the others. How often they should be rotated is another thing altogether.

Recommendations for tire rotation vary from every 3,500 miles to every 15,000 miles. For once, I disagree with many of the owner's manuals, which would have you rotating your tires as often as every three months. With good tires, every 15,000 miles is generally fine for most cars.

While the tires are being rotated, get the wheels checked for balance and alignment. And make sure the mechanic checks the brakes too.

The Electric Future?

Question: **When are we going to get electric cars?**

Answer: **Ask General Motors.**

Most women who love their cars love the environment too. And as so often happens with affairs of the heart, these two loves clash. Only three out of the 150 women in the focus groups said that the environment was not a concern for them.

What to do? Automotive emissions can contribute up to two-thirds of urban smog. Give up cars? Only one woman was ready to do that. The alternative, of course, is to clean them up.

Nearly two-thirds (62%) say they look for cars with high gas mileage and thus low emission ratings, but an even higher number—87%—say they'd buy an electric car if one was in production.

Electric cars use no gasoline. The energy to power the car is provided by electricity stored in batteries—either lead-acid batteries as in the car you now drive, or other kinds, such as sodium-sulfur, zinc-air, and nickel-cadmium. Instead of an internal combustion engine, wires lead directly from the battery to small electric motors inside each of the wheels, providing an automatic all-wheel drive.

The result: a car with very few moving parts and therefore very little to service. Except, of course, for the battery. Though researchers are fast developing pumped-up batteries that store far more power than the one currently in your car, they would still last only two or three years and then need replacing. This is why there's much talk now about hybrids: cars that run on a combination of a battery and a small gas turbine engine to recharge the battery as the car runs. It's a good compromise for the time being, and one that will undoubtedly be used.

As the regulations now stand, California will require that at least 2% of all new vehicles sold in that state have zero emissions by 1998. That means no carbon monoxide, no nitrous oxides, nothing noxious coming out of the tail pipe—in fact, in the case of electric cars, no tail pipe. That percentage will slowly rise over the years. Several states in the Northeast are considering similar regulations. And automakers are objecting like crazy.

First, they claim, the technology is not there yet. Second, the cars will be too expensive. Third, they'll have too little power. And fourth, they won't solve the pollution problem since coal-fired electrical generating plants will still pollute the air.

Then General Motors shot much of its own argument in the foot by developing the experimental Impact coupe, which was not a "conversion" of a gasoline car to electricity but was designed as an electric car from the wheels up. The Impact was revolutionary: It performed as well as a Miata on acceleration and speed, and it looked great, like a swoopy silver bullet.

Apparently, then, the technology *is* available, and so is the power and speed. So let's take a closer look at the automakers' arguments.

Technology

Batteries as they now exist provide only a 100-mile range on a single charge for an electric car. (Gasoline cars provide a 300-mile range between fillings.) Yet a hundred miles is well within what most people drive on any one day. At the end of the day, commuters would plug the car in to the electrical outlet in their garage and be ready to go again the next morning. In fact, the car wouldn't even need all night to recharge. Recharging times are down to as low as twenty minutes with some batteries.

Battery life is a bigger problem, since they're expensive to replace. Two possible long-term solutions: a replaceable cassette that could be inserted into the main body of the battery, then exchanged at filling stations, and an advanced type of battery known as a fuel cell, which uses hydrogen in metallic, noncombustible form.

On the other hand, maybe batteries last longer than Detroit now thinks. In 1912 a certain Mrs. French from Victoria, British Columbia, purchased a Detroit Electricar (until World War I, electric cars were more numerous than gasoline ones, and more popular with women, since they were easier and cleaner to operate and didn't need to be cranked). In 1938 her husband wrote to the Edison Battery Company complimenting them on the quality of their batteries: The car still ran on its original, from 1912.

Expense

Automakers' estimates of how much electric cars would cost are based on limited production. In mass production, prices would come way down. In fact, with so few moving parts, the price should be far lower than that of gasoline cars.

But even before mass production, women say they'd pay more for electric cars. Less committed than men to the showy, noisy, smelly power of the internal combustion engine, and possibly more concerned about its effect on the air we breathe, women like the idea of a car that doesn't pollute. So much so that 76% would be willing to pay $1,000 more, and 10% as much as $5,000 more.

Power

Though some women share the male obsession with speed and mechanical power, most don't. So what if an electric car won't tear up the asphalt? A whopping 86% say that a top speed of 100 mph would be just fine by them, and 51% say they'd be content with a top speed of only 70 mph.

Since women buy half the cars out there, automakers should really start listening.

Pollution

It's perfectly true that coal-powered electrical plants generate pollution, but this pollution is far easier to control when it comes from a single stack instead of millions of tail pipes. Coal is still the main fuel used to generate electricity, but hydroelectric plants are far cleaner. Nuclear plants have their attendant risks, and solar power is nowhere near the stage where it could be used for large-scale generation of electricity. Again, the long-term goal is to use metal-bound hydrogen in fuel cells, where the only by-product is water.

Of course, the four reasons automakers give in their arguments against electric cars aren't quite the whole story. There's another factor they don't mention: Mass-producing electric cars would require huge capital investment. It means a total redesign of manufacturing and assembly plants. And because there are fewer parts, parts makers would be out of business. Economically, then, this would be a costly changeover. That means good-bye to happy shareholders and corporate bonuses for a few years, as the changeover takes place.

In the meantime, emissions from gasoline cars are getting better and better—that is, lighter and lighter. New cars are relatively pollution-free compared to those of just twenty years ago. The auto industry argues that if all cars on the road were new, we'd solve the pollution problem—an argument that is, at best, self-serving, since of course we'd all have to buy those new cars from them. It's also shortsighted, since the ever-increasing number of cars on the road means that although each car may be producing fewer emissions, the total remains the same or higher. Moreover, the automakers don't even address the fact that oil is a nonrenewable resource, and one we have to fight for, as in the Gulf War.

In the short run, gasoline cars will prevail, along with other, cleaner internal-combustion fuels such as compressed natural gas (CNG), now being used in some states by fleets such as UPS. But in the long run, mass-produced electric cars are on the way. Not yet, except as delivery vans and other service vehicles, but possibly within the next ten years, and certainly within the next twenty.

"And what about solar cars?" many women ask. I wish the news were better. It's true that a specially designed solar-powered race car can reach speeds up to 70 mph (I was there in Australia when a Honda solar car did that), but solar technology has a very long way to go until it can be used to transport four people and luggage at reasonable speed in reasonable safety and comfort. Sorry, but we'll have to wait.

Questionnaire

➡ **"I don't think this questionnaire could have been written by a man."**

—Legal assistant, New York

All the women in the focus groups answered this questionnaire at the start of each group.

The answers constitute a first-time database on how women really relate to their cars. This will be an ongoing database, so please feel welcome to fill out the questionnaire, add any comments you wish, tear out these pages, and send them to me at:

    P.O. Box 9553
    Seattle, WA 98109

All participation is of course on an anonymous basis unless you request otherwise.

1. **Rate each of the following words for how your car makes you feel:**

	Very much	Somewhat	Not really	Not at all
Independent				
Sexy				
Responsible				
Free				
Capable				
Aggressive				
Classy				
Carefree				

Anything else? _____

2. **Do you like your car?. . . . A lot / Some / A little / Don't**

3. **Do you like driving?. . . . A lot / Some / A little / Don't**

4. **Do you think there's such a thing as a sexy car? Yes / No**
   If Yes, what's the sexiest car you can think of?
   _____

5. **What kind of car do you drive most? (circle one):**
   sedan / coupe / sports car / minivan / four-by-four / pickup / wagon

6. **What kind of car would you most like to drive?**
   sedan / coupe / sports car / minivan / four-by-four / pickup / wagon

7. **Is the car you drive**
   your car / his car / the family car / other (specify)_____

8. **Do you ever dream about cars and/or driving? Yes / No**
   If Yes, what?_____

9. **Did you ever have sex in a car? Yes / No**

10. What do you carry most in your car? (Choose no more than two.)

    __children
    __groceries
    __professional equipment (specify)_____
    __adult passengers
    __sports equipment (specify)_____
    __you alone
    __animals
    __other (specify)_____

11. Who actually purchased the car (you, a relative, a sugar daddy, a fairy godmother)?_____

12. What do you think of flashy red sports cars?
Love 'em / Like 'em / So-so / Hate 'em

13. Do you ever daydream about cars and/or driving? Yes / No
If Yes, what?_____

14. Does your car make you feel:
   • very safe / safe enough / not so safe / vulnerable
   • very happy / happy enough / not so happy / unhappy
   • younger than you are / your age / older than you are
   • more in control of your life / no difference / less in control

15. What specific car would you most like to own?_____
Why?_____

16. Have you ever had fantasies of being a racecar driver? Yes / No
If Yes, did you win? Yes / No

17. What pleases you most about your car?_____
_____

18. What annoys you most about your car?_____
_____

19. To what degree does your car express your personality?
a lot / to some degree / a little / not at all

20. What's the fastest you've ever driven? _____ mph
When was that? _____ (year)

21. **To what degree would you *like* a car to be an expression of your personality?**
a lot / to some degree / a little / not at all

22. **Do you think most women want something different from a car than most men? Yes / No**
If Yes, what?_____
_____

23. **As a driver, do you consider yourself:**
- very aggressive / mildly aggressive / somewhat yielding / timid
- very slow / fairly slow / somewhat fast / very fast
- excellent / good / average / not so good / bad
- impatient / somewhat impatient / fairly patient / very patient
- very cautious / fairly cautious / somewhat incautious / reckless

24. **What's your favorite car color?**_____

25. **Do you drive better or worse than the man in your life?**
better / same / worse / no man, thanks

26. **Is speed important to you?**
Very / somewhat / a little / not at all

27. **Do you drive faster or slower than the man in your life?**
faster / same / slower / no man, thanks

28. **Does your car have: stick shift / automatic shift**
Which do you prefer: stick shift / automatic shift

29. **How much research do you do before you buy a car?**
a lot / some / a little / none

30. **Rank the following things you might look for in a new car from 1 to 9, 1 being least important, 9 most important:**

__handling
__price
__styling
__safety
__comfort
__power
__fuel consumption
__prestige
__reliability

31. Have you ever been in an accident as a driver (more than a fender-bender)? Yes / No
If Yes, when, and what happened?_____
_____

32. Are you concerned about the environment?
Yes / No
If Yes, does this affect your decision on which vehicle to drive? Yes / No

33. What make of car do you most trust, and
why?_____
_____

34. Do you know more or less about cars than the man in your life?
more / same / less / no man, thanks

35. What make of car do you least trust, and why?_____
_____

36. Would you trust a woman salesperson more than a male one?
more / the same / less

37. Rate the following sources of information for buying a new car,
(4 being high, 1 being low, 0 being not applicable):

__friends' recommendations
__print advertisements
__partner's recommendations
__*Consumer Reports* and/or other buying services
__family recommendations
__television commercials
__dealers' recommendations

Any other sources?_____

38. How much do you negotiate when buying a car?
a lot / some / a little / not at all

39. Do you enlist the help of others to buy a car? Yes / No
If Yes, who?_____

40. Do you think you got a good deal on your current car? Yes / No

41. Do you think you would have gotten a better deal if you'd been male?
Yes / No

42. Do you think of automobile dealers as:

	Very	Somewhat	A little	Not at all
Helpful				
Aggressive				
Intimidating				
Honest				
Other (specify)				

43. Have you ever changed a tire? Yes / No
If not, do you know how? Yes / No
If not, would you want to know how? Yes / No

44. How often does your car get washed?
weekly / monthly / quarterly / biannually / annually, perhaps

Who usually washes it?
yourself / your partner / a service / your child
How?
by hand / in an automatic carwash

45. Have you ever changed the oil? Yes / No
If not, do you know how? Yes / No
If not, would you want to know how? Yes / No

46. Do you think mechanics deal fairly with you? Yes / No
If No, do you think it's because you're a woman? Yes / No

47. Would you trust a woman mechanic more than a male one? Yes / No

48. Have you ever changed the spark plugs? Yes / No
If not, do you know how? Yes / No
If not, would you want to know how? Yes / No

49. Would you buy an alternate-fuel car (an electric or a hybrid)
- if it cost the same as a gasoline car? Yes / No
- if it cost $1,000 more? Yes / No
- if it cost $5,000 more? Yes / No
- if it had a top speed of 100 mph? Yes / No
- if it had a top speed of 70 mph? Yes / No

50. Do you have a name for your car? Yes / No
If Yes, what?_____

Have you ever had a name for previous cars? Yes / No
If Yes, what?_____

51. Do you talk to your car? Yes / No
If Yes, what do you say to it?_____

52. Do you pat / kiss / stroke your car? (circle if Yes)

53. Do you know how to check the air in the tires? Yes / No
And how to add more or take some out? Yes / No

54. What age did you start driving? _____

55. Do you ever yell at other drivers? Yes / No
If Yes, what?_____

56. Do you have totems of any kind in your car? Yes / No
If Yes, what?_____

57. Do you have fuzzy dice in your car? Yes / No
What do you feel about fuzzy dice?_____

58. How old are you? _____
What's your occupation?_____
_____

59. What make, model, and year of car do you drive?_____
_____

60. What's the most memorable thing that's ever happened to you in a
car?_____
_____
_____

Many thanks for your participation
—LH

Tech Talk Translated

All those arcane terms guys keep throwing around do actually mean something. How meaningful these meanings are is quite another question: Some mean a lot, others are of interest only to engineers. Here's a quick guide to the most common, many of which you've already encountered in this book.

0–60: How long it takes for a professional test-driver to get a car to 60 mph from a dead stop. A guy thing. Four seconds is really fast; seven seconds is sports-car respectable; over ten seconds is kind of slow.

Body roll: The tendency of a car—and thus its driver—to lean during cornering. Less body roll is better.

Cab-forward design: A car on which the windshield reaches out over the front wheels, and all four wheels are near the corners of the car, with less overhang. This creates more interior room without making the whole car larger.

Catalytic converter: The pollution-control device on the tail pipe. It chemically decomposes unburned waste matter in the exhaust, thus reducing the amount sent out of the tail pipe.

cd: Coefficient of drag (always lower-case). This is a

measure of the car's wind resistance, established in wind-tunnel testing. A cd of 1.0 would be a brick wall. A cd of 0.0 would be thin air. So the lower the cd—0.20 is pretty low—the more aerodynamic the car, and the easier it cuts through wind resistance. This may mean that it goes like the wind, or seems to, but it's really of importance only in race cars and airplanes. In a passenger car, even the lowest cd won't make a whole heck of a lot of difference unless you're going something like 150 mph.

Compression ratio: A formula for how much the air in the engine has been compressed. The more it's compressed, the more power you get.

Concept cars: Aka dream cars or blue-sky cars—design exercises that are very popular in auto shows. Sometimes they see the light of day, in much altered form, as production cars. More often, they are sent to the great dream-car graveyard in the sky.

DOHC: Dual overhead camshaft (usually upper-case). As opposed, of course, to SOHC—single overhead camshaft. Also known as twin-cam engines. (Camshafts used to be below the cylinder heads, inside the engine block; placing them above the cylinder heads gives more direct contact with the valves.)

EPA estimates: Mileage estimates based on tests administered by the Environmental Protection Agency. Actual mileage (miles traveled per gallon of gas) varies depending on the driver, the load, and road conditions.

Ergonomics: The tech term for the art of placing everything in the right place for your body: all the controls within easy reach, as if the car is made for you.

Four-by-four: Not a piece of wood, but any vehicle that can be driven in four-wheel drive. Usually sport-utility vehicles such as Jeeps or pickups.

Fuel injection: A means of delivering precisely measured amounts of fuel directly to the intake valves of the cylinders. More efficient than the carburetors formerly used.

Fully loaded: Sounds like a car with a full complement of passengers and baggage, but in fact it's a car with all the available options, such as leather seats, CD player, and electrically powered windows, doors, locks, and seats.

Gaskets: After all you've heard about cars blowing gaskets (let alone people blowing their gaskets), they're disappointingly simple. They're thin rubber plates inserted between two metal parts either to seal the join perfectly or to cushion against wear.

Gear ratio: The engine speed as compared to the speed of the output shaft of the transmission, in any given gear.

Horsepower: A measure of energy that has nothing to do with horses, despite all that talk about the number of horses under the hood. The real definition is just about meaningless to most people, but just so you can impress your males, one horsepower is the energy required to lift 550 pounds to a height of one foot within one second.

Lean-burn engine: Used in many models in Japan, but not yet in America, these engines run on air-fuel mixtures of up to 25 to 1 instead of 15 to 1, producing higher mileage.

Manifold: Either the exhaust manifold or the air-intake manifold—a set of pipes, one for each cylinder, which in the case of the exhaust, blend into one at the manifold, and in the case of the air-intake, branch into many at the manifold.

Multivalve engines: Instead of two valves per cylinder, these have three, four, or even five valves per cylinder, which makes them more powerful and yet more fuel-efficient at the same time.

Muscle car: Any car with lots of "muscle"—that is, horsepower—relative to its size and cost. Usually used only for American cars. The Camaro is a muscle car, so is the Mustang (thus the term "pony car").

Odometer: A device that measures how many miles the car has traveled, and shows you the total in a little window beneath the gauges. There's also a trip odometer that can be set to zero at the beginning of a trip by pushing a button just below it. This can come in very useful when you're following the kind of directions that read "Go five miles and then . . ."

Oversteer: The tendency of certain cars, usually rear-wheel drive, to turn more sharply in a corner than the driver intends. Feels as if the car is trying to get its rear end through the turn before its front end. This is what they mean by "the rear end breaking loose" or "sliding out."

Power curve: The curve created on a graph by tracing the engine's peak power at different rpms. Related to torque.

Redline: The point on the tachometer where the markings turn from black to red, indicating that you're taking the car to its maximum rpm in any gear. Drive over the redline and you're putting too much strain on the engine. Many cars now have an automatic fuel cutback that kicks in when you reach the redline, so that you can't damage the engine even if you try.

RPM: Revolutions per minute—the speed at which the engine, specifically the crankshaft, is turning.

Solenoid: An electrical device that converts the DC current of the battery into AC current for the starter. It used to be separate from the starter but is integrated into the starter in newer cars.

Specs: Short for specifications—all the numerical measurements of a car's size, engine, and performance.

Supercars: Aka exotic cars—sports cars capable of going outrageous speeds, such as the 218-mph Jaguar XJ220. They're very expensive (the XJ220 costs $750,000) and statements solely of image, since there's nowhere to drive at such speeds except in the Indy 500.

Tachometer: Tach, for short—the gauge next to the speedometer, measuring rpm. (See *redline.*) Very important in race cars, but most passenger-car drivers don't use the tach or even need it. Still, it makes drivers feel more professional.

Throttle: Technically, a device for controlling how much fuel is in the air-fuel mixture your car runs on, but the word is used loosely as a synonym for pressure on the gas pedal, as in "full throttle."

Top speed: Another guy thing—the maximum speed the car is capable of in testing, though if anybody but a professional driver takes it up to this speed, they're liable to end up taking an unexpected off-road excursion.

Torque: Measured in foot-pounds (lbs-ft), meaning the number of pounds of pressure per square foot. In a car, it's a measure of rotational force, and maximum torque figures are usually given together with the engine speed at which they occur, such as 155 ft-lbs @ 5500 rpm. Strong torque at low rpm gives good acceleration from a standstill and is a good thing to have if you're towing a boat or a camper.

Transfer case: A transmission-like device that sends power to all four wheels in a sport-utility or other four-wheel-drive vehicle, providing what is essentially an additional set of more powerful gears.

Turbocharging: Increasing power by rerouting hot exhaust gases through a turbine (a kind of powerful fan), thus forcing more air into the cylinders and getting higher compression. When they talk of the turbocharger "kicking in," they mean that the turbine has started to work, giving a sudden burst of extra power.

Turning the rotors: The rotors in question are the discs on your disc brakes. The brake pads can wear grooves in the rotors after a few years, but as long as the rotors aren't warped, they can be ground lightly on a lathe ("smoothed" or "turned") instead of replaced.

Two-plus-two: Any car with a rear seat that can fit only adults with no legs, usually a sports car trying to be a four-seater but not quite making it.

Understeer: The tendency of certain cars (usually front-wheel drive) to corner less sharply than the driver intended. Feels as if the car wants to go straight ahead rather than round the corner.

Vapor lock: Air bubbles formed in the fuel line, blocking it, when the fuel boils in extreme heat. With the fuel feed blocked, of course, the car stops running. If it happens, just let the car cool down.

Wheelbase: The distance from the center of the front wheel to the center of the rear wheel. A longer wheel base generally gives increased stability, which is why many new cars have their wheels practically at the corners of the car. The short wheelbase of small sport-utilities combined with their height can make them tippy.

Automotive Trivia

Few people know that several automakers' names are acronyms.

Alfa: Societa Anonima Lombarda Fabbrica Automobili, which is Italian for the Lombardy Automobile Manufacturing Company

BMW: Bayerische Motoren Werke, which is German for Bavarian Motor Works

Fiat: Fabbrica Italiana di Automobili Torino, which is Italian for the Italian Automobile Manufacturers of Milan

MG: Morris Garage (only the British would be so terse)

Saab: Svenska Aeroplan A.B., which is Swedish for the Swedish Airplane Corporation (yes, they do make airplanes as well as cars.)

The Automotive Rolodex

Automakers

Here are the addresses and phone numbers of all automakers currently selling new cars in the United States. Call first and ask for the name of the current customer-relations manager, then write—and keep copies of your correspondence.

Acura
1919 Torrance Boulevard
Torrance, CA 90501-2746
Tel: 310/783-2000

Alfa Romeo
Box 598026
Orlando, FL 32859-8026
Tel: 407/856-5000

Aston Martin Lagonda
1290 East Main
Stamford, CT 06902
Tel: 203/359-2259

Audi
3800 Hamlin Road
Auburn Hills, MI 48326
Tel: 810/340-5000

Bentley
Box 476
Lyndhurst, NJ 07071
Tel: 201/460-9600

BMW
Box 1227
Woodcliff Lake, NJ 07675-1227
Tel: 201/307-4000

Buick
902 East Hamilton Avenue
Flint, MI 48550
Tel: 800/521-7300

Cadillac
30009 Van Dyke
Warren, MI 48090
Tel: 800/458-8006

Chevrolet
30007 Van Dyke
Warren, MI 48090
Tel: 800/222-1020

Chrysler
12000 Chrysler Drive
Highland Park, MI 48288
Tel: 800/992-1997

Dodge
12000 Chrysler Drive
Highland Park, MI 48288
Tel: 800/992-1997

Ferrari
250 Sylvan Avenue
Englewood Cliffs, NJ 10732
Tel: 201/816-2600

Ford
Box 43301
Detroit, MI 48243
Tel: 313/446-8321

General Motors
3044 West Grand Boulevard
Detroit, MI 48202
Tel: 313/556-5000

Geo
30007 Van Dyke
Warren, MI 48090
Tel: 800/222-1020

GMC Truck
31 East Judson Street
Pontiac, MI 48058
Tel: 800/462-8782

Honda
1919 Torrance Boulevard
Torrance, CA 90501-2746
Tel: 310/783-2000

Hyundai
10550 Tabert Avenue
Fountain Valley, CA 92728-0850
Tel: 714/965-3000

Infiniti
18501 South Figueroa
Carson, CA 90248
Tel: 800/662-6200

Isuzu
13181 Crossroads Parkway
North
City of Industry, CA 91746
Tel: 310/699-0500

Jaguar
555 MacArthur Boulevard
Mahwah, NJ 07430-2327
Tel: 201/818-8500

Jeep-Eagle
12000 Chrysler Drive
Highland Park, MI 48288
Tel: 313/956-5741

Kia
2 Cromwell
Irvine, CA 92718
Tel: 714/470-7000

Land Rover
Box 1503
Lanham, MD 20706
Tel: 301/731-9040

Lexus
19001 South Western Avenue
Torrance, CA 90509
Tel: 800/255-3987

Lincoln-Mercury
Box 43322
Detroit, MI 48243
Tel: 313/446-8321

Lotus
1655 Lakes Parkway
Lawrenceville, GA 30243
Tel: 404/822-4566

Mazda
7755 Irvine Center Drive
Irvine, CA 92718
Tel: 714/727-1990

Mercedes-Benz
1 Mercedes Drive
Montvale, NJ 07645-0350
Tel: 201/573-0600

Mitsubishi
Box 6400
Cypress, CA 90630
Tel: 714/372-6000

Nissan
18501 South Figueroa
Carson, CA 90248
Tel: 800/647-7261

Oldsmobile
920 Townsend
Lansing, MI 48921
Tel: 800/442-6537

Plymouth
12000 Chrysler Drive
Highland Park, MI 48288
Tel: 800/992-1997

Pontiac
1 Pontiac Plaza
Pontiac, MI 48058-3484
Tel: 800/276-6842

Porsche
Box 30911
Reno, NV 89501
Tel: 702/348-3000

Rolls-Royce
Box 476
Lyndhurst, NJ 07071
Tel: 201/460-9600

Saab
Box 9000
Norcross, GA 30093
Tel: 404/279-0100

Saturn
Box 7025
Troy, MI 48007-7025
Tel: 800/522-5000

Subaru
Box 6000
Cherry Hill, NJ 08034
Tel: 609/488-8500

Suzuki
3521 East Imperial Highway
Brea, CA 92621-6722
Tel: 714/996-7040

Toyota
19001 South Western Avenue
Torrance, CA 90509
Tel: 310/618-4000

Volkswagen
3800 Hamlin Road
Auburn Hills, MI 48326
Tel: 810/340-5000

Volvo
Box 913
Rockleigh, NJ 07647
Tel: 201/768-7300

Consumer and Lobby Groups

AAA
(American Automobile
Association)
1000 AAA Drive
Heathrow, FL 32746-5063

Center for Auto Safety
2001 S Street NW
Washington, DC 20009
(Nonprofit consumer organization, founded by Ralph Nader)

Consumer Federation of America
1012 14th Street, #1105
Washington, DC 20005

Council of Better Business
Bureaus
Automotive Programs
1515 Wilson Boulevard, #600
Arlington, VA 22209

Insurance Institute for Highway
Safety
1005 North Glebe Road
Arlington, VA 22201
(Funded by insurance industry)

Mothers Against Drunk Driving
(MADD)
669 Airport Freeway
Hurst, TX 76053

National Automobile Dealers
Association
8400 Westpark Drive
McLean, VA 22102

National Institute for Automotive
Service Excellence
13505 Dulles Technology Drive
Herndon, VA 22071-3415

Federal

Department of Justice
Consumer Litigation, Civil Division
550 11th Street NW
Washington, DC 20530

Director of Consumer Affairs
Office of Consumer Affairs
Office of the President
Washington, DC 20506

Environmental Protection Agency
401 M Street SW
Washington, DC 20460

National Highway Traffic Safety
Administration
Director of Public and Consumer
Affairs
400 7th Street SW
Washington, DC 20590
(NHTSA Auto Safety Hotline:
800/424-9393)

About the Author

Lesley Hazleton lives on a houseboat in Seattle, drives fast cars, and flies slow planes. She discovered cars in 1988, and hasn't stopped writing about them since. She writes a regular auto column for *Mirabella*, has also written about autos for the *New York Times*, *Town and Country*, *Connoisseur*, *Lear's*, *Travel Holiday*, and *Parade* magazine, and is a contributing editor of *Self*. Her previous car book was *Confessions of a Fast Woman*.

Index